# LETTERS OF
# SAINT PAUL

# LETTERS OF
# SAINT PAUL

ST PAULS

*Pauline*
BOOKS & MEDIA
Boston

*Nihil Obstat:*   Msgr. Daniel Murray
                  Rector St. Charles Borromeo Seminary, Overbrook, PA

                  Rev. Robert Hayden
                  Vice Rector Immaculate Conception Seminary, Huntington, NY

*Imprimi Potest:*  Most Rev. Emil A. Wcela
                   Vicar Eastern Vicariate, Diocese of Rockville Centre, NY

*Imprimatur:*   Most Rev. Daniel E. Pilarczyk
                President, National Conference of Catholic Bishops
                March 22, 1991

*Rescript:*
In accord with canon 825, §1 of the *Code of Canon Law*, the National Conference of
Catholic Bishops hereby approves for publication the Books of the New Testament, a
translation by Mark A. Wauck, submitted by Alba House.

   Most Rev. William H. Keeler
   President, National Conference of Catholic Bishops, Washington, DC
   May 6, 1994

Cover design by Rosana Usselmann

*Photo credit:* Pompeo Batoni (1708–1787). *Portrait of St. Paul.* National Trust / Art
Resource, NY.

Translation, introductions, and footnotes by Mark A. Wauck
Foreword by Rev. Jeffrey Mickler, S.S.P.
Appendix I compiled by Sr. Mary Mark Wickenhiser, F.S.P.
Appendix II and Appendix III by Sr. Kathryn James Hermes, F.S.P.

ISBN 0-8198-4524-8 (Daughters of St. Paul)
ISBN 0-8189-1272-3 (Society of St. Paul)
ISBN 978-0-8189-1272-6 (Society of St. Paul)

Published by Pauline Books & Media, 50 Saint Paul's Avenue, Boston, MA 02130-3491.
www.pauline.org. Printed in the U.S.A.

Pauline Books & Media is the publishing house of the Daughters of St. Paul, an international congregation of women religious serving the Church with the communications media.

   2 3 4 5 6 7 8 9                                         12 11 10 09 08

# CONTENTS

Foreword . . . . . . . . . . . . . . . . . . *vii*

The Letter to the Romans . . . . . . . . . . . . . *1*

The First Letter to the Corinthians . . . . . . . . . 48

The Second Letter to the Corinthians . . . . . . . . 91

The Letter to the Galatians . . . . . . . . . . . 124

The Letter to the Ephesians . . . . . . . . . . . 142

The Letter to the Philippians . . . . . . . . . . 159

The Letter to the Colossians. . . . . . . . . . . 172

The First Letter to the Thessalonians . . . . . . . . 185

The Second Letter to the Thessalonians . . . . . . 195

The First Letter to Timothy . . . . . . . . . . . 202

The Second Letter to Timothy . . . . . . . . 217

The Letter to Titus . . . . . . . . . . . . . . 227

The Letter to Philemon. . . . . . . . . . . . . . . *234*

The Letter to the Hebrews . . . . . . . . . . . . *238*


Appendix I: Prayers . . . . . . . . . . . . . . . . *280*

Appendix II: The Heart of Saint Paul:
             Living "In Christ" . . . . . . . . . . *285*

Appendix III: Topical Index . . . . . . . . . . . . *288*

# FOREWORD

Saint Paul is one of the most influential figures in human history. For the Christian, he is a man of lofty spiritual stature who spread the story of the crucified and resurrected Jesus throughout the Mediterranean world of the first century. Ultimately he laid down his life as a martyr in the service of the Gospel. His writings are considered divinely inspired and have served the followers of Jesus well throughout all the succeeding centuries. His written words have been reflected on, studied, and, most importantly, acted upon by millions of believers. This translation of his letters, with its fresh and lively style, is meant to stimulate in new ways the people already familiar and in love with the writings of Paul, as well as to launch those unfamiliar with them into a first-time reading of his works.

Paul is a saint for everyone. Students can identify with Paul who spent years studying with Gamaliel and learned from Peter and others about the Lord of life. Working men and women can identify with this industrious tradesman who supported himself by making tents. Sailors can see in Paul someone who sailed the Mediterranean and did not abandon shipmates in time of crisis. Athletes will find in Paul's sports metaphors some helpful lessons for life. Communicators of all kinds can take heart from the efforts and frustrations Paul faced in keeping contact with his fledgling communities and with Christian leaders in Jerusalem. Most of all, however, people striving to be great lovers of God and neighbor will find in these letters soul-shaping wisdom and practical ways of sharing the Gospel with the world.

Although John is called the "beloved disciple," Paul can rightly be called the "apostle of love." His reflection on love in 1 Corinthians 13 is both exalted and down to earth, challenging yet inspiring. It is a reminder of what it means to be a servant of the God of love. However, every letter Paul wrote is filled with a sense of love, and the actions of his life show the sincerity of his belief.

Paul used familial terms to describe his relationship with members of the believing communities that he served. They were his family. In his earliest letter, 1 Thessalonians, he calls the Thessalonians "brothers beloved by God." He describes his approach to the Thessalonians as "a nursing mother comforting her child." He affirmed that he had the same attitude toward them as "a father with his own children." One way to approach these letters is to think of them as messages from a wise and trusted friend, messages that transcend time and speak to us today. Generation after generation of believers have heard excerpts from these letters proclaimed in the liturgy, but few people read each of Paul's letters from beginning to end. The publishers sincerely hope this edition will encourage people to read Paul's words carefully and to share them with others. Savoring these letters as a whole will embed them in our hearts and minds, expand our capacity to love, and deepen our faith.

*Rev. Jeffrey Mickler, Ph.D., SSP*

# THE LETTER TO THE
# ROMANS

By the late 50s A.D., probably about the year 57, Paul had come to believe that the time was coming for him to seek out new fields of missionary activity. He had been proclaiming the good news and establishing churches in the areas surrounding the Aegean sea as well as some inland parts of Asia Minor for the better part of ten years, and had had considerable success. He was now completing work on a very special project, the collection among the new Gentile churches which he planned to offer to the mother church in Jerusalem as a symbol of that new unity of Jew and Gentile, that universal salvation, which the good news of Jesus had brought. But even as he prepared for what he knew could be, and indeed turned out to be, a very dangerous trip to Jerusalem, he was already looking ahead.

The new field Paul had selected for his ministry was Spain. To undertake to proclaim the good news in so distant a land would take planning and preparation, and so as he wintered over in Corinth before his final trip to Jerusalem he spent part of his time composing a letter of introduction to the church in Rome. His hope was that the large Roman church would be able to assist him in his plans, and so he wished to acquaint them with his vision of the good news in so far as it concerned its proclamation to the Gentiles. The letter was to be carried by a trusted patroness, Phoebe.

First-century Rome had a very large Jewish community, and the good news had been proclaimed there very early on, probably in the early 40s A.D. or even earlier. As was usual, however, the church in Rome had come to be Gentile in its major part. It was to this church, established and nourished by others, unacquainted with the controversial Apostle to the Gentiles except by reputation, that Paul turned for help. The instrument he chose with which to introduce himself has come down to us as the Letter to the Romans, generally considered to be Paul's masterwork.

Romans is certainly Paul's greatest effort at a sustained exposition of the gospel he had devoted his life to. It is not, however, a complete exposition of his gospel. The letter is concerned with the place of Israel and the Gentiles in God's plan of salvation, a subject which was still controversial. It would therefore be mistaken to seek a systematic "theology of Saint Paul" in Romans. On the other hand, because it was written — more or less — at leisure, rather than in the heat of some crisis in the life of a particular church, it presents the most systematic and considered view of Paul's ideas on almost any topic, with the possible exception of Ephesians.

Paul opens with a somewhat extended greeting, followed by a thanksgiving which, in its final two verses, presents the theme of the letter. He then goes on to present the dilemma facing the human race — all, both Jew and Gentile, are in need of God's grace. Included in this presentation, of course, is precisely what some found so controversial, the idea that both Jews and Gentiles are in fundamentally the same plight. Paul next presents God's solution to this dilemma: restoration to fellowship with God through faith in Christ. Included in this section is an extended midrashic discussion of Abraham's example of faith as well as a discussion of the extraordinary nature of God's redemption. Chapters 6 through 11 present detailed answers to a variety of objections which could be raised to Paul's version of the good news, probably based on actual objections he had been confronted with.

The final chapters include a lengthy exhortatory section on the life in Christ, a plea for the Romans' assistance in Paul's plans for the future, and a commendation of Phoebe. The letter concludes with an unusually long list of greetings to specific individuals, probably intended to establish his ties to the community and to serve as references.

### OUTLINE OF THE LETTER TO THE ROMANS

| | | |
|---|---|---|
| A. | 1:1–7 | Greeting |
| B. | 1:8–17 | Thanksgiving and Theme of the Letter |
| C. | 1:18–3:20 | The Problem: Both Jew and Gentile Are in Need of God's Grace |
| | 1:18–32 | The Gentiles Have Incurred God's Just Wrath |

|        | 2:1–29      | The Jews Too Fall Short in God's Sight and Have No Special Status |
|--------|-------------|------------------------------------------------------------------|
|        | 3:1–20      | The Dilemma of God's Faithfulness and Israel's Unfaithfulness |
| D.     | 3:21–5:21   | God's Solution: Restoration to Fellowship with God through Faith in Christ |
|        | 4:1–25      | The Example of Abraham's Faith |
|        | 5:1–21      | The Extraordinary Nature and Consequences of God's Redemption |
| E.     | 6:1–11:36   | Objections to Paul's Gospel Answered |
|        | 6:1–7:6     | Are We Now Free to Sin? |
|        | 7:7–25      | The Role of the Torah in God's Saving Plan |
|        | 8:1–39      | Life in the Spirit, Life in Hope |
|        | 9:1–11:36   | The Place of Jews and Gentiles in God's Plan |
| F.     | 12:1–15:13  | Practical Counsels for the Life in Christ |
| G.     | 15:14–33    | Paul Appeals for the Romans' Aid in His Plans for Future Evangelization |
| H.     | 16:1–23     | Commendation of Phoebe and Closing Greetings |
| I.     | 16:25–27    | Praise of God's Glory |

## A. Greeting

**1** ¹ Paul, a servant of Christ Jesus, called to be an apostle set apart for the proclamation of God's good news ² which He promised beforehand through His prophets in the Holy Scriptures — ³ the good news about His Son Jesus Christ our Lord, who was born from the line of David according to the flesh ⁴ and was designated Son of God in power according to the Spirit of holiness by his resurrection from the dead. ⁵ Through him we have received the grace of apostleship to bring about the obedience of faith among all nations for the sake of his name. ⁶ And you too are among those called to belong to Jesus Christ. ⁷ To all those in Rome who are beloved of God and are called to be saints, grace and peace be with you from God our Father and the Lord Jesus Christ.

## B. Thanksgiving and Theme of the Letter

⁸ First of all, I give thanks to my God through Jesus Christ for all of you, because your faith is being proclaimed

---

1:5     "The obedience of faith." Obedience to a written code, the Torah, is replaced with obedience of the spirit, brought about through faith.

1:7     The Greek root for such words as "saints," "holy," and "sanctify" translated the Hebrew concept of being "set apart" or "consecrated," especially as an offering to God.

throughout the world. 9 God is my witness — Whom I
serve with my spirit by proclaiming the good news of His
Son — that I continually mention you 10 in my prayers
and ask that somehow by God's will I'll finally manage to
come to you, 11 for I long to see you and to share with you
some spiritual gift in order to strengthen you, 12 that is, so
we may be mutually encouraged by one another's faith,
both yours and mine. 13 *a* I want you to know, brothers,
that I've often planned to come to you (although I've been
prevented from doing so thus far) in order to receive some
fruit among you as I've done among the rest of the Gentiles.
14 For I'm obligated to both Greeks and barbarians, to the
wise and foolish alike, 15 and so I'm eager to proclaim the
good news to you who live in Rome as well.

16 For I'm not ashamed of the good news — it's God's
saving power for everyone who believes, first the Jew and
then the Greek as well. 17 In this good news God reveals
His saving righteousness, from faith to faith, as it is written,
*Whoever is righteous by faith shall live.*

---

*a* *Ac 19:21.*

---

1:17      Hb 2:4.

## C. THE PROBLEM: BOTH JEW AND GENTILE ARE IN NEED OF GOD'S GRACE

### The Gentiles Have Incurred God's Just Wrath

[18] God's wrath is revealed from Heaven against all the wickedness and evil of those who suppress the truth by their evil, [19] because what can be known about God is evident to them, since God has revealed it to them. [20] From the creation of the world God's invisible attributes — His eternal power and divine nature — have been accessible to human knowledge through what can be perceived, and so they have no excuse. [21] [b] They knew God and yet they didn't honor Him as God or give Him thanks; instead, their reasoning became foolish and their senseless hearts were darkened. [22] They claimed they were wise but they became foolish, [23] exchanging the glory of the immortal God for an image in the likeness of mortal man, birds, four-footed animals, or reptiles.

[24] And so God handed them over to the impure desires in their hearts, which led them to degrade their bodies with one another. [25] They exchanged the truth of God for falsehood, they worshipped and did service to creatures instead

---

[b] *Eph 4:17–18.*

1:18   "God's wrath" refers to the Divine retribution for evil, which is consequent upon God's holiness and righteousness.

1:20   The doctrine that God can be known from His works was common in rabbinic theology. "Through what can be perceived." Lit., "through created things."

1:23   Dt 4:16–18.

of to the Creator, Who is blessed forever, amen. 26 This is why God handed them over to dishonorable passions; indeed, even their women exchanged natural relations for those which are against nature, 27 and similarly their men also forsook natural relations with women and burned with desire for one another — men committed shameful deeds with other men, and received a fitting punishment for their perversion in their own persons. 28 And since they refused to acknowledge God, God handed them over to corrupted reasoning to do things they shouldn't do. 29 They're filled with all sorts of wrongdoing, evil, greed, and malice; full of envy, murder, strife, deceit, and mean spiritedness; they gossip, 30 slander, hate God, are insolent, arrogant, and boastful; they invent evil, are disobedient to their parents, 31 are foolish, disloyal, inhuman, and merciless. 32 Although they know that God's law says those who do such things deserve death, not only do *they* do them, they approve of *others* who do them.

## The Jews Too Fall Short in God's Sight and Have No Special Status

2 1 *c* But this is why all you who pass judgment on others have no excuse! For to the extent that you pass judgment on others you condemn yourself, since you who judge do the very same things. 2 Now we know that God's judgment against those who do such things is in accordance with the

---

*c* *Mt 7:1; Lk 6:37.*

truth. ³ Do you think, then, that you — who pass judgment on those who do such things yet do the same things yourself — do you think you can escape God's judgment? ⁴ Or do you despise the richness of His kindness, forbearance, and patience, not understanding that the purpose of God's kindness is to lead you to repentance? ⁵ By your hardness and your impenitent heart you're storing up wrath for yourself on the day of wrath, when God's righteous judgment will be revealed. ⁶ He'll reward each according to their works — ⁷ those who through perseverance in good works seek glory, honor, and immortality will receive everlasting life, ⁸ whereas those who act out of selfish ambition and disobedience to the truth and who obey evil will receive wrath and anger. ⁹ There will be tribulation and anguish upon every person who does evil, Jews first and then Greeks, ¹⁰ but glory, honor, and peace for everyone who does what's good, Jews first and then Greeks. ¹¹ God doesn't play favorites — ¹² those who sin outside the Torah will also perish outside the Torah, and those who sin under the Torah will be judged by the Torah. ¹³ For those who hear the Torah aren't the ones who are righteous before God — those who observe the Torah will be vindicated. ¹⁴ When Gentiles who don't have the Torah do by nature what the Torah commands, even though they don't have the Torah they're a law

---

2:6    Ps 62:12; Pr 24:12.

2:9–15    Paul uses an allusion to Jr 31:31–33 to show that the Gentiles are also God's people. In this passage, God tells Israel that He will make a new covenant with them, since they have broken the covenant which He made with them at Sinai (as Paul has been saying). By this new covenant the Torah will be written on their hearts, and not just on stone tablets. Paul observes, in this connection, that experience with conscience shows that a "natural" version

for themselves. [15] They show that what the Torah requires is written on their hearts. Their consciences also bear witness, their conflicting thoughts accusing or even defending them [16] on the day when, according to my gospel, God judges men's secrets through Christ Jesus.

[17] But if you call yourself a Jew and rely upon the Torah and boast about God, [18] if you know God's will and can discern what's right as a result of your instruction in the Torah, [19] if you're confident that you're a guide for the blind, a light for those in darkness, [20] an instructor for the ignorant, a teacher for children, if you really believe that in the Torah you have the embodiment of knowledge and truth — [21] how can you teach others, yet fail to teach yourself? You preach against theft, but do you steal? [22] You say people shouldn't commit adultery, but do you commit adultery? You abhor idols, but do you rob temples? [23] You boast about the Torah, but do you dishonor God by violating the Torah? [24] For as it is written, *God's name is blasphemed among the Gentiles because of you.* [25] Circumcision will only benefit you if you observe the Torah, but if you violate the Torah your circumcision becomes uncircumcision. [26] So then, if a Gentile keeps the precepts of the Torah, won't his uncircumcision be regarded as circumcision? [27] Then the man who is uncircumcised in the physical sense but keeps the Torah will pass judgment on you who, in spite of the written law and circumcision, violate the Torah.

---

of the Torah is written on the hearts of the Gentiles as well. Thus, from a moral standpoint Jews and Gentiles are on the same level and are both in need of redemption.

2:24    Is 52:5.

28 For external observance isn't what makes you a Jew, nor is circumcision an external matter of the flesh. 29 Rather, the true Jew is a Jew in an internal sense, and circumcision is a matter of the heart, spiritual rather than literal; the true Jew receives his praise from God rather than from men.

## The Dilemma of God's Faithfulness and Israel's Unfaithfulness

3 1 What advantage does the Jew have, then? Is there any value in circumcision? 2 The advantage is great in every respect! First of all, the Jews were entrusted with God's messages. 3 What does it matter if some of them were unfaithful? Can their faithlessness cancel out God's faithfulness? 4 By no means! God must be faithful, even if every man were a liar, as it is written,

> *That You may be vindicated in Your words,*
> *and be victorious when You're judged.*

5 But if our wickedness highlights God's righteousness, what shall we say? Is God unjust for inflicting His wrath? (I speak in a human manner.) 6 By no means! Otherwise, how could God judge the world? 7 But if through my falsity God's truth abounds to His glory, why am I still being condemned as a sinner? 8 And why not say, as some slanderously claim that we *do* say, "Let's do evil that good may come of it!" Those who say such things are justly condemned!

---

3:4      Ps 51:4.

⁹ What then? Are we Jews better off? Not at all! for I've already argued that everyone is under the power of sin, Jew and Greek alike. ¹⁰ As it is written,

> *No one is righteous, not even one,*
> ¹¹     *no one understands, no one seeks God.*
> ¹² *All have turned away, together they've*
>           *become worthless,*
>       *no one does what's right, not even one.*
> ¹³ *Their throats are open graves.*
>       *with their tongues they deceive,*
>     *The venom of asps is under their lips,*
> ¹⁴     *their mouths are full of curses and bitterness.*
> ¹⁵ *Their feet rush quickly to shed blood,*
> ¹⁶     *in their wake is ruin and misery,*
> ¹⁷ *The way of peace they know not,*
> ¹⁸     *there is no fear of God before their eyes.*

¹⁹ Now we know that whatever the Torah says is directed to those under the Torah, so that every excuse may be cut off and the whole world may be subject to God's judgment. ²⁰ *ᵈ For no one is held to be righteous in God's sight* based upon

---

*ᵈ Gal 2:16.*

3:9ff.     Paul has already stated that God will be faithful even though Israel has been unfaithful, but the dilemma remains: since Israel is in need of reconciliation, what form will God's faithfulness, His saving righteousness, take?

3:10–12   Ps 14:1–3; 53:1–3.

3:13      Ps 5:9; 140:3.

3:14      Ps 10:7.

3:15–17   Is 59:7–8.

3:18      Ps 36:1.

3:20      Ps 143:2.

observance of the Torah, for the Torah gives only the consciousness of sin.

## D. GOD'S SOLUTION: RESTORATION TO FELLOWSHIP WITH GOD THROUGH FAITH IN CHRIST

21 But now God's saving righteousness has been revealed apart from the Torah, although the Torah and the Prophets bear witness to 22 *ᵉ* God's plan for restoring us to His fellowship through faith in Jesus Christ for *all* who believe. There can be no distinction; 23 all have sinned and therefore are deprived of God's glory. 24 They are restored to fellowship with God by His freely given grace through the redemption that comes in Christ Jesus. 25 God put him

---

*ᵉ* Gal 2:16.

---

3:21–31 Paul has shown that both Jews and Gentiles are on the same level. Now he outlines the solution to the dilemma of God's faithfulness and man's unfaithfulness: God has revealed in Jesus His intent to offer reconciliation, through faith in Jesus. Since redemption is contingent only upon faith and not upon observance of the Torah, redemption is now available to *all* who put their faith in Jesus.

3:22 The Greek verb behind the phrase "restoration to fellowship" was often used in a secular context to mean "to acquit" or "to declare innocent." However, Paul's use of the word (usually translated "justification") takes on a very specific and original sense when he uses it, as he does here, in the context of our redemption. Even God cannot declare the guilty to be innocent when they are not so in fact. What He does is even more wonderful: in spite of our guilt, a guilt we could never expiate on our own, God unilaterally offers us pardon, reconciliation, and restoration to His fellowship through the redemptive death of Jesus His Son. When we place our faith in Jesus the merits of his expiatory death are "credited to us as righteousness," and so through faith we are restored to fellowship with God.

3:25 According to Judaic sacrificial theology "the life of the flesh is in the blood... it is the blood that makes an atonement for the soul" (Lv 17:11). Thus the reference to blood is properly understood within a sacrificial context, whereby the shedding of blood brings life. Cf. also 5:8–9.

forward to serve as an expiation for sins with his blood, and that expiation is ours through faith. In this way God demonstrated His saving righteousness, by overlooking past sins ²⁶ in His divine forbearance — as a demonstration of His saving righteousness at the present time, showing that He Himself is righteous and will restore to His fellowship whoever puts his faith in Jesus.

²⁷ What basis can there be for boasting, then? All boasting is excluded. Is it excluded on the basis of works? No, boasting is excluded on the basis of faith. ²⁸ For we consider that a person is restored to fellowship with God by faith, and not by observing the Torah. ²⁹ After all, is God only the God of the Jews? Isn't He also the God of the Gentiles? Yes, of the Gentiles as well, ³⁰ ᶠ since God is one, and He'll restore both circumcised and uncircumcised to His fellowship based on their faith. ³¹ Well then, does that mean that our faith nullifies the Torah? By no means! On the contrary, the principle of faith upholds the Torah.

## The Example of Abraham's Faith

4 ¹ What, then shall we say? Has Abraham been found to be our forefather acording to the flesh? ² If Abraham was restored to fellowship with God by his own efforts he

---

ᶠ *Gal 3:20.*

---

3:31    As Paul will go on to show, the Christian upholds the Torah in a new and deeper sense: we observe the Torah "in the new way of the Spirit," rather than the old way of observing a written code (7:6). This places the Torah within the true context of God's plan for our redemption.

has something to boast about, but he has no such boast, not before God! 3 *g* For what does Scripture say? *Abraham believed God, and it was credited to him as righteousness.* 4 Now a worker's wages are credited to him not as a gift but as something that's owed to him, 5 whereas in the case of someone who doesn't work but puts his faith in the God Who pardons sinners, God accepts his faith for the purpose of restoring him to fellowship. 6 And so David speaks of how blessed the person is whom God receives into fellowship without regard to his works,

> 7 *Blessed are they whose iniquities are forgiven,*
> *whose sins are covered;*
>
> 8 *Blessed the man whose sin God does not count*
> *against him.*

9 Is this blessedness only for the circumcised, or also for the uncircumcised? We say, *Abraham's faith was credited to him as righteousness,* 10 but when was it credited to him? Before he was circumcised or after he was circumcised? It was before he was circumcised, not after. 11 He received circumcision as a sign or seal indicating that through faith he had been restored to fellowship with God while still uncircumcised. This was so he would be the father of all the uncircumcised who believe and are credited with righteousness, 12 as well as being the father of the circumcised who are not only

---

*g* Gal 3:6.

| | |
|---|---|
| 4:3 | Gn 15:6. |
| 4:7–8 | Ps 32:1–2. |
| 4:9 | Gn 15:6. |

circumcised but also follow the steps of faith that our father Abraham followed when he was still uncircumcised.

13 [h] For the promise to Abraham and his descendants that they would inherit the world was based not on Abraham's observance of the Torah but on the fact that he had been restored to fellowship with God through faith. 14 [i] If the heirs are those who observe the Torah, then faith is pointless and the promise is null and void. 15 For the Torah paves the way for God's wrath, whereas where there's no law there can be no violation of the law. 16 [j] The reason the promise was based on faith was so that it would be a free gift and would be secured for all his descendants, not just for those who observe the Torah but also for those who follow Abraham's example of faith. (Abraham is the father of all of us, 17 as it is written, *I have made you the father of many nations*.) He is our father in the sight of God, God Who gives life to the dead and calls into existence what doesn't exist. 18 Abraham believed, hoping against hope, that he would become *the father of many nations* as he had been told, *So shall your descendants be*. 19 Nor did his faith weaken when he considered his own body, which was already as good as dead since he was about a hundred years old, or when he considered Sarah's barrenness. 20 His faith in God's promise never wavered; instead, his faith grew stronger and he gave glory to God, 21 since he was fully convinced that

---

[h] *Gal 3:29.*   [i] *Gal 3:18.*   [j] *Gal 3:7.*

4:17        Gn 17:5.
4:18        Gn 15:5.
4:19        Gn 17:7.

God was able to do what He had promised. 22 That's why Abraham's faith *was credited to him as righteousness.* 23 But the words "it was credited to him" weren't written for his sake alone — 24 they were also written for our sake, and righteousness will be credited to us who have faith in the One Who raised our Lord Jesus from the dead. 25 He was handed over for our offenses and was raised to restore us to fellowship with God.

## The Extraordinary Nature and Consequences of God's Redemption

5 1 Now that we've been restored to His fellowship by faith we're at peace with God through our Lord Jesus Christ. 2 Through him we've obtained access [by faith] to God's grace in which we now stand, and we rejoice in our hope of sharing in God's glory. 3 Not only that, we even rejoice in our afflictions, since we know that affliction produces steadfastness, 4 steadfastness produces proven character, and proven character produces hope. 5 And this hope is no illusion, because God's love has been poured out in our hearts through the Holy Spirit which has been given to us. 6 For while we were still helpless Christ died for the wicked at the appointed time. 7 It's hardly likely that someone would die even for a righteous man, although someone might have the courage to die for a good man, 8 but the proof of God's love for us is that Christ died for us

---

4:22    Gn 15:6.

while we were still sinners. 9 Now that we've been restored to fellowship with God by Jesus' blood we can be far more certain that he'll also save us from God's wrath. 10 For if we were reconciled to God through the death of His Son while we were still God's enemies, now that we've been reconciled we have a much greater assurance that we'll be saved by His Son's life. 11 Not only that, we even boast of God through our Lord Jesus Christ, through whom we've now received reconciliation.

12 Therefore, just as through one man sin entered the world, and through sin, death, and in this way death spread to all men because they all sinned — 13 sin was indeed in the world before the Torah was received, although sin isn't charged against anyone in the absence of a law. 14 But death reigned from Adam until Moses even over those who hadn't sinned in the same way as Adam, who was a figure of the one who was to come.

15 But God's free gift is not at all like the offense. For while it's true that many died because of one man's offense, nevertheless God's grace and the free gift through the grace of the one man Jesus Christ have overflowed to far greater effect for the many. 16 Nor is God's free gift proportionate to the effect of that one man's sin, for the judgment that followed the single offense brought condemnation, whereas the gift that followed many offenses brought pardon. 17 It may be true that as a result of one man's offense death began its reign through that one man, yet how much greater is

---

5:9     The "far more" shows that in spite of the emphasis Paul put on restoration to fellowship the real center of his thought was the life in Christ *after* restoration.

the gift! For those who receive God's abundant grace and the free gift of righteousness shall reign in life through the one man Jesus Christ. 18 So then, just as one man's offense resulted in condemnation for all, so too one man's obedience results in pardon and life for all. 19 For just as many were made sinners as a result of one man's disobedience, so too through one man's obedience many will be made righteous. 20 The Torah came in so as to increase the offense, but where sin increased grace increased even more, 21 so that just as sin reigned in death so too would grace reign in reconciliation leading to eternal life through our Lord Jesus Christ.

## E. Objections to Paul's Gospel Answered

### Are We Now Free to Sin?

6 ¹ What shall we say, then? Should we remain in sin so grace will increase? 2 By no means! How can we who died to sin still live in it? 3 Don't you know that those of us who were baptized into Christ Jesus were baptized into his death? 4 *ᵏ* Therefore, we were buried with him through our

---

ᵏ *Col 2:12.*

---

5:19    The centrality of obedience for Paul's understanding of Christ's redemptive death flowed naturally from the Judaic concept of complete loyalty to the Torah as well as the Suffering Servant figure in Deutero–Isaiah, but it was also firmly founded in Jesus' own experience.

6:3ff.    It is believed that following baptism the new Christian received ethical instruction. Paul reminds the Romans that through baptism they are called to a new life, one which is dead to sin.

baptism into his death so that just as Christ was raised from the dead by the Father's glory we too might be able to lead a new life. 5 For if in baptism we've become sharers in a death like his, we'll also share in a resurrection like his. 6 We know that our old self was crucified with him in order to do away with the sinful self, so we'd no longer be slaves to sin, 7 for a person who has died is set free from sin. 8 But if we've died with Christ we believe that we'll also come to life with him, 9 for we know that Christ rose from the dead and will never die again — death no longer has any power over him. 10 For the death he died he died to sin once and for all, and the life he lives he lives for God. 11 Thus, you too should consider yourselves dead to sin and living for God in Christ Jesus.

12 Therefore, don't let sin reign in your mortal bodies so that you obey bodily desires. 13 Don't yield your members to sin as weapons of evil; instead, offer yourselves to God as raised from the dead and now living, and offer your members to God as weapons of righteousness. 14 For sin has no power over you, since you're under grace, not under law.

15 What shall we do then? Since we're under grace instead of under law shall we sin? By no means! 16 Don't you know that if you offer yourselves to someone as obedient

---

6:6      Lit., "our old man."

6:12     "Mortal bodies." It is important to remember that for Paul "body" could refer to more than just the physical aspects of human beings — it referred to the human person as a totality. Therefore the sins of the body included non–sensual sins such as greed and pride, although in our disordered state (the effect of sin) sins of the flesh (in the modern sense) naturally bulk large.

slaves, you're slaves of the one you obey, be it sin which leads to death or obedience which leads to righteousness? [17] But thanks be to God, for you who were once slaves to sin have become obedient from the heart to the pattern of teaching which was handed down to you — [18] you've been set free from sin and have become slaves of righteousness. [19] (I'm speaking in terms suitable to the weakness of your human nature.) For just as you once allowed your bodily members to become slaves of impurity and ever greater wickedness, so now you offer your bodily members as slaves to righteousness so that they may be sanctified. [20] When you were slaves of sin you were free of righteousness — [21] so what benefit did you derive from those things you're now ashamed of? Those things lead only to death. [22] But now that you've been freed from sin and have become slaves of God the benefit you derive is sanctification, which leads to eternal life. [23] The wages of sin is death, whereas God's free gift is eternal life in Christ Jesus our Lord.

7 [1] Don't you know, my brothers — for I'm speaking to people who understand legal matters — that law has power over you only as long as you're alive? [2] For example, a woman is by law bound to her husband while he's alive, but if he dies she's released from the law with respect to her husband. [3] So then, she'll be branded an adulteress if she marries another man while her husband is alive, but if her husband dies she's free as far as the law is concerned and she won't be an adulteress if she marries another man. [4] And so it is, my brothers — you've been put to death with respect to the Torah through Christ's body. You may now

belong to another, to him who was raised from the dead, so that we may produce fruit for God. 5 For when we were in the flesh the sinful desires stirred up by the Torah were at work in our bodily members so as to bear fruit for death. 6 Now, however, we've been freed from the Torah; we've died to what had held us fast so that we'll be able to serve in the new way of the Spirit, rather than in the old way of observing a written code.

## The Role of the Torah in God's Saving Plan

7 What shall we say, then? Is the Torah sin? By no means! But I never would have known what sin is if it hadn't been for the Torah. I never would have known what it is to covet if the Torah hadn't said, *You shall not covet!* 8 Sin took advantage of the opportunity provided by the commandment to produce all sorts of covetousness in me, for apart from law, sin is dead. 9 I once was alive apart from law, but when the commandment came sin came to life 10 and I died — it turned out that, for me, the commandment that was supposed to bring life brought death, 11 for sin took advantage of the opportunity provided by the commandment to deceive me and kill me by means of the commandment. 12 So the Torah itself is holy, and the commandment is holy, just, and good.

13 Well then, did something good cause death? By no means! It was sin that brought about my death by *using* what

---

7:7      Ex 20:17; Dt 5:21.

was good, so that the reality of sin might be revealed and so sin would, through the commandment, reach the extreme of sinfulness. ¹⁴ We know that the Torah is spiritual, but I am of the flesh, sold and subjected to sin. ¹⁵ ¹ I don't even choose my own actions, because instead of doing what I want to do I do what I hate. ¹⁶ Now if I don't want to do the very thing that I actually do, then I agree that the Torah is, in fact, good. ¹⁷ So then I'm no longer the one doing these things — it's sin dwelling within me that's to blame. ¹⁸ I know that the good doesn't dwell within me, that is, in my flesh, because although I want to do what's right I'm unable to do it, ¹⁹ for instead of doing the good that I want to do, I do the evil thing that I *don't* want to do. ²⁰ Now if I do the very thing that I don't want to do, that means it's not me doing it, it's sin dwelling within me that's doing it. ²¹ So it turns out to be a law that when I want to do what's right, evil awaits me, ²² for although I agree with God's law in my inmost self ²³ I can see that there's another law in my bodily members which wars against the law of my

---

¹ *Gal 5:17.*

---

7:14    Here Paul uses "flesh," as he often does, to refer to our lives as lived "in sinful self–reliance," oriented away from God, as if He didn't matter. Such an orientation may very well involve a type of "practical materialism" but, as we can see from Paul's inclusion of greed and pride under the heading of "sins of the flesh," Paul's anthropology had not reached the stage of an explicitly formulated body/soul distinction as it was later developed. Cf. 8:4.

7:15    "Choose." Traditionally translated "understand." As the context of this extended passage shows, what is at issue is not intellectual understanding — after all, I clearly understand that my actions are wrong and desire to follow the law — but the ability to carry out the choices I make. This meaning of the underlying Greek verb is apparent in other passages of the Bible as well.

7:23ff.    Cf. 6:12.

reason and holds me captive to the law of sin in my bodily members. 24 What a miserable state I'm in! Who can save me from this body which is leading me to death? 25 Thanks be to God through our Lord Jesus Christ! So then, I myself serve God's law with my mind, but in the flesh I serve the law of sin.

## Life in the Spirit, Life in Hope

8 1 Thus there's no condemnation now for those who are in Christ Jesus. 2 For the law of the Spirit of life in Christ Jesus has freed you from the law of sin and death. 3 What the Torah was unable to do because the flesh had weakened it, God has done — by sending His own Son in the likeness of sinful flesh and as an offering for sin, He has condemned sin in the flesh. 4 He did this so that the just requirement of the Torah would be fulfilled in us, who live according to the Spirit instead of according to the flesh. 5 The thoughts of those who live according to the flesh are in accordance with the flesh, while the thoughts of those who live according to the Spirit are in accordance with the Spirit. 6 To have a mind conformed to the flesh leads to death, but to have a mind conformed to the Spirit leads to life and peace, 7 because the flesh's way of thinking is hostile to God — it

---

8:1ff.     The dilemma that the Torah places us in — that knowledge of the law doesn't free us from sin (7:7–25) — is resolved by Christ's redemptive death, which opens for us life in the Spirit, thus freeing us from sin and death.

8:3     "In the likeness of sinful flesh," i.e., a normal human being in appearance; thus, to all appearances he would be subject to sin.

doesn't obey God's law, in fact it can't. ⁸ And so those who are in the flesh are unable to please God. ⁹ But you're not in the flesh — you're in the Spirit, since the Spirit of God dwells within you. And if anyone doesn't have Christ's Spirit, he doesn't belong to Christ. ¹⁰ But if Christ is in you, even though your body is dead because of sin, then your spirit is alive because of righteousness. ¹¹ *ᵐ* And if the Spirit of God Who raised Christ from the dead dwells within you, then the One Who raised Christ from the dead will give life to your dead bodies through His Spirit that dwells within you.

¹² So then, my brothers, we are under an obligation, but it's not to the flesh and we're not obligated to live according to the flesh; ¹³ for if you live according to the flesh you'll die, but if by the Spirit you put to death the deeds of the body you'll live. ¹⁴ For all those who are led by the Spirit of God are sons of God. ¹⁵ *ⁿ* You didn't receive a spirit of slavery which caused you to be afraid; you received a spirit of adoption, by which we cry, "Abba, Father!" ¹⁶ The Spirit itself bears witness with our spirit that we're God's children. ¹⁷ And if we're children, then we're also heirs — heirs of God, co-heirs with Christ, if we suffer with him so as to be glorified with him as well.

¹⁸ I consider that the sufferings of the present time simply don't compare with the glory to come, which will be revealed to us. ¹⁹ Creation awaits the revelation of the sons of God with eager anticipation, ²⁰ for creation was subjected to futility, not of its own will but because of the one who

---

*ᵐ 1 Cor 3:16.* *ⁿ Gal 4:5–7; Mk 14:36.*

made it subject, with the hope 21 that creation itself would be freed from its slavery to corruption and be brought to the glorious freedom of the children of God. 22 For we know that all creation has been groaning in labor pains up till the present; 23 ° moreover, we ourselves who have the Spirit as the first fruits are also groaning within ourselves as we await our adoption as sons, the redemption of our bodies. 24 For it was through this hope that we were saved, but a hope that can be seen isn't truly a hope — after all, who hopes for what they can already see? 25 But if we hope for what we do not yet see, then we wait patiently.

26 Likewise the Spirit also helps us in our weakness, for we don't know how to pray as we should; instead, the Spirit himself pleads for us with inexpressible groanings, 27 and the One Who is able to see what's in the heart knows what the Spirit wishes, because the Spirit intercedes for the saints in accordance with God's will. 28 Now we know that God works in every way for the good with those who love God and are called in accordance with His plan. 29 Those God knew beforehand He also predestined to be conformed to the image of His Son, so that he might become the firstborn of many brothers. 30 Now those He predestined, God also called, and those He called He restored to His fellowship, and all those whom He restored to fellowship He also glorified.

---

° 2 Cor 5:2–4.

8:28    Many manuscripts read: "We know that everything works for the good for those who love God."

³¹ What then shall we say in view of this? If God is for us, who can be against us? ³² If God didn't spare His own Son but instead gave him up for all of us, won't He also freely give us everything along with His Son? ³³ Who will accuse God's chosen ones? God Himself pardons them! ³⁴ Who will condemn them? Christ died and rose for us and is now at God's right hand interceding for us! ³⁵ Who will separate us from Christ's love? Affliction, distress, persecution, famine, destitution, danger, or the sword? ³⁶ As it is written,

> *For your sake we're being put to death all day long,*
> *we're regarded as sheep for the slaughter.*

³⁷ But in all these things we are winning an overwhelming victory through the One Who loved us. ³⁸ I'm convinced that neither death nor life, neither angels nor principalities, neither things present nor to come nor powers, ³⁹ neither height nor depth nor any other created being will be able to separate us from God's love in Christ Jesus our Lord.

## The Place of Jews and Gentiles in God's Plan

9 ¹ I'm speaking the truth now in Christ, I'm not lying: my conscience bears me witness in the Holy Spirit ² that I'm in great sorrow and the pain in my heart is unceasing.

---

8:36    Ps 44:22.

8:39    It is generally agreed that "height" and "depth" are astrological terms, but here they probably refer to heavenly or angelic beings.

9:1    Paul now confronts a formidable objection to his gospel: true, God's plan appears to be succeeding among the Gentiles, but isn't it failing among the Jews, most of whom

3 For I could wish that I myself were accursed and cut off from Christ for the sake of my brothers, my kinsmen according to the flesh. 4 They are Israelites, and to them belonged the adoption as sons, the glory of God's presence, the covenants, the giving of the Torah, the Temple worship, and the promises; 5 theirs were the patriarchs, and from them came the Messiah according to the flesh — may God Who is over all be blessed forever, amen!

6 But it's not as if God's word has failed. For not everyone who comes from the line of Israel truly belongs to Israel, 7 and the fact that they're descended from Abraham doesn't mean they're all his children; rather, *Through Isaac shall your descendants be named.* 8 That means that it isn't Abraham's children in the physical sense who are God's children, it's the children of the promise who are considered to be Abraham's descendants. 9 Now this is the wording of the promise: *I'll come at about this same time next year and Sarah will have a son.* 10 Moreover, Rebecca too conceived children from one

have not put their faith in Jesus? Paul goes on to explain this seeming anomaly, but his anguish at Israel's lack of faith is apparent.

9:4      "The glory of God's presence," esp. during the Exodus. "The Temple worship" refers to the splendor of Israel's liturgical services. "Of God's presence" and "Temple" are not in the original.

9:6–8      "Not everyone who comes from the line of Israel..." Membership in Israel is contingent upon the mystery of God's call and is not an entitlement based on physical descent. The "children of the promise" (v. 8) attained this status through faith (4:13). Although Paul continues to speak of God's freedom to show mercy to whomever He wishes without explaining His ways to any creature (vv. 16–24), it becomes clear by the end of Chapter 9 that the problem is not that God has rejected Israel but that Israel has lost out through lack of faith (vv. 30–33).

9:7      Gn 21:12.

9:9      Gn 18:10.

man, our father Isaac, [11] and though they still hadn't been born and hadn't done anything for good or ill, nevertheless so that God's intended selection might continue [12] based on God's call rather than on any deeds, she was told, *The older will serve the younger,* [13] as it is written,

> *Jacob I loved,*
> > *but Esau I hated.*

[14] What shall we say, then? Shall we accuse God of being unjust? By no means! [15] For God said to Moses,

> *I'll show mercy to whomever I show mercy.*
> > *and I'll be compassionate to whomever*
> > > *I'm compassionate to.*

[16] So then, the deciding factor is not a man's desire or his exertions, but God's mercy. [17] For Scripture says to Pharaoh, *For this very reason have I raised you up: to demonstrate My power through you and to proclaim My name in every land.* [18] So then, He shows mercy to whomever He wishes, and hardens whomever He wishes.

[19] You'll say to me, then, "Then why does God still blame anyone? Who can resist His will?" [20] But on the contrary, who are you, a man, to talk back to God? *The clay can't*

---

9:12     Gn 25:23.

9:13     Ml 1:2–3. Paul's point is that the true Israelite is not determined by physical descent. Esau, the elder twin brother, was not to be the father of God's people despite his physical descent. It is God's will, rather, that the true Israelite is such by faith in Jesus, the Messiah.

9:15     Ex 33:19.

9:17     Ex 9:16.

9:20     Is 29:16; 45:9.

*say to the potter,* "Why did you make me like this?" 21 Doesn't
*the potter who forms the clay* have the right to make from
the same lump of clay one vessel for special occasions and
another for everyday use? 22 Perhaps God wanted to show
His wrath and make known His might, and has been ex-
tremely patient with the objects of His wrath which are
destined to be destroyed, 23 and did this in order to make
known the wealth of His glory for the objects of His
mercy which He had previously prepared for glory. 24 It
is precisely such objects of His mercy that we are, called
from among not only Jews but also Gentiles, 25 as He also
says in Hosea,

> *Those who were not My people I will call My people,*
> *and she who was not beloved I will call beloved;*
> 26 *And in the very place where they were told,*
> *'You're not My people.'*
> *they will be called sons of the Living God.*

27 Isaiah cries out over Israel, *Even though the number of the
sons of Israel may be like the sand of the sea, only a remnant will
be saved;* 28 *for the Lord will act swiftly to carry out His sentence
upon the earth.* 29 And just as Isaiah foretold,

> *If the Lord of Hosts hadn't left us descendants,*
> *we would have become like Sodom,*
> *we would have become like Gomorrah.*

---

9:21      Jr 18:6; Ws 15:7.
9:25      Ho 2:23.
9:26      Ho 1:10.
9:27–28   Is 10:22–23.
9:29      Is 1:9.

30 What shall we say, then? That Gentiles who weren't seeking righteousness have attained righteousness, a righteousness based on faith, 31 whereas Israel, which sought a righteousness based upon law, has not been able to fulfill that law. 32 Why? Because Israel relied upon their own efforts, rather than on faith. They stumbled over the stumbling stone, 33 as it is written,

> *Behold I am laying in Zion a stumbling stone,*
> *a rock that will cause men to fall,*
> *but whoever believes in him will not be*
> *put to shame.*

10 ¹ Brothers, my heart's desire and my prayer for them to God is for their salvation. ² I'll bear them witness — they're zealous for God, but their zeal is based on a misconception, ³ for by failing to understand God's saving righteousness and trying to establish their own righteousness they haven't submitted themselves to God's saving righteousness. ⁴ For Christ brings the Torah to an end, so that everyone who has faith may be righteous.

⁵ This is what Moses wrote about the righteousness that comes from observance of the Torah: *Whoever observes it will live by it.* ⁶ But the righteousness which comes from faith

---

9:33    Is 28:16.

10:1ff.    Having explained how God's plan is being fulfilled despite Israel's lack of faith, Paul is nevertheless still in anguish over his "kinsmen." He continues to pray for Israel's salvation, even as he indicts them for their obstinacy (Chapter 10).

10:5    Lv 18:5.

10:6–8    Dt 30:12–14.

says: "*Don't say* in your heart, *Who will ascend into Heaven
(that is, to bring Christ down)?* 7 or *Who will descend into the
Abyss (that is, to bring Christ up from the dead)?*" 8 What
does it say?

> *The word is near you,*
> *in your mouth and in your heart,*

(that is, the word of faith we preach). 9 Because if you profess
with your mouth that Jesus is Lord and believe in your heart
that God raised him from the dead, you'll be saved. 10 For
with your heart you believe and are restored to fellowship
with God, and your profession through your mouth leads
you to salvation. 11 Scripture says, *No one who believes in him
will be put to shame.* 12 The same Lord is Lord of all and he
bestows riches upon everyone who calls upon him, 13 for
*whoever calls upon the Lord's name will be saved.*

14 But how can they appeal to him if they haven't put
their faith in him? And how can they put their faith in him
if they haven't heard of him? How will they hear unless
someone preaches? 15 Who will preach if no one is sent out?
As it's written, *How beautiful are the feet of those who bring good
news!* 16 But not all have responded to the good news, for as
Isaiah says, *Lord, who has believed what they've heard from us?*
17 So faith comes from what's heard, and what's heard comes

---

10:11–13  The quotations from Is 28:16 and Jl 2:32 clearly refer to God, but Paul quite
matter of factly applies them to Jesus. Many commentators see instances such as this as
highly significant in evaluating Paul's Christology.

10:15    Is 52:7.
10:16    Is 53:1.

through Christ's word. <sup>18</sup> But I ask, haven't they heard? They certainly have!

> *Their voice has gone out to every land,*
> *their words to the ends of the inhabited world.*

<sup>19</sup> But I ask, didn't Israel understand? First Moses says,

> *I'll make you jealous of those who aren't a nation,*
> *I'll make you angry with a foolish nation.*

<sup>20</sup> Then Isaiah makes bold to say,

> *I was found by those who weren't seeking Me,*
> *I showed Myself to those who didn't ask for Me.*

<sup>21</sup> But regarding Israel He says, *All day long I held out My hands to a disobedient and obstinate people.*

# 11

<sup>1 p</sup> I ask, then, has God rejected His people? By no means! After all, I too am an Israelite, a descendant of Abraham from the tribe of Benjamin. <sup>2</sup> *God has not rejected His people* whom He knew beforehand. Don't you know what Scripture says in the story of Elijah? How Elijah appeals to God against Israel: <sup>3</sup> *Lord, they've killed Your prophets, torn down Your altars, and I alone am left, and now they're*

---

<sup>p</sup> Ph 3:5.

10:18   Ps 19:4.
10:19   Dt 32:21.
10:20–21  Is 65:1–2.

11:1ff.   Paul now outlines the reasons for hoping that Israel will be saved after all. First of all, the remnant of Israel (personified in Paul himself) has not been rejected. Second, Israel's lack of faith has already contributed to God's plan, for it has been instrumental in bringing salvation to the Gentiles. Finally, God has not withdrawn His call; His offer of salvation is still open.

11:3   1 K 19:10, 14.

*trying to kill me!* 4 But what is the Divine answer to him? *I've kept seven thousand men for* Myself, *who haven't bent a knee to Baal.* 5 That's how it is at the present time as well — there's a remnant chosen by grace. 6 But if they were chosen by grace then they weren't chosen because of their works, since then grace would no longer be grace. 7 What does this mean, then? Israel failed to find what it was looking for. The chosen *did* find it, but the rest became hardened, 8 as it is written,

> God gave them a numbness of spirit,
>> eyes that are unable to see
>> and ears that are unable to hear,
> to this very day.

9 And David says,

> Let their table become a snare and a trap,
>> a stumbling block and retribution to them;
> 10 May their eyes be darkened so as not to see,
>> and their back forever bent.

11 So I ask, have they stumbled so as to be lost forever? By no means! Rather, their offense brought salvation to the Gentiles, which will cause them to become jealous. 12 Now if their offense brought riches to the world and their failure riches to the Gentiles, imagine how much more their full number will bring!

---

11:4      1 K 19:18.

11:8      Dt 29:4; Is 29:10.

11:9–10   The rabbis equated "table" with "altar," raising the possibility that Paul is applying Ps 69:22–23 to the Jewish Temple cultus.

13 Now I'm speaking to you Gentiles. As long as I'm an apostle to the Gentiles I'll go on praising my ministry 14 in the hope of somehow arousing the jealousy of my kinsmen and saving some of them. 15 For if their rejection brought reconciliation to the world, would their acceptance be anything less than life from the dead? 16 If the first fruits are holy, so is the whole lump of dough, and if the root is holy then so are the branches.

17 But if some of the branches have been broken off and you, a wild olive, have been grafted into their place to share in the rich root of the olive tree, 18 don't despise the branches. If you boast, remember that you're not supporting the root — it's the root that supports you. 19 Perhaps you'll reply, "The branches were broken off so *I* could be grafted in." 20 That's quite true. They were broken off because they didn't believe, and you are in their place because of your faith. Rather than being proud you should stand in awe, 21 for if God didn't spare the natural branches He won't spare you either. 22 Here you can see God's kindness as well as His severity. With those who have fallen He's severe, but with you God is kind as long as you remain in His kindness; otherwise you'll be cut off too. 23 But even those who fell will be grafted back in, unless they persist in their unbelief, for God has the power to graft them back in again. 24 For if you were cut off from what is by nature a wild olive tree and, contrary to nature, were grafted into a cultivated olive tree, imagine how much more readily the branches which belong to the olive tree by nature will be grafted back into their own tree.

25 I want you to understand this mystery, my brothers, so you won't become smug and consider yourselves to be wise. Israel has been partially hardened until the full number of the Gentiles enters, 26 and in this way all Israel will be saved, as it is written,

> *The Deliverer will come from Zion*
> > *and he'll banish ungodliness from Jacob,*
> 27 *This will be My covenant with them,*
> > *when I take away their sins.*

28 With respect to the good news God regards them as enemies for your sake, but with respect to the choice God made they are beloved for the sake of their forefathers, 29 for God's gift and His calling are irrevocable. 30 Just as you were once disobedient to God but have now received mercy because of *their* disobedience, 31 so too have they been disobedient because of the mercy you received so that they may also receive mercy [now]. 32 For God has consigned all to disobedience so that He may show mercy to all.

33 O the depth and richness of God's wisdom and knowledge! How unfathomable are His judgments, how inscrutable His ways!

> 34 *For who has known the mind of the Lord?*
> > *Who has been His counsellor?*
> 35 *Who has been the giver*
> > *and God the One Who returned the gift?*

---

11:26–27  Is 59:20–21 (Septuagint); Is 27:9 (Septuagint).

11:34    Is 40:13(Septuagint).

11:35    Jb 41:11.

36 *q* For all things are from Him, through Him, and in Him. To Him be glory forever, amen.

## F. PRACTICAL COUNSELS FOR THE LIFE IN CHRIST

12 ¹ So I beg you by God's mercy, my brothers, to offer your whole lives as a living sacrifice which will be holy and pleasing to God — this is your spiritual worship. ² Don't pattern yourselves after the ways of this world; transform yourselves by the renewal of your minds, so you'll be able to discern what God's will is, and what is good, pleasing, and perfect.

³ By the grace that's been given to me I say to each one of you, don't think more highly of yourselves than you ought to. Instead, aim for a sober and accurate appraisal, based on the measure of faith that God has provided to each of you. ⁴ *r* For just as we have many members in one body and all the members don't have the same functions, ⁵ in the same way we, many as we are, are one body in Christ, and each one of us is a part of the other. ⁶ *s* We all have different gifts and should use them in accordance with the grace that has been given to us — prophecy should be exercised in proportion to the faith received, ⁷ if we have

---

*q 1 Cor 8:6.   r 1 Cor 12:12.   s 1 Cor 12:4–11.*

12:1   Lit., "offer your bodies." Here again we see that "body" refers to the whole person, both mind and body, for Paul goes on in the remainder of the verse to call this offering "your spiritual worship."

the gift of serving it should be used in service, the teacher
should use his gift to teach, 8 whoever is gifted in exhorting
should encourage, whoever makes contributions should be
generous, whoever gives aid should do so eagerly, whoever
shows kindness should do so cheerfully.

9 Love should be genuine; hate what's evil, hold fast
to what's good. 10 Be devoted to one another in brotherly love, try to outdo one another in showing respect.
11 Don't hang back when zeal is called for — serve the
Lord, aglow with the Spirit. 12 Rejoice in your hope, bear
up when you're afflicted, persevere in prayer. 13 Contribute
to the needs of the saints, strive to be hospitable. 14 ' Bless
those who persecute you — bless, and don't curse them.
15 Rejoice with those who rejoice, weep with those who
weep. 16 Have an equal regard for one another; associate
with the lowly and don't be proud. Don't have an exaggerated opinion of your own wisdom. 17 " Don't pay back
evil with evil, *set your sights on what all consider to be honorable.*
18 If possible live in peace with everyone to the extent that
you're able to. 19 Don't take revenge, my beloved — leave
that to God's wrath, for it is written, *Vengeance is Mine, I
shall repay,* says the Lord. 20 Instead, *if your enemy is hungry,
feed him, if he's thirsty, give him to drink, for by doing this you'll
be heaping burning coals on his head.* 21 Don't let evil defeat
you; instead, overcome evil with good.

---

' *Mt 5:44; Lk 6:28.*   " *Mt 5:39.*

   12:17    Pr 3:4.
   12:19    Dt 32:35.
   12:20    Pr 25:21–22 (Septuagint).

13 ¹ Every person should be subject to the governing authorities. For all authority comes from God and the existing authorities have been appointed by God. ² Therefore, whoever resists authority resists God's order, and those who resist will bring judgment upon themselves. ³ For only wicked conduct need fear the rulers, not good conduct. Do you want to be free from fear of whoever is in authority? Then do what's good and you'll be praised by him, ⁴ because he's God's servant for your good. But if you do what's evil you should fear, for not without reason does the one in authority wield the sword. For he's God's servant, the avenger who brings wrath to the evildoer. ⁵ Therefore it's necessary to submit not only because of God's wrath but also for the sake of conscience. ⁶ ᵛ This is why you pay taxes, for the authorities are God's servants, busily engaged at this very thing. ⁷ Pay everyone what you owe — taxes to the tax collectors, customs duties to the customs officials; respect those to whom it's due, honor those to whom honor is due.

⁸ ʷ See that you owe nothing, except for your obligation to love one another, for whoever loves his neighbor has fulfilled the Torah. ⁹ For *You shall not commit adultery, you shall not murder, you shall not steal, you shall not covet* and any other commandments can be summed up in one sentence

---

ᵛ *Mt 22:21; Mk 12:17; Lk 20:25.*   ʷ *Mt 22:34–40; Mk 12:28–34; Lk 10:25–28.*

13:1–5   Paul only counsels obedience to the state in its proper sphere — maintaining order and suppressing crime. He does not suggest that the state has unlimited authority.

13:9      Ex 20:13–15; Dt 5:17–19.

— *You shall love your neighbor as yourself.* 10 Love does no harm to a neighbor, so love is the fullness of the Torah.

11 Do this, because you know what time it is, you know it's already time for you to rise from your sleep, for now your salvation is nearer than when you first believed. 12 The night is almost over, and the day is near. Be done with the deeds of darkness and clothe yourselves with the weapons of light. 13 Let us conduct ourselves decently as we would during the day, not in carousing and drunkenness, not in promiscuity and indecent behavior, not in strife and envy. 14 Instead, clothe yourselves with the Lord Jesus Christ and give no thought to doing what the flesh desires.

14 1 x Welcome the person whose faith is weak, and don't enter into quarrels over your differing opinions. 2 One person may believe it's permissible to eat everything, while another whose faith is weak will eat only vegetables. 3 The person who eats everything shouldn't despise the one who doesn't, and the person who doesn't eat everything shouldn't condemn the one who does, for God has accepted him. 4 Who are you to judge someone else's servant? He stands or falls before his own masters, and he will stand, because the Lord is able to make him stand. 5 One person considers a certain day to be more important than another, while another considers every day to be the same. Let everyone make up their own minds. 6 The person who observes a certain day as special is thinking of the Lord, and the person who eats everything eats with the Lord in

---

x  *Col 2:16.*

mind, because he gives thanks to God for this; and whoever doesn't eat does so for the Lord and also gives thanks to God. [7] We none of us live for ourselves and we none of us die for ourselves, [8] for if we live we live for the Lord and if we die we die for the Lord. And so whether we live or whether we die we belong to the Lord. [9] This is why Christ died and came to life — so he'd be Lord of both the dead and the living. [10] [y] Why do you condemn your brother? Why do you despise your brother? After all, we'll all stand before God's judgment seat, [11] for it is written,

> *As I live, says the Lord, every knee shall bend to me,*
> *and every tongue shall give praise to God.*

[12] So then each of us will render an account of ourselves to God.

[13] Therefore, let's not condemn each other any longer; instead, resolve that you'll do nothing that would cause a brother to stumble or fall. [14] I know and am certain in the Lord Jesus that nothing is in itself unclean, but if someone thinks that it is unclean then it's unclean for him. [15] If your brother is distressed by what you eat then your conduct is no longer based on love. Don't allow what you eat to cause the downfall of someone for whom Christ died. [16] So don't let our good be blasphemed. [17] After all, the Kingdom of God doesn't consist of eating and drinking — it consists of righteousness, peace, and joy in the Holy Spirit. [18] Whoever serves God in this way will be acceptable to

---

[y] *2 Cor 5:10; Mt 15:11; Mk 7:15.*

14:11   Is 42:53 (Septuagint).

God and respected by men. ¹⁹ So then let's strive for what leads to peace and edification for one another; ²⁰ don't destroy God's work for the sake of food. All foods are indeed clean, but it's evil if the person eating it considers it to be an offense. ²¹ It's good to avoid eating meat, drinking wine, or doing anything else that would cause your brother to stumble. ²² Keep what you believe in this matter between yourself and God. Blessed is he who can make his decision with a clear conscience. ²³ But the person who is uncertain is condemned if he eats, because his decision isn't based on faith. Whatever doesn't come from faith is sin.

**15** ¹ We who are strong ought to bear with the failings of the weak and should not seek to please ourselves. ² Each of us should try to please our neighbor for their own good and for their edification. ³ Christ didn't try to please himself; instead, as it is written, *The reproaches of those who reproached You fell upon me.* ⁴ For whatever was written in the past was written for our instruction, so that by our steadfastness and the encouragement of the Scriptures we might have hope. ⁵ May God, the source of steadfastness and encouragement, grant that you may live in harmony with one another in accordance with Christ Jesus, ⁶ so that with one mind and one mouth you may glorify the God and Father of our Lord Jesus Christ.

⁷ Therefore, accept one another as Christ has accepted you, for the glory of God. ⁸ For I tell you that Christ became a servant for the circumcised in order to show that

---

15:3    Ps 69:9.

God is truthful and to confirm the promises He made to the patriarchs, 9 and so that the Gentiles might glorify God for His mercy, as it is written,

> *Therefore I'll praise you among the Gentiles,*
>   *Your name will I praise.*

10 And again it says,

> *Rejoice with His people, you Gentiles!*

11 And again,

> *Praise the Lord, all you Gentiles,*
>   *let all the peoples praise Him.*

12 And again Isaiah says,

> *The root of Jesse shall come,*
>   *who will rise to rule the Gentiles,*
>   *and the Gentiles will hope in him.*

13 May God, the source of hope, fill you with all joy and peace through your belief in Him, so that you'll overflow with hope by the power of the Holy Spirit.

## G. Paul Appeals for the Romans' Aid in His Plans for Future Evangelization

14 My brothers, I myself am fully satisfied that you yourselves are full of goodness, filled with every sort of knowledge, and able to instruct one another. 15 Still, on

---

15:9   2 S 22:50; Ps 18:99.
15:10   Dt 32:43.
15:11   Ps 117:1.
15:12   Is 11:10.

some points I've written to you rather boldly as a reminder, because God has given me the grace [16] to be a minister of Christ Jesus to the Gentiles and to perform a priestly service for God's good news, so that the offering of the Gentiles may be acceptable to God and sanctified by the Holy Spirit. [17] Therefore it is in Christ Jesus that I have reason to boast of my work for God, [18] for I don't dare speak of anything except what Christ has done through me to win the obedience of the Gentiles by word and deed, [19] by the power of signs and wonders, and by the power of the Holy Spirit. As a result, all the way around from Jerusalem to Illyricum I've completed the proclamation of God's good news. [20] And so my ambition is to proclaim the good news where Christ's name has never been heard so that I won't be building on someone else's foundations, [21] but as it is written,

> *Those who were never told of Him shall see,*
> *and those who haven't heard will understand.*

[22] This is why I've been prevented from coming to you so many times, [23] but now since I no longer have any opportunities in these regions and since for many years I've had a great desire to come to see you, [24] while I'm on my way to Spain I hope to pass through and see you and be helped on my way by you, after I've enjoyed being with you for a while. [25] [z] Right now, however, I'm on my way to Jerusalem

---

[z]  *1 Cor 16:1–4.*

15:16    Paul portrays himself as a priest, and the Gentiles as the offering being presented to God.

15:21    Is 52:15

to help the saints, 26 for Macedonia and Achaia have been pleased to make a contribution to the poor among the saints in Jerusalem. 27 *a* They were pleased to do it, and in fact they're indebted to the saints, for if the Gentiles have come to share in their spiritual blessings they have an obligation to help the saints with their material blessings. 28 So when I've finished this and have safely turned this sum over to them, I'll go to Spain by way of you, 29 and I know that when I come to you I'll come in the fullness of Christ's blessing.

30 I beg you, my brothers, by our Lord Jesus Christ and the love of the Spirit, to join me in my struggle by praying to God for me 31 that I may be delivered from the unbelievers in Judea and that my service in Jerusalem may be acceptable to the saints 32 so that, God willing, I'll come to you full of joy and will find rest with you. 33 May God Who gives peace be with you all, amen.

## H. COMMENDATION OF PHOEBE AND CLOSING GREETINGS

**16** 1 I commend to you our sister, Phoebe, who is a minister in the church at Cenchreae. 2 Receive her in the Lord in a manner worthy of the saints and help her with anything she may need from you, for she has been a benefactor to many people, including myself.

3 Greet Prisca and Aquila, my co-workers in Christ Jesus. 4 They risked their own necks to save my life, and

---

*a* 1 Cor 9:11.

not only I but also the Gentile churches thank them.
5 Also greet the church at their house. Greet my beloved
Epaenetus who is the first fruits of Asia for Christ. 6 Greet
Mary, who has worked so hard for you. 7 Greet Androni-
cus and Junias, my kinsmen and fellow prisoners; they are
prominent among the apostles and were in Christ before
me. 8 Greet Ampliatus, my beloved in the Lord. 9 Greet
Urbanus, our co-worker in Christ, and my beloved Stachys.
10 Greet Apelles, who is tried and true in the Lord. Greet
those who belong to Aristobulus' family. 11 Greet my kins-
man Herodion. Greet those in Narcissus' family who are
in the Lord. 12 Greet Tryphaena and Tryphosa, laborers
in the Lord. Greet the beloved Persis, who has worked so
hard in the Lord. 13 *b* Greet Rufus, chosen in the Lord, and
his mother, who is also *my* mother. 14 Greet Asyncritus,
Phlegon, Hermes, Patrobas, Hermas, and the brothers who
are with them. 15 Greet Philologus, Julia, Nereus, and his
sister, as well as Olympas and all the saints who are with
them. 16 Greet one another with a holy kiss. All Christ's
churches greet you.

17 My brothers, I urge you to watch out for those who
cause dissension and raise obstacles which are contrary to
what you were taught. Shun them, 18 for such persons are
serving their own appetites instead of our Lord Christ, and
by smooth speech and flattery they deceive the unsuspect-
ing. 19 Word of your obedience has reached everyone and
so I rejoice for you, but I want you to be wise regarding

---

*b* Mk 15:21.

what's good and innocent regarding what's evil. 20 Then God Who gives peace will quickly smash Satan beneath your feet. The grace of our Lord Jesus be with you.

21 *c* My co-worker Timothy greets you, as do Lucius, Jason and Sosipater, my kinsmen. 22 Tertius, the writer of this letter, greets you in the Lord. 23 *d* My host Gaius greets you, along with the whole church at his house. Erastus, the city treasurer, greets you, as does our brother Quartus. [24]

# I. PRAISE OF GOD'S GLORY

25 To Him Who is able to strengthen you according to my gospel and the proclamation of Jesus Christ, according to the revelation of the mystery which was kept secret for long ages 26 but is now revealed through the writing of the Prophets and made known by order of the eternal God to bring the obedience of faith to all nations — 27 to the God Who alone is wise be glory forever through Jesus Christ, amen.

---

*c Ac 16:1. d Ac 19:29; 1 Cor 1:14; 2 Tm 4:20.*

16:24    Some textual witnesses insert the following verse: "The grace of our Lord Jesus Christ be with you all. Amen."

16:25–27    While the best manuscript tradition places this concluding doxology here, some manuscripts place it at the end of Ch. 14 or 15. A few manuscripts omit it entirely.

# THE FIRST LETTER TO THE

# CORINTHIANS

After leaving Thessalonica Paul traveled south through Greece, eventually winding up in Corinth. In that bustling commercial center and seaport he found fertile ground for the good news, and the church that he established there was as alive as the city itself. As reported in Acts (the portions relevant to the Corinthian correspondence are 18:1–18, 24–28), Paul followed his usual procedure of first preaching in the local synagogue and then turning to the Gentiles after encountering resistance among the Jews. The letter itself confirms that the majority of Corinthian converts must certainly have been Gentiles.

After leaving Corinth and returning to Antioch, Paul set out once again. This time he spent about three years in the Ephesus area, and it was toward the end of his stay in Ephesus that he wrote the present letter, in A.D. 55 or 56. Apparently he wrote it partially in response to a letter the Corinthians had sent him requesting guidance and partially as a result of information he had received from members of "Chloe's household." This information had been very troubling, for it painted a picture of a church torn by internal divisions, at odds over basic principles governing behavior at the liturgy, and confused about everyday ethical questions.

The resulting correspondence is fascinating both for the detailed information it gives concerning the inner life of one of the earliest Christian communities as well as for what it tells about Paul himself. While lacking the sustained power of Romans, perhaps, 1 Corinthians covers a wide range of issues of continuing importance — liturgical, ethical, spiritual, and doctrinal.

## OUTLINE OF THE FIRST LETTER TO THE CORINTHIANS

| | | |
|---|---|---|
| A. | 1:1–3 | Greeting |
| B. | 1:4–9 | Thanksgiving |
| C. | 1:10–6:20 | Paul Addresses Problems within the Corinthian Church |
| | 1:10–3:23 | Divisions and Factions |
| | 4:1–21 | A Reminder of Paul's Authority |
| | 5:1–6:20 | Dealing with Immorality in the Community |
| D. | 7:1–11 | Paul Answers the Corinthians' Questions |
| | 7:1–40 | Regarding Marriage |
| | 8:1–13 | Regarding the Eating of Food That Had Been Previously Offered to Idols |

9:1–27         Paul's Defense of His Ministry as an Apostle

10:1–11:1      A General Moral Exhortation

E.   11:2–14:40   Paul Addresses Certain Problems Which Have Arisen in the Liturgical Gatherings

11:2–16        Women's Headdress

11:17–34       Their Manner of Celebrating the Lord's Supper

12:1–14:40     Regarding the Purpose and Relative Importance of Spiritual Gifts

F.   15:1–58      Doctrinal Teaching: The Resurrection of the Dead

G.   16:1–18      Paul's Plans and Other Practical Considerations

H.   16:19–24     Farewell

## A. Greeting

**1** [1] Paul, called by the will of God to be an apostle of Christ Jesus, and our brother Sosthenes, [2] to the church of God in Corinth, to those who have been sanctified in Christ Jesus, who are called to be saints, with all those people everywhere who call upon the name of our Lord Jesus Christ — their Lord and ours — [3] may the grace and peace of God our Father and the Lord Jesus Christ be with you.

## B. Thanksgiving

[4] I constantly give thanks to God for you because of the grace God has given you in Christ Jesus. [5] In him you have been enriched in every way, in speech and in knowledge, [6] for our testimony about Christ has become established in you to such an extent [7] that there's no grace you lack, as you await the revelation of our Lord Jesus Christ [8] who will sustain you until the end, so that you'll be blameless on the day of our Lord Jesus Christ. [9] God is faithful, and it was God Who called you to the fellowship of His Son, our Lord Jesus Christ.

# C. Paul Addresses Problems
# Within the Corinthian Church

## Divisions and Factions

10 I beg you, brothers, in the name of our Lord Jesus Christ, to all speak as one. Let there be no divisions among you — be united in thought and purpose. 11 For some members of Chloe's household have informed me, brothers, that there's quarreling among you. 12 *a* Here's what I mean: each of you says, "I follow Paul," "I follow Apollos," "I follow Kephas," or "I follow Christ." 13 Can Christ be divided? Was Paul crucified for you, or were you baptized in Paul's name? 14 *b* I thank God that I baptized none of you except Crispus and Gaius, 15 so no one can say they were baptized in my name. 16 I baptized Stephanas' household, too; other than that I know of no one else I baptized. 17 Christ didn't send me to baptize, he

---

*a* Ac 18:24–28.   *b* Ac 18:8; 19:29; Rm 16:23.

---

1:12    "Kephas." This is the Aramaic for "Peter." It is known from tradition that Peter traveled widely and so it is entirely possible that he may have stayed for a time in Corinth. On the other hand, a faction among the Corinthians may have used Peter's name simply because of his prominence. This possibility is illustrated in Galatians, where Paul refers to Peter as a person well known to the Galatians, but only by name and reputation as far as we can tell — there is nothing in the letter to suggest that Peter had ever visited the Galatians.

1:17    The word "wisdom" had both positive and negative connotations in Judaism, but Paul is using it here in its negative sense. As the letter progresses it becomes clear that some of the Corinthians had developed an inordinate pride in their speaking and reasoning ability. Paul recalls them to that humility which is inseparable from the true spirit of Christ and is itself "wisdom." The Corinthians had forgotten that their call was based on God's freely

sent me to proclaim the good news, but not with words of "wisdom," lest Christ's cross be deprived of its power.

¹⁸ For the message of the cross is foolishness to those who are on their way to destruction, but for those who are being saved — for us — it's the power of God. ¹⁹ For it's written,

> I'll destroy the wisdom of the wise,
> and the insights of the intelligent I'll reject.

²⁰ Where is the wise man? Where is the scribe? Where is the skilled debater of this age? Hasn't God turned the wisdom of this world to foolishness? ²¹ For since, in God's wisdom, the world was unable to come to knowledge of God with its own wisdom, God chose through the foolishness of our proclamation to save those who believe. ²² Jews ask for signs and Greeks look for wisdom, ²³ but we proclaim Christ crucified — a stumbling block for Jews and foolishness to Greeks, ²⁴ but for those who have been chosen, both Jew and Greek alike, Christ the power of God and the wisdom of God, ²⁵ for God's foolishness is wiser than human wisdom, and God's weakness is stronger than human strength.

²⁶ For consider the fact that *you* were called. Not many of you were wise according to the flesh, nor powerful or well-born, ²⁷ but God chose the foolish things of the world to shame those who are wise, the weak of the world to

---

given grace which flew in the face of human "wisdom" and their own unworthiness. Paul constantly returns to this ironic contrast between the true wisdom which is regarded as foolishness and the foolishness which is acclaimed as wisdom.

1:19     Is 29:14 (Septuagint).

1:24, 30  Cf. 10:4 for a discussion of Jesus as the Wisdom of God.

shame the strong; 28 God chose the base-born and con-
temptible of the world, things that are nothing, to shame
what *is*, 29 so that the flesh would have nothing to boast of
before God. 30 Through God you are in Christ Jesus, and
through God Christ became our wisdom, righteousness,
sanctification, and redemption, 31 so that as it is written,
*Whoever boasts, let him boast in the Lord.*

2 1 When I came to you, brothers, I didn't proclaim the mystery of God to you in high-sounding
language or with a display of wisdom. 2 I had made up my
mind to know nothing while I was among you except Jesus
Christ, and the fact that he was crucified. 3 I came to you
in weakness, fear, and trembling, 4 and my message and
proclamation were delivered not with plausible words of
"wisdom" but with a demonstration of the Spirit and of
power, 5 so that your faith would be based on the power
of God rather than on human wisdom.

6 Yet among the mature we do preach wisdom, but
a wisdom which is not of this age nor of the rulers of this
age, who are losing their power. 7 Instead we preach *God's*

---

1:31    Jr 9:24.

2:1    The "mystery of God" which Paul proclaimed was God's saving righteousness, His plan for bringing salvation to both Jews and Gentiles. Some manuscripts read
"testimony" for "mystery."

2:6–3:3  Paul introduces a fundamental distinction. The Christian is called to live according to God's Spirit, which has been given to us so we can understand God's will for
us. To live in the Spirit is to be oriented toward God. In their petty, prideful factionalism,
however, the Corinthians have shown themselves to be still of the "flesh," understood not
as matter but as a basic orientation which relies upon human abilities ("wisdom") and
ignores God, which is to say, True Wisdom. Thus, those who are "of the flesh" are spiritually blind, unable to discern wisely.

wisdom, a wisdom which is secret and hidden and which God ordained before the ages for our glory. 8 None of the rulers of this age understood this, for if they *had* they never would have crucified the Lord of glory. 9 But as it is written,

> *What eye has not seen nor ear heard,*
>> what human heart has not conceived,
> What God has prepared for those who love Him,

10 this God has revealed to us through His Spirit, for the Spirit is able to search out everything, even the depths of God's intentions. 11 For who can know what someone else intends? Surely only that person's own spirit knows! So, too, no one knows what God intends except the Spirit of God. 12 But the Spirit we have received is not the spirit of this world but the Spirit that comes from God and enables us to know what it is that God has freely bestowed upon us. 13 And we proclaim this in words taught by the Spirit rather than by human wisdom, words which explain spiritual matters to those who have the Spirit. 14 The unspiritual man is unable to accept what comes from the Spirit of God, since for him it's foolishness. He's unable to understand such matters because they can be evaluated only spiritually. 15 The spiritual man, on the other hand, *is* able to evaluate all such matters and is subject to no one else's judgment.

---

2:8    The "rulers of this age" are almost certainly to be understood as angelic powers, here seen as hostile to God's saving plan. By leading their subjects, the human race, to crucify the Lord they unwittingly brought God's plan to fruition and showed their inability to fathom God's wisdom. In turn, God's plan will bring about their downfall and break their power over the human race. Cf. also below at 6:3.

2:9    Is 64:4; 52:15.

16  *For who knows the mind of God,*
         *who can advise Him?*

But we have the mind of Christ.

**3** ¹ I wasn't able to speak to you, brothers, as I would to the spiritually mature. Instead, I spoke to you as to children of this world, infants in Christ. ² ᶜ I gave you milk to drink, because you were not yet able to eat solid food. The fact is, you're still not able to eat solid food, ³ you still belong to this world. For when there's jealousy and strife among you, don't you show that you belong to this world? Aren't you behaving in accordance with human standards? ⁴ When someone says, "I'm a follower of Paul," while someone else says, "I follow Apollos," aren't you showing yourselves to be mere men? ⁵ After all, what is Apollos? What is Paul? We're only the ministers through whom you came to believe — we each simply performed the task assigned to us by the Lord. ⁶ I planted, Apollos watered, but it was God Who caused the growth. ⁷ Thus, neither the one who planted nor the one who watered amounts to anything — only God Who caused the growth is of importance. ⁸ The one who plants and the one who waters are both equal, and each will receive a reward corresponding to their labor. ⁹ We are God's co-workers. You are God's field, you are God's building.

¹⁰ In accordance with the grace God has given me I laid the foundation the way a wise master builder would, while another is building upon those foundations. But each

---

ᶜ *Heb 5:12–13.*

2:16    Is 40:13 (Septuagint).

builder must take care how he proceeds. 11 No one can lay any other foundation than the one which was laid, which is Jesus Christ. 12 You can build on the foundation with gold, silver, precious stones, wood, hay, or straw, 13 but the nature of each person's work will be made known, for it will be revealed on the day of the Lord. It will be revealed with fire, for the fire will show what sort of work each has done. 14 If anyone's work lasts, he'll receive a reward; 15 if anyone's work is burned up, he'll be punished — he himself will be saved, but it will be through fire. 16 *d* Don't you know that you're the Temple of God, and that the Spirit of God dwells within you? 17 If anyone destroys God's Temple, God will destroy him, for God's Temple is holy, and you are that Temple!

18 Don't deceive yourselves! If any of you think you're wise in this age, become foolish, so you'll be *truly* wise. 19 The wisdom of this world is foolishness to God, for it is written,

> *He catches the wise in their cunning,*

20 and again,

---

*d* 2 Cor 6:16.

3:13–15 "The day of the Lord" will introduce the final judgment. "Fire" is seen not only as a means of punishment and destruction but also as having power to cleanse the sinner. Here too we see Paul's fundamental optimism — he almost always speaks of saving the sinner rather than of punishing the sinner in a vindictive spirit.

3:16    Paul normally uses the image of the Church as the Temple only when referring to his ministry. His preferred image for the Church is the Body of Christ.

3:19    Jb 5:13.

3:20    Ps 94:11.

> *The Lord knows the thoughts of the wise,*
>   *He knows that they're futile.*

21 So no one should put their pride in mere men — everything is yours. 22 Paul, Apollos, Kephas, the world, life, death, the present, the future — it's all yours, 23 but you belong to Christ, and Christ belongs to God.


## A Reminder of Paul's Authority

4 1 This is how you should regard us — as Christ's servants and stewards of God's mysteries. 2 Naturally, stewards must be examined and be shown to have been faithful. 3 For me it's of no importance if I'm judged by you or by some human tribunal — I don't even judge myself. 4 I'm not aware of anything against me, but that doesn't mean I'm acquitted, because the Lord is the one who will judge me. 5 So don't pass judgment before the proper time, before the Lord comes and brings to light what's hidden in darkness and reveals the motives of our hearts. Then God will commend each of us.

6 I've applied all this to myself and Apollos for your sake, brothers, so that through us you'll learn what "Don't go beyond what's written" means, and won't arrogantly despise one person in favor of another. 7 For who says you're so important? What do you have that you didn't receive? And if you received it, why do you boast as if it were your own? 8 Already you've become self-satisfied, already you think you're rich! You've become kings and

left us behind! I wish you *had* become kings, so we could reign with you! 9 For it seems to me that God has made us apostles the lowliest of all, as if we were condemned to death, because we've become a spectacle to the world, both to angels and to men. 10 We are fools for Christ, while you are wise in Christ; we are weak, but you are strong; you are honored, while we are despised. 11 Right up to the present moment we suffer hunger and thirst, we're poorly clothed and roughly treated, we wander about without a home. 12 ⸲ We labor and work with our own hands. When we're cursed we give blessings in return, when we're persecuted we endure it, 13 when we're reviled we respond cheerfully; we've become the world's garbage heap, the scum of the earth right up to the present.

14 I'm not writing this to shame you, but to admonish you as my beloved children. 15 For though you may have innumerable guides in Christ, you don't have numerous fathers — *I* was the one who begot you in Christ Jesus through the good news. 16 So I urge you to become imitators of me. 17 That's why I sent Timothy to you — he's my beloved and faithful child in the Lord and will remind you of the way I walk in Christ, which is what I teach everywhere, in every church. 18 Some of you have become arrogant, as if I weren't coming to you, 19 but I'll come to you quickly if the Lord is willing and I'll find out what sort of power these arrogant people have, not just how well they speak. 20 For the Kingdom of God is not a matter of words

---

⸲ Ac 18:3.

but of power! 21 What do you want? Should I come to you
with the rod, or in a spirit of love and gentleness?

## Dealing with Immorality in the Community

5 1 It's actually reported that there is fornication among
you, fornication of a kind that's unheard of even among
the Gentiles — a man is living with his father's wife! 2 But
you're puffed up with pride! Shouldn't you be grieving, instead? The perpetrator of this deed should be removed from
among you! 3 For though I'm absent in body I'm present
in spirit, and I've already passed judgment on the man who
did this as if I *were* present, 4 in the name of the Lord Jesus.
When you've assembled and my spirit is present with the
power of our Lord Jesus, 5 you are to hand that man over
to Satan for the destruction of the flesh, so his spirit may be
saved on the day of the Lord. 6 *f* You have nothing to boast
about! Don't you know that "A little yeast leavens all the
dough"? 7 Get rid of the old yeast so you'll be a new batch

---

*f* *Gal 5:9.*

5:1      Dt 22:30. In rabbinical theology "fornication" was often used in a technical
sense to refer to unlawful marriages within forbidden degrees of consanguinity.

5:2      "Puffed up with pride." Perhaps the Corinthians felt they were exhibiting
true Christian freedom.

5:6–8    Paul here presents in a very compact form his vision of the Christian life as
a prolonged celebration of the Passover festival. Christ, the new Paschal Lamb, has been
sacrificed; the Church, the new Israel, is embarked upon a New Exodus from slavery to
sin and spiritual death to freedom and life; like the Old Israel, Christians must discard the
old leavening of wickedness and celebrate the New Passover with the unleavened bread
of moral renewal. This Passover/Exodus imagery will reappear twice again in the letter.

5:7      Ex 12:15.

of dough, as indeed you *are* unleavened. Christ our Paschal Lamb has been sacrificed, 8 so let's celebrate the feast not with the old yeast, the yeast of wickedness and evil, but with the unleavened bread of sincerity and truth.

9 In the letter I wrote to you I warned you not to associate with the immoral, 10 not meaning, of course, the immoral of this world — the greedy, thieves, idolaters — because then you'd have to leave this world! 11 What I meant was that, if someone who bears the name "brother" is immoral, greedy, idolatrous, abusive, a drunkard, or a robber, don't associate with them, don't even *eat* with them. 12 What business is it of mine to judge outsiders? Isn't it those within the church whom you're to judge? 13 *God* will judge outsiders. *Remove the evil person from among you!*

6 1 Do any of you dare bring your disputes with one another before the unrighteous for a decision, instead of bringing the matter before the saints? 2 Don't you know that the saints will judge the world? And if you're the ones who will judge the world, are you incapable of judging minor matters? 3 Don't you know that we'll be passing judgment on angels? And here we're speaking of everyday affairs! 4 So then, if you have ordinary lawsuits of this sort, why bring them before those who have no standing in the church? 5 I say this to shame you. Isn't there even one person among you wise enough to settle disputes between brothers? 6 But instead brothers sue brothers, and before unbelievers!

---

5:13    Dt 17:7 (Septuagint).

6:2–3    In Jewish mythology of that time each nation was thought to have a ruling angel. Paul says that Christians will judge those angels.

⁷ Actually, having lawsuits against one another is already a defeat for you; wouldn't it be better to submit to the injustice? Wouldn't it be better to let yourselves be cheated? ⁸ Instead, you're the ones who wrong and cheat others, even brothers! ⁹ Don't you know that the unjust will not inherit the Kingdom of God? Make no mistake, neither fornicators, nor idolaters, nor adulterers, nor perverts, nor sodomites, ¹⁰ nor thieves, nor the greedy, nor drunkards, nor those who slander others, nor robbers will inherit the Kingdom of God. ¹¹ And that's what some of you were. But you were washed clean, you were sanctified, you were admitted to fellowship with God in the name of the Lord Jesus Christ and by the Spirit of our God.

¹² "Everything is permissible for me," but not everything is beneficial. "Everything is permissible for me," but I won't be enslaved by anything. ¹³ "Food is for the stomach, and the stomach is for food," but God will do away with both. The body, on the other hand, is not for fornication — it's for the Lord, and the Lord is for the body. ¹⁴ Now God raised the Lord, and He'll raise us, too, through His power. ¹⁵ Don't you know that your bodies are parts of Christ's

---

6:9        Perverts. The Greek word, literally, means "soft." Paul is referring to effeminate homosexuals, who were despised in Greek society. "Sodomites" refers to "masculine" homosexuals. Paul may have felt it was necessary to be this specific in writing to his Gentile converts. Paul's Jewish converts would not have needed such a graphic explanation.

6:12–20  Paul returns here to the topic of sexual immorality. Apparently some in the community were prepared to extend their freedom in dietary matters to sexual ethics as well, as if it were simply a matter of satisfying a bodily appetite such as hunger. Paul's reply rejects any division of man into distinct spheres of body and spirit, and so too the corollary that sins of the flesh don't affect the spirit. Paul's argument is essentially a *reductio ad absurdum* which presupposes that spirit and flesh are parts of a complexly interdependent unity.

body? Shall I take parts of Christ's body, then, and make them part of a prostitute's body? God forbid! 16 Don't you know that whoever joins himself with a prostitute becomes one body with her? For Scripture says, *The two shall become one flesh.* 17 But whoever joins himself to the Lord becomes one spirit with him. 18 Flee fornication! Every other sin you commit remains outside your body, but whoever is guilty of fornication sins against his own body. 19 *g* Or don't you know that your bodies are Temples of the Holy Spirit within you, Who comes to you from God, and that you don't belong to yourselves? 20 You were bought for a price, so glorify God in your bodies!

## D. Paul Answers the Corinthians' Questions Regarding Marriage

7 ¹ Regarding the things you wrote about — it's good for a man not to touch a woman, 2 but to prevent immorality every man should have his own wife, and every woman her own husband. 3 The man should fulfill his duties to his wife, and likewise the woman for her husband.

---

*g* 2 Cor 6:16.

---

6:16.     Gn 2:24.

7:1ff.     At the same time that some members of the Corinthian church were indulging in gross immorality and advocating libertinism, others were urging an exaggerated asceticism, especially in the context of marriage. Paul opposes both extremes and exhibits his usual firm common sense. Although an expectation that the "end" is near provides the background for his remarks, he once again transcends this hope and enunciates principles which are essentially timeless.

⁴The woman has no authority over her body — her husband does. Likewise, however, the man has no authority over *his* body — his wife does. ⁵ Don't deny one another, except perhaps for a short time by mutual agreement in order to devote yourselves to prayer, and then come together again lest Satan use your lack of self-control to tempt you. ⁶ But I say this as a concession; it's not a command. ⁷ I wish everyone were like myself, but all have their own gift from God, one of one sort, another of a different kind.

⁸ To those who are unmarried and to widows I say, it's good for them to remain as I do. ⁹ But if they're unable to exercise self-control they should marry, for it's better to marry than to burn. ¹⁰ ʰ Those who are married, I command you — not I, but the Lord — a wife shall not separate from her husband, ¹¹ but if she does separate, she must either remain unmarried or be reconciled with her husband, nor should a husband leave his wife. ¹² As for the rest, *I* say — not the Lord — if any brother has a non-believing wife who agrees to live with him, he may not leave her. ¹³ And if any wife has a non-believing husband who agrees to live with her, *she* may not leave *him*. ¹⁴ For a non-believing husband is sanctified by his wife, and a non-believing wife is sanctified by her husband. Otherwise, your children would be unclean, but we know that they're holy. ¹⁵ If a non-believer separates, however, let him go — a brother

---

ʰ *Mt 5:32; 19:9; Mk 10:11–12; Lk 16:18.*

7:9        "Than to burn." This phrase probably means "to burn with passion," but it may possibly mean to fall into sin and be condemned to Hell.

or sister isn't bound in such cases, for God has called you to peace. 16 Does a wife know for sure that she'll be able to save her husband? Does a husband know that he'll be able to save his wife?

17 The main point is the Lord assigned some role to each of you; each of you should therefore continue to live as you were when God called you — this is the instruction I give in all the churches. 18 Were you circumcised when you were called? Then don't try to remove the marks of circumcision. Were you *uncircumcised* when you were called? Then don't have yourself circumcised. 19 Neither circumcision nor uncircumcision is of any importance; what's important is to obey God's commandments. 20 Each of you should remain in the state you were in when you were called. 21 Were you a slave when you were called? Don't worry about it, but if you get the chance to become free, take advantage of it. 22 For any slave who was called in the Lord is a freedman of the Lord. Likewise, whoever was free when they were called is a slave of Christ. 23 You were bought for a price, so don't become slaves of men. 24 Each of you, brothers, should remain before God in the same state in which you were called.

25 Regarding girls who are betrothed — I have no command from the Lord, but I'll give you my opinion as one who through the Lord's mercy is trustworthy. 26 In view of the present distress this is what I think — it's best

---

7:16    There is some basis for interpreting this verse: "But perhaps a woman will be able to save her husband, or a husband will be able to save his wife."

to remain as you are. 27 Do you have a wife? Then don't seek to be free of your obligations. Are you without a wife? Then don't go looking for a wife. 28 But if you *do* marry, you've committed no sin. Nevertheless, people who marry will be afflicted with worldly concerns, and I'd prefer to spare you that. 29 This is what I'm saying, brothers. Time is short; from now on those who have wives should live as if they didn't, 30 those who are weeping as if they weren't weeping, those who are rejoicing as if they weren't rejoicing, those who are buying as if they had nothing, 31 and those who make use of the world as if they weren't making full use of it, for the world as we know it is passing away. 32 I want you to be free from anxiety. The unmarried man concerns himself with the Lord's affairs, with how to please the Lord, 33 while the married man concerns himself with worldly affairs — how to please his wife — 34 and is divided. Likewise, girls who are betrothed and unmarried women are concerned with the Lord's affairs — how to be holy in body and spirit — while a married woman is concerned with affairs of the world, such as how to please her husband. 35 I'm saying this for your own good, not simply to rein you in — I want you to preserve good order so you'll be able to devote yourselves to the Lord without distractions.

36 If anyone thinks he's behaving improperly toward his betrothed, if his passions are strong and it must be so, he should do what he wishes — he's committing no sin; they should get married. 37 But whoever has his heart firmly set, who is under no compulsion but has control over his desires and has decided in his heart to have her remain a virgin, he

does well. 38 And so the one who marries his betrothed does well, and the one who doesn't marry does better.

39 A woman is bound as long as her husband is alive, but if her husband dies she's free to marry whoever she wishes to, as long as he's in the Lord. 40 But in my opinion she'll be happier if she remains as she is, and I think that I too am in accord with God's Spirit.

## Regarding the Eating of Food That Had Been Previously Offered to Idols

8 1 Regarding meat that was offered to idols — we know that "we all have knowledge." Knowledge leads to arrogance, but love builds up. 2 Anyone who thinks he knows something still doesn't know as he ought to know, 3 but whoever loves God is known by God. 4 So concerning meat that was offered to idols, we know that "there are no idols in the world" and that "there is no God but One." 5 For even if there are so-called gods in heaven or on earth, as indeed there are many so-called "gods" and "lords," 6 there is still only one God for us, the Father from Whom everything comes and for Whom we live, and there's one Lord, Jesus Christ, through whom all things are and through whom we exist.

7 But not everyone knows this. Some, because up till now they've been accustomed to idols, eat meat as if it re-

---

8:1ff.    Paul takes advantage of a specific issue (eating food that had previously been sacrificed to idols) to set out a fundamental principle of Christian morality — concern for the conscience of "weaker" persons.

ally had been offered to idols, and since their conscience is weak they're defiled. ⁸ Now food will not commend us to God — if we don't eat we won't be any worse off, and if we do eat we won't be any better off. ⁹ But be careful that your freedom doesn't somehow cause those who are weak to fall. ¹⁰ For if someone sees you who have knowledge reclining at table in an idol's temple, and his conscience is weak, won't he be encouraged to eat meat that's been offered to idols? ¹¹ And so your knowledge would lead to the weak person's downfall — who is himself a brother for whom Christ died. ¹² Therefore, whoever sins against his brothers in this way and injures their weak consciences is sinning against Christ. ¹³ Thus, if food causes my brother to sin I'll never eat meat again, so I won't cause my brother to sin.

## Paul's Defense of His Ministry as an Apostle

9 ¹ Am I not free? Am I not an apostle? Haven't I seen Jesus our Lord? Aren't you my work in the Lord? ² If I'm not an apostle to others, I certainly am to you, for you're the seal of my apostleship in the Lord!

³ This is my defense to those who sit in judgment over me. ⁴ Have we no right to eat and drink? ⁵ Have we no right to travel with a Christian wife, as do the other apostles, the brothers of the Lord, and Kephas? ⁶ Are Barnabas and I the only ones who have no right to be free from the necessity

---

9:1ff.    Paul now returns to a matter he first raised in Chapter 4. Apparently, in their "wisdom," some of the Corinthians felt able to pass judgment on Paul and other Christian missionaries. This is Paul's defense of his worth as an apostle, but even more than that, Paul sets out the principles that form the basis for his ministry.

to work? 7 Who serves as a soldier at his own expense? Who plants a vineyard but doesn't eat its fruit? Who shepherds a flock but doesn't get any of the flock's milk? 8 Am I saying this on human authority, or doesn't the Torah also say this? 9 For in the Law of Moses it's written, *You shall not muzzle the ox when it's threshing.* Is it for oxen that God is concerned? 10 Isn't He saying this for us all? For it was written for us that the plowman should plow in hope and the thresher should thresh in hope of gaining a share. 11 If we have sown spiritual seed for you, is it so shocking that we should reap material benefits from you? 12 If others share in this claim on you, don't we have even more of a right to do so?

Nevertheless, we've made no use of this right; instead, we endure everything rather than place an obstacle in the way of Christ's good news. 13 Don't you know that those who perform the Temple services get their food from the Temple, and those who serve at the altar share in what's offered on the altar? 14 *i* So, too, the Lord commanded those who proclaim the good news to gain their living from the good news. 15 And yet I've made use of none of these things, nor am I writing this in order to have it done for me — I'd rather die than let anyone deprive me of my boast! 16 For proclaiming the good news is not my boast, since I do so under compulsion — woe to me if I *don't* proclaim the good news! 17 If I do it of my own free will, then I

---

*i* Mt 10:10; Lk 10:7.

---

9:9   Dt 18:1–3.

get a reward, but if not, I've simply been entrusted with a commission. ¹⁸ What then is my reward? My reward is to proclaim the good news free of charge without asserting my rights in the good news.

¹⁹ For though I'm totally free I've made myself a slave to all in order to win over as many as possible. ²⁰ I became a Jew for the Jews in order to win the Jews over; for those under the Torah I acted as if *I* were subject to the Torah — although I'm *not* subject to the Torah — in order to win over those who *are* under the Torah; ²¹ for those outside the Torah I became like one outside the Torah in order to win over those outside the Torah, although rather than being outside God's law I'm subject to Christ's law. ²² For those who were weak I became weak in order to win over the weak. I've become all things to all men so that by all means I might win some of them over. ²³ I do all this for the sake of the good news so that I'll be able to share in it.

²⁴ Don't you know that all the runners in the stadium race, but only one gets the prize? Run to win! ²⁵ Everyone who competes in an athletic contest trains rigorously, but while *they* do it to win a *perishable* crown *we're* competing for an *im*perishable crown. ²⁶ So I don't run as if I didn't know where the finish line is; when I box I don't just punch wildly. ²⁷ On the contrary, I discipline myself and bring my body under control, because I don't want to preach to others and then find *myself* disqualified.

## A General Moral Exhortation

10 ¹ I want you to bear in mind, brothers, that our ancestors were all under the cloud and they all passed through the sea. ² They were all baptized into Moses in the cloud and in the sea; ³ they all ate the same spiritual food ⁴ and they all drank the same spiritual drink. For they drank of the spiritual rock that followed them, and that rock was Christ. ⁵ Nevertheless, God was displeased with most of them, for He struck them down in the desert. ⁶ Now these events were warnings for us, not to long for evil things like those evil people did. ⁷ Don't be idolaters, like some of them were, as it's written, *The people sat down to eat and drink, and got up to dance.* ⁸ Don't turn to fornication like some of them did — in one day twenty-three thousand fell in the desert. ⁹ Let's not test Christ like some of them did, and were killed by the snakes. ¹⁰ Don't grumble, like some of them did,

---

10:1ff.    Paul begins his moral exhortation with a renewed appeal to the image of the Church as the New Israel embarked upon a New Exodus from sin and death to life — the experience of the Passover and Exodus is the experience of the Christian life. The Corinthians must bear in mind that passing through the waters of baptism is no guarantee that they will reach the Promised Land.

10:4    At Ws 11:4 the water the Israelites received from the rock is identified with Wisdom. If Paul has this passage in mind he is identifying Jesus with the Wisdom of God, continuing a theme alluded to at 1:24, 30. This is a further identification of Jesus as the New Torah, for the rabbis had come to equate the Torah with the revelation of the Divine and creative Wisdom. This is significant for Christology, for Wisdom was at the beginning with God. It is also significant for ethics and the spiritual life, Paul's chief concern in this passage, for it is the basis of Paul's vision of the Christian life as a living of Christ's life rather than as mere obedience to a written code.

10:7    Ex 32:6.

10:9    Some manuscripts read "the Lord" for "Christ."

and were killed by the Destroyer. <sup>11</sup> These things happened to them as warnings, but they were written down for *our* instruction, for the end of the ages has come to us. <sup>12</sup> So anyone who thinks they're standing should be careful not to fall. <sup>13</sup> The only temptations you've received are normal human ones. God is trustworthy and won't allow you to be tested beyond your strength — along with the temptation He'll also provide a way out, so you'll be able to endure it.

<sup>14</sup> Therefore, beloved, flee idolatry. <sup>15</sup> I'm speaking as if to the wise — judge for yourselves what I say. <sup>16</sup> *j* The blessing cup we bless, isn't it a sharing in Christ's blood? The bread we break, isn't it a sharing in Christ's body? <sup>17</sup> Because there's one bread, we who are many are one body. <sup>18</sup> Look at the people of Israel. Aren't those who eat the sacrifices sharers in the altar? <sup>19</sup> What am I saying? That food offered to an idol is of any significance, or that an idol has any significance? <sup>20</sup> No, what I'm saying is that the things the Gentiles sacrifice they sacrifice to demons rather than to God, and I don't want you to become sharers with demons. <sup>21</sup> You can't drink the Lord's cup *and* the cup of demons; you can't share in the Lord's table *and* the table of

---

*j* Mt 26:26–28; Mk 14:22–24; Lk 22:19–20.

---

10:14–22    As he so often does, Paul stresses the communal/covenant aspect of the Eucharist — his remarks are best understood in light of the Passover/Exodus experience. The events of the Passover and Exodus were constitutive for Israel as the people of God and are seen by Paul as types of the sacraments. Sharing in the sacramental life of the Church, especially in the Eucharist, is in this sense constitutive for the New Israel. Cf. also 5:7, 10:2–4; 11:20–34.

10:20    Dt 32:17 (Septuagint).

demons. ²² Are we to provoke the Lord to jealousy? Are we stronger than he is?

²³ "Everything is permitted," but not everything will benefit you. "Everything is permitted," but not everything will build you up. ²⁴ Everyone should look out for his neighbor's good rather than his own. ²⁵ Eat whatever's in the meat market without making inquiries for the sake of your conscience, ²⁶ *for the earth and everything in it belongs to the Lord.* ²⁷ If any of the unbelievers invite you over and you wish to go, eat whatever's put before you without making inquiries for the sake of your conscience. ²⁸ But if anyone tells you, "This was offered in sacrifice," then don't eat it for the sake of the person who informed you and for conscience's sake — ²⁹ I don't mean your *own* conscience, I mean the other person's. For why should my freedom be limited by someone else's conscience? ³⁰ If I share in the food gratefully, why should I be criticized for something I give thanks for? ³¹ Whether you eat or drink or whether you don't, do everything for the glory of God. ³² Give no offense to the Jews, the Greeks, or to the church of God, ³³ just as I try to please everyone in everything *I* do. I look out for the good of the many, rather than my own good, so that they'll be saved.

**11** ¹ Be imitators of me, just as I imitate Christ.

---

10:26   Ps 24:1.

## E. Paul Addresses Certain Problems Which Have Arisen in the Liturgical Gatherings

### Women's Headdress

2 I commend you because you always remember me and hold fast to the traditions just as I handed them down to you. 3 But I want you to understand that Christ is the head of every man, the husband is the head of his wife, and God is the head of Christ. 4 Any man who prays or prophesies with his head covered disgraces his head, 5 while any woman who prays or prophesies with her head *un*covered disgraces *her* head — it's the same as if her head were shaved. 6 For if a woman leaves her head uncovered, she may as well have her hair cut off, but since it's shameful for a woman to cut her hair off or be shaved, then she should cover her head. 7 A man, on the other hand, should *not* cover his head, since he's the image and glory of God, while woman is the glory of man. 8 For woman was made from man, not man from woman, 9 and woman was created for man, not man for woman. 10 Therefore a woman should wear a sign of authority on her head for the sake of the angels. 11 Nevertheless, in the Lord woman is not independent of man, nor is man independent of woman, 12 for just as woman comes from man, so too man comes from woman, and everything

---

11:8–9   Gn 2:18–23.

11:10    Based on Qumran parallels, it is possible that the angels were thought to be present at liturgies and that therefore proper decorum should be maintained.

comes from God. ¹³ Judge for yourselves, is it proper for a woman to pray to God with her head uncovered? ¹⁴ Doesn't nature itself teach us that it's shameful for a man to wear his hair long, ¹⁵ while a woman's long hair is her glory? For her hair is given to her as a covering. ¹⁶ But if anyone is disposed to keep arguing — we have no such custom, nor do the churches of God.

## Their Manner of Celebrating the Lord's Supper

¹⁷ But in giving these instructions I *don't* commend the fact that your assemblies lead to harm rather than to good. ¹⁸ In the first place, when you assemble as a church I hear that there are divisions among you, and in part I believe it — ¹⁹ after all, it's necessary for there to be factions among you so that it will be apparent which of you are genuine. ²⁰ But when you assemble it's not to eat the Lord's supper, ²¹ for when you eat each of you goes ahead with his own supper — one is hungry, while another is drunk. ²² Don't you have homes to eat and drink in? Do you despise God's church and shame those in need? What shall I say to you? Shall I commend you? I certainly don't commend you for this!

²³ For I received from the Lord what I handed down to you, that on the night he was betrayed the Lord Jesus took

---

11:17   At 11:2 Paul had praised the Corinthians for following tradition and for consulting him in doubtful matters, such as women's headdress. Now, however, Paul comes to a serious matter in which their conduct is not so praiseworthy.

bread, 24 and after blessing it he broke it and said, "This is my body which is for you. Do this in remembrance of me!" 25 In the same way he took the cup after they had eaten and said, "This cup is the new covenant in my blood. Do this, whenever you drink it, in remembrance of me!" 26 For whenever you eat this bread and drink this cup you proclaim the death of the Lord, until he comes.

27 Therefore, if anyone eats the bread or drinks from the cup of the Lord unworthily, he'll be answerable for the body and blood of the Lord. 28 Each of you should first examine yourself and then eat the bread and drink from the cup, 29 for whoever eats and drinks without recognizing the body eats and drinks judgment to himself. 30 That's why so many of you are weak and ill, and a considerable number have died, 31 but if we examined ourselves we wouldn't be subject to judgment. 32 But when we're punished by the Lord we receive guidance so that we won't be condemned with the world. 33 Therefore, my brothers, when you assemble to eat, wait for each other. 34 If anyone is hungry, let him eat at home, so your assembly won't lead to condemnation. I'll give you instructions about the other matters when I come.

---

11:29   In the context, "recognizing the body" refers both to recognizing in the Eucharist the saving sacrifice of Jesus' body and blood as well as the Church's unity with Christ in the Eucharist. Every individual Christian shares the responsibility for maintaining that unity.

## Regarding the Purpose and
## Relative Importance of Spiritual Gifts

**12** $^1$ Regarding spiritual gifts — brothers, I don't want you to lack understanding in this matter. $^2$ You know that when you were Gentiles whenever you were seized by a spirit you used to be led off to dumb idols. $^3$ This is why I want you to know that no one speaking under the influence of God's Spirit can say, "Cursed be Jesus!" and no one can say, "Jesus is Lord!" except under the influence of the Holy Spirit.

$^4$ $^k$ There are various gifts, but the same Spirit, $^5$ there are various ministries, but the same Lord, $^6$ and there are various ways to be active, but the same God Who causes all these effects in everyone. $^7$ Some manifestation of the Spirit is given to each for the common good. $^8$ To one it may be given to speak wisdom through the Spirit, to another it's given to speak deep knowledge according to the same Spirit. $^9$ To still another faith may be given through the same Spirit, while to another the one Spirit will give healing gifts. $^{10}$ To one may be given the ability to perform miracles, to another the gift of prophecy, to one the gift of distinguishing spirits, to another various tongues, to still another the interpretation of tongues. $^{11}$ One and the

---

$^k$  Rm 12:6–8.

---

12:1–26 The idea animating this important passage is that the Church as a Body is a unity, not a mere aggregate of individuals. Spiritual gifts must therefore be understood as being essentially at the service of the Church rather than being the possessions of individual Christians.

same Spirit causes all this, distributing individually to each as He wishes.

12 [1] For just as the body is one but has many members, all the members of the body — many though they are — are one body, and so it is with Christ. 13 We've *all* been baptized in one Spirit into one body, whether Jew or Greek, slave or free, and we've all drunk of one Spirit. 14 For the body isn't one member — it's made up of many members. 15 If the foot should say, "I'm not a hand, so I'm not part of the body," it would still be part of the body for all that, 16 and if the ear should say, "I'm not the eye, so I'm not part of the body," it would still be part of the body for all that. 17 If the whole body were an eye, how could it hear? If the whole body were an ear, how could it smell? 18 But as it is, God arranged the members of the body — each one of them — as He wished them to be. 19 If they were all just one member, what sort of body would that be? 20 As it is, though, there are many members, but one body. 21 The eye can't tell the hand, "I have no need of you," nor can the head tell the feet, "I have no need of you." 22 On the contrary, the members of the body which seem the weakest are much more necessary, 23 the members of the body which seem less honorable are the ones we grant the most honor to, and our private parts we treat with more modesty, 24 whereas there's no need to treat our more presentable parts that way. But God has formed the body in such a way as to give greater honor to the members which lack it, 25 so that

---

[1] Rm 12:4–5.

there will be no discord in the body and the members will feel the same concern for one another. 26 If one member suffers, all the members suffer; if one member is honored, all the members rejoice.

27 You are the body of Christ, and each individual is a member. 28 *m* God has appointed some in the church to be, first, apostles, second, prophets, third, teachers, then miracle workers, those with the gift of healing, helpers, administrators, and those with various tongues. 29 Are all members apostles? Are all prophets? Are all teachers? Do all work miracles? 30 Do all have the gift of healing? Can all speak in tongues? Can all interpret tongues? 31 But strive for the greatest gifts.

And I'll show you an even better way.

13 1 If I can speak both human and angelic tongues but don't have love, I'm nothing but a gong sounding or a cymbal clashing. 2 *n* If I have the gift of prophecy, understand every mystery, and possess all the deepest knowledge, if I have such complete faith that I can move mountains but I don't have love, I'm nothing. 3 And if I give all my possessions away and hand my body over to be burned but I don't have love, it does me no good at all.

---

*m Eph 4:11. n Mt 17:20; 21:21; Mk 11:23.*

---

13:1ff.    This passage builds on what preceded it. Just as the gifts of the Spirit are for building up the life of the Church, so Paul reminds the Corinthians that the essence of that life of the Spirit "in Christ" is love. Individual achievements and gifts are to be measured against their success in strengthening the community's life of love "in Christ." This emphasis on the Church over the individual continues the Old Testament tradition that individuals were inspired by the Spirit for the good of Israel.

13:3    "To be burned." Some manuscripts read "that I may boast."

⁴ Love is patient, love is kind, it isn't jealous, doesn't boast, isn't arrogant. ⁵ Love is not dishonorable, isn't selfish, isn't irritable, doesn't keep a record of past wrongs. ⁶ Love doesn't rejoice at injustice but rejoices in the truth. ⁷ Love endures all things, love has complete faith and steadfast hope, love bears with everything.

⁸ Love never ends. Prophecy will pass away, speaking in tongues will cease, knowledge will pass away. ⁹ Our knowledge is incomplete and prophecy is incomplete, ¹⁰ but when what's perfect comes the imperfect will pass away. ¹¹ When I was a child I spoke like a child, thought like a child, reasoned like a child. When I became a man, I put an end to childish ways. ¹² Right now we see indistinctly, as in a mirror, but then we'll see face to face. At present my knowledge is incomplete, but then I'll truly understand, as God understands me. ¹³ So these three — faith, hope, and love — remain, but the greatest of them all is love.

14 ¹ Strive for love and set your hearts on the gifts of the Spirit, but especially desire to receive the gift of prophecy. ² The person who speaks in tongues speaks to God and not to men, since no one can understand him — he proclaims mysteries through the Holy Spirit. ³ But whoever prophesies strengthens, encourages, and comforts others. ⁴ You strengthen yourself when you speak in tongues, but when you prophesy you strengthen the church. ⁵ I want you all to speak in tongues but I'm especially desirous that you should prophesy. It's far better to prophesy than to speak in tongues, unless someone translates what you're saying so the whole church will be strengthened.

⁶ Look at it this way, brothers. If I come to you speaking in tongues what good will it do you, unless I proclaim some revelation, deep knowledge, prophecy or teaching? ⁷ Similarly, if inanimate objects that produce sounds, such as the flute or the lyre, don't produce distinct notes, how will anyone know what's being played? ⁸ If I sound an uncertain trumpet blast, who will prepare for battle? ⁹ So, too, when you speak in tongues — unless you can give an intelligible account of it, how will anyone know what you're saying? You may as well be speaking to the air! ¹⁰ Or take another example — there are many different types of speech in the world, and all are intelligible, ¹¹ but if I don't know what the sounds mean I'll be like a foreigner to the person who's speaking, and he'll be a foreigner to me. ¹² So, since you're eager for gifts of the Spirit, strive to have an abundance of those which build up the church. ¹³ Therefore, whoever speaks in tongues should pray to be able to interpret them. ¹⁴ For when I'm praying in tongues my spirit is praying but my mind is idle. ¹⁵ What should I do? I'll pray with my spirit, but I'll also pray with my mind; I'll sing with my spirit, but I'll also sing with my mind. ¹⁶ Otherwise, if you praise God in the Spirit, how will someone without special gifts be able to raise the "Amen!" to your thanksgiving, since he doesn't know what you're saying? ¹⁷ You may be thanking God well enough, but no one else is being strengthened. ¹⁸ I give thanks to God that I'm able to speak in tongues more than any of you, ¹⁹ but in church I'd rather speak five words from my mind which provide instruction for others, than ten thousand words in tongues.

²⁰ Brothers, don't be childish in your thinking — be like children with regard to evil, but be mature in your thinking. ²¹ In the Torah it's written,

> *Through foreigners*
> *and through the lips of foreigners*
> *I'll speak to this people,*
> *and even so they won't listen to me,*

says the Lord. ²² Therefore, speaking in tongues is a sign to non-believers rather than to believers, while prophecy is for believers rather than non-believers. ²³ So if the whole church were to gather together and be speaking in tongues and uninstructed people or non-believers should come in, they'd say you were out of your minds, wouldn't they? ²⁴ But if you were all prophesying when the non-believer or uninstructed person came in he'd be convinced of his errors and be called to account by all of you. ²⁵ The secrets of his heart would be revealed — he'd fall on his face and worship God, proclaiming, "God is truly with you!"

²⁶ What should you do, brothers? When you gather, each of you should have a song, some teaching, a revelation, a message in tongues, or an interpretation — everything should be done with a view toward strengthening the church. ²⁷ If anyone wants to speak in tongues, let two or, at most, three do so, but have them take turns and have one of them translate. ²⁸ If there's no one there to translate, they should be silent in church — let them speak to themselves or to God. ²⁹ Let two or three prophets speak while the

---

14:21   Is 28:11–12.

others pass judgment, <sup>30</sup> but if someone sitting there receives a revelation, the first speaker should stop talking. <sup>31</sup> You can all prophesy one at a time, so that you'll all learn and receive encouragement. <sup>32</sup> The prophetic spirit should be controlled by the prophets, <sup>33</sup> for God is made manifest in peace, not in disorder.

As in all the churches of the saints, <sup>34</sup> women should remain silent in church, for they're not permitted to speak. They should be subordinate, as the Torah says, too. <sup>35</sup> If they want to learn about something they should ask their husbands at home, because it's disgraceful for a woman to speak in church. <sup>36</sup> Did the word of God come from you? Are you the only ones it came to?

<sup>37</sup> If anyone thinks he's a prophet or that he's been favored with gifts of the Spirit he'll realize that what I'm writing to you is a command of the Lord. <sup>38</sup> Anyone who doesn't accept that should be ignored. <sup>39</sup> Therefore, brothers, set your hearts on prophecy, but don't hinder speaking in tongues. <sup>40</sup> Everything should be done in a proper and orderly fashion.

## F. Doctrinal Teaching: the Resurrection of the Dead

**15** <sup>1</sup> I want to remind you, brothers, of the good news I proclaimed to you, the good news you received

15:1ff. As a prolegomena to his discussion of resurrection from the dead, Paul reviews the content of the good news he had previously proclaimed to the Corinthians. He specifically notes that he proclaimed to them what he himself had received,

and in which you stand firm. ² You'll be saved through the good news if you hold fast to the message I proclaimed to you, unless you believed in vain. ³ For I handed down to you as of primary importance what I, in turn, had received, namely that Christ died for our sins in accordance with the Scriptures, ⁴ that he was buried, that he was raised on the third day in accordance with the Scriptures, ⁵ and that he appeared to Kephas and then to the Twelve. ⁶ Then he appeared to more than five hundred brothers at once, the majority of whom are still with us, although some have died. ⁷ Then he appeared to James, then to all the apostles. ⁸ Last of all he appeared to me as well, to one born at the wrong time, as it were, ⁹ for I'm the least of the apostles, not even worthy to be *called* an apostle, because I persecuted God's church. ¹⁰ But through the grace of God I am what I am, and the grace He gave me has not been without result — I've worked harder than any of them, although it wasn't me working — it was the grace of God working in me. ¹¹ So whether it was me or them, this is what we proclaimed and this is what you believed.

¹² Now if Christ is proclaimed as raised from the dead, how can some of you say that there's no resurrection of the dead? ¹³ If there's no resurrection from the dead, then Christ wasn't raised either, ¹⁴ and if Christ wasn't raised then

---

so that vv. 3–7 can be traced to a very early formulation of the Church's *kerygma*. This was, of course, not the whole *kerygma*; Paul summarized those portions which pertained to the topic he wished to elucidate. A much fuller statement of the Church's *kerygma* can be found in Peter's speech at Acts 2:14–36.

15:3     Is 53:5–12.
15:4     Ps 16:10.

everything we proclaimed is in vain, and so is your faith. [15] Moreover we'll have been found to be false witnesses against God, for we testified that God raised Christ, whom He couldn't have raised if the dead in fact are not raised. [16] For if the dead are not raised, then Christ wasn't raised either, [17] and if Christ wasn't raised our faith is worthless and you're still in your sins, [18] and those who died in Christ have also perished. [19] If our hope in Christ is for this life only, we're the most pitiable of men.

[20] As it is, Christ *was* raised from the dead, the first fruits of those who have died. [21] For since death came through a man, resurrection from the dead *also* came through a man, [22] for just as in Adam all men die, so too in Christ they'll also come to life again. [23] Each will be raised in the proper order — Christ the first fruits, then at his coming those who belong to Christ will rise. [24] Then the end will come, when he'll deliver the Kingdom to his God and Father, when he'll do away with every ruler, authority, and power. [25] For Christ must reign until he's put all his enemies under his feet. [26] The last enemy to be done away with will be death, [27] for *God has put everything under his feet.* When it says that "everything" has been made subject to him it's clear that "everything" doesn't include God. [28] When everything is made subject to him, then the Son himself will be subjected

---

15:20    The "first fruits" was a harvest offering to God, but Paul is probably thinking once again of the Passover and Exodus. At Dt 26:1–11 the offering of the first fruits is explicitly described as a thank offering for the mighty works of the Lord in bringing Israel out of Egypt and into the Promised Land.

15:25    Ps 110:1.

15:27    Ps 8:6.

to the One Who subjected everything to the Son, so that God will be all in all.

²⁹ Otherwise, what's the point in people being baptized for the dead? If the dead aren't actually raised, why are people baptized for them? ³⁰ Why do we run risks every hour of the day? ³¹ Every day I die. I do! I swear it by the pride I have in you in Christ Jesus our Lord! ³² If in human terms I fought with wild beasts in Ephesus, what good did it do me? If the dead aren't raised,

> *Let's eat and drink,*
> *for tomorrow we'll die!*

³³ Don't be led astray,

> "Bad company ruins good morals!"

³⁴ Come to your senses and stop sinning! Some of you don't know God — I say this to your shame.

³⁵ Perhaps some one will say, "How can the dead be raised? What kind of bodies will they have?" ³⁶ You fool! What you sow doesn't come to life unless it dies! ³⁷ What you sow isn't your body as it will be — it's a bare kernel, like wheat or something of that sort. ³⁸ God gives it the body He's chosen for it, and each type of seed has its own body. ³⁹ Not all flesh is the same; human flesh is of one sort, the flesh of domestic animals is of another; the flesh of birds is of one kind, while fish have another type. ⁴⁰ There are

---

15:29    Apparently the Corinthians engaged in a form of baptism by proxy on behalf of dead relatives. Paul points out the inconsistency of engaging in such a practice while denying the resurrection of the dead.

15:32    Is 22:13.

15:33    This is a quotation from the Greek poet Menander.

also heavenly bodies and earthly bodies, but the glory of heavenly bodies is one thing and the glory of earthly bodies is something else. ⁴¹ The sun has one type of brightness, the moon another, and the stars yet another, for stars differ according to their brightness.

⁴² So it is with the resurrection of the dead.

> What is perishable when it's sown is imperishable
>     when it's raised.
> ⁴³ What's sown in dishonor is raised in glory,
>     What's sown in weakness is raised in power;
> ⁴⁴ A physical body is sown, a spiritual body is raised.

Now if there's a physical body, there's also a spiritual body. ⁴⁵ So it is written,

> Adam, the first man, became a living being;
>     the last Adam became a life-giving spirit.
> ⁴⁶ But the spiritual isn't first;
>     first comes the physical, then comes the spiritual.
> ⁴⁷ The first man was made of dust,
>     the second man came from Heaven.
> ⁴⁸ Those who are of the dust
>     are like the man of dust,
> And those who are of Heaven
>     are like the man from Heaven,
> ⁴⁹ And just as we've borne the image of the man of
>         dust,
>     so too we'll bear the image of the man from
>         Heaven.

---

15:45   Gn 2:7.

⁵⁰ This is what I mean, brothers — it's impossible for flesh and blood to inherit the Kingdom of God, nor can what's perishable inherit what's imperishable.

51 *ᵒ*    Behold, I'll tell you a mystery —
    not all of us will die,
But all of us will be transformed,
52    in a moment, in the twinkling of an eye,
At the sound of the last trumpet call,
    when the trumpet sounds,
The dead will be raised imperishable
    and we'll be transformed.
53 For this corruptible body must be clothed
    in incorruptibility,
    and this mortal body must be clothed
    in immortality.
54 And when this corruptible body is clothed
    in incorruptibility
    and this mortal body is clothed in immortality
The following passage of Scripture will come to pass,
55 Death is swallowed up in victory.
Death, where is your victory?
Death, where is your sting?
56 Sin is death's sting,
    and the Torah is sin's power,
57 But thanks be to God, Who gives us victory
    through our Lord Jesus Christ.

---

*ᵒ 1 Th 4:15–17.*

---

15:54–55   Is 25:8; Ho 13:14 (Septuagint).

58 Therefore, my beloved brothers, be firm and steadfast.
Constantly increase your work for the Lord, in the knowledge that your labor in the Lord is not in vain.

## G. Paul's Plans and Other Practical Considerations

16 1 Regarding the collection for the saints — do just as I
commanded the churches in Galatia to do. 2 On the
first day of every week each of you is to lay aside and save
whatever you're able to, so that a collection won't have to
be made when I come. 3 When I arrive I'll send whomever
you approve to carry your gift to Jerusalem with letters of
introduction. 4 If it seems proper for me to go too, they'll
accompany me.

5 [p] I'll come to you when I go through Macedonia,
for I'll be going through Macedonia, 6 and I may stay
with you awhile or even spend the winter with you, so
you'll be able to send me on to wherever I'm going. 7 I
don't want to see you now just in passing — I'm hoping
to spend some time with you if the Lord will permit it,
8 [q] but I'll stay in Ephesus until Pentecost, 9 for a particularly effective door of opportunity has been opened for me,
though I have many adversaries.

10 If Timothy comes, see that he's made welcome
among you, for he's doing the Lord's work just as I am,

---

[p] *Ac 19:21.* [q] *Ac 19:8–10.*

11 so no one should look down on him. Send him on in peace so he'll be able to come to me, for I'm waiting for him along with the brothers.

12 Regarding our brother Apollos — I strongly urged him to go to you with the brothers, but it was not at all God's will for him to go now — he'll come to you when he has the chance.

13 Be watchful, stand firm in the faith, be manly, be strong! 14 Let all your work be done in love.

15 You know that those in Stephanas' household were the first converts in Achaia and that they've devoted themselves to the service of the saints. I beg you, 16 obey them and all who labor and work as they do. 17 I rejoice that Stephanas, Fortunatus, and Achaicus came, because they make up for your absence — 18 they've refreshed my spirit as well as yours. Give such men recognition.

## H. FAREWELL

19 The churches of Asia greet you. Aquila and Prisca greet you fervently in the Lord along with those in the church at their house. 20 All the brothers greet you. Greet one another with a holy kiss.

21 This greeting is my own writing — Paul's. 22 If anyone doesn't love the Lord, let him be cursed! *Marana tha*! 23 The grace of the Lord Jesus be with you. 24 May my love be with all of you in the Lord Jesus.

---

16:22    *Marana tha*. Aramaic for, "Come, Lord!"

# THE SECOND LETTER TO THE

# CORINTHIANS

Second Corinthians is undoubtedly one of Paul's most difficult letters. Unlike in Romans, theological complexity is not the main difficulty — in fact, specifically theological concerns occupy a relatively minor portion of the whole. Rather, its difficulty stems from its intensely personal character and its seeming lack of unity. This is not to deny the letter its share of theological insights (see Chapters 3–5 especially), but they must be viewed within the context of the letter as a whole, which is the crisis in Paul's relations with the Corinthians.

Paul had remained in Corinth for about two years, and his ministry there had been rewarded with great success. He had then, after a brief return trip to Palestine and Antioch, based himself in Ephesus, an important city on the western coast of Asia Minor, across the Aegean sea from Corinth. Problems had arisen in the Corinthian church, however, and Paul had been required to visit at least once, to send emissaries, and to write letters. Apparently Paul's visit had been a stormy one, involving a challenge to Paul's authority. After leaving Corinth, Paul had written a letter in which he demanded that his main antagonist be disciplined. This "painful letter" (as he himself termed it) had had the effect he had hoped for, and his emissary, Titus, had returned with the good news that the Corinthians were once more wholeheartedly behind Paul. Against this background, Paul wrote 2 Corinthians. The date of composition falls in A.D. 56–57. The place of composition could have been Ephesus, Macedonia, or both.

There is universal agreement that the material contained in 2 Corinthians is genuinely Pauline. What is questioned, however, is whether the letter was originally written as we have it or whether it may be a collection of several letters written by Paul to the Corinthians, some of which may be alluded to within 2 Corinthians. Scholars who question the letter's unity point to its repetitions, sudden changes of subject, and wide variations of tone. Certainty in this matter appears to be impossible, but what these questions undoubtedly illustrate is the inner complexity of the document. The following divisions are commonly made by those who question the original unity of 2 Corinthians: 1:1–7:16 (a defense of Paul's ministry, written in conciliatory tones); 6:14–7:1 (a warning against relations with unbelievers); Chapter 8 (an appeal for the collection for the Jerusalem church); Chapter 9 (a renewed appeal regarding the collection); Chapters 10–13 (a defense of Paul's ministry, but written in an impassioned, almost combative style, full of irony and sarcasm).

Those who maintain that the letter is a unity advance no less weighty considerations. They point to the unity of theme through much of the letter, maintain (correctly) that Paul was prone to rapid shifts of topic, and suggest that the letter may have been written over a period of time, as new information arrived. Specifically, Chapters 10–13 with their harsh condemnation are believed by some to have been written at a later date than the first nine chapters in response to fresh news about trouble in Corinth. This trouble was occasioned by the arrival of Jewish Christian missionaries who denigrated both Paul's person and his message.

The most likely view is probably that the first nine chapters were written as one letter, that Chapters 10–13 were added on at a slightly later date, and the whole was then delivered as one letter. However, in view of the letter's complexity, it has been deemed advisable to provide a brief synopsis of the letter before presenting the outline which will be used in the translation.

The letter opens with a brief greeting (1:1–2). Normally the greeting would be followed by a thanksgiving, but instead the next section (1:3–14) opens with an adaptation of a Jewish blessing which leads into an introduction of the themes which will dominate this letter: the importance of sharing in Christ's sufferings and Paul's own record of selfless sacrifice on behalf of the Corinthians. Verses 12–14 give what is almost certainly a glimpse of the complaints that had been made about Paul. Apparently some had accused Paul of being boastful and even of having used the Corinthians to puff up his own importance. Paul briefly asserts the rectitude of his conduct and that he has been guided by the grace of God.

Paul next explains in some detail (1:14–2:13) why he changed his travel plans and didn't come to Corinth after having said he would. The Corinthians appear to have felt that Paul had lost interest in them and that he had showed his fickleness by neglecting them and canceling the promised visit. Again, in view of recent stormy relations, they may have feared that Paul was avoiding them. Paul protests that his change of plans was motivated by his love for them and a desire to avoid causing the Corinthians further pain (after the previous painful visit). Second Corinthians 7:5–16 is considered to be either an actual continuation of this section or a resumption of the general theme, in which Paul insists upon his continued concern for the Corinthians, even in the midst of all his sufferings.

Beginning at 2:14 Paul makes a full-scale defense of his style of apostleship, couched in conciliatory tones. It appears that he is already aware that missionaries who are critical of him — probably from a Jewish Christian perspective — have arrived in Corinth, but he refrains from criticism. Paul first stresses that his ministry was received from God and that that is the fundamental source of the confidence (apparently irritating to some) which allows him to ignore his own unworthiness. In addition, the surpassing glory of the New Covenant — in comparison to the Old Covenant, which his rivals may have stressed — drives him on. He is undaunted by his weakness because, paradoxically, it shows that his work is from God and can't be from him alone. It also shows that he is an apostle of Jesus, who died for all. What may seem like boasting, therefore, is simply Paul's effort to bring salvation to everyone — he's completely dominated by the vision of Christ's love. He concludes (at 6:13) by protesting his steadfast efforts to avoid giving offense and appealing for the Corinthians' love. However, at 7:2–4 we find a renewed appeal for their love in terms which are very similar to those at 6:13.

Separating the main body of his defense from the tag at 7:2–4 is a warning against relations with unbelievers (6:14–7:1). Opinion is divided as to whether this was inserted later or whether it belongs in the present context. To the idea that this section is un-Pauline, it may be noted that 1 Corinthians 5:9–13 gives good grounds for believing that this admonition was not out of character for Paul.

Chapters 8 and 9 appeal to the Corinthians to show generosity in giving to Paul's collection on behalf of the "saints" in Jerusalem. (The term "saints" indicates that those so designated have been chosen and set off by God.) This project was of exceptional importance for Paul, not only from a humanitarian standpoint but probably more importantly from a theological standpoint, for Paul saw this as an important symbol of the end times, when the Gentiles would become one in solidarity with Israel. He had devoted his life to this ministry and even the sensitive relations between himself and the Corinthians could not deter him from making these appeals, especially since at the time he wrote he had recently received Titus' encouraging report. Both chapters are written in a basically similar tone and display Paul's sensitive awareness of the need not to offend the Corinthians and to avoid any appearance of impropriety in the collection and handling of the money.

The final chapters, 10–13, are a renewed defense of Paul's ministry, but the contrast to the earlier defense is striking. Here Paul is impassioned and embattled. Far from refraining from criticism as in the earlier section, he goes so far as to call his opponents "false apostles, dishonest workers who disguise themselves as apostles of Christ" (11:13). Stung by accusations of weakness, Paul launches into an extended "boastful" account of his credentials and warns that when he comes to Corinth he will come with God's power in Christ.

## OUTLINE OF THE SECOND LETTER TO THE CORINTHIANS

A.  1:1–2          Greeting

B.  1:3–14         Statement of the Letter's Theme: Paul's Record Is of Selfless Service in God's Grace

C.  1:15–2:13      A Review of Recent Troubled Relations Between Paul and the Corinthians

D.  2:14–7:16      The Nature of Apostleship the Source of Paul's Confidence

    3:4–4:6        The Superiority of the New Covenant of the Spirit

    4:7–5:10       Sharing in Jesus' Death and Life

    5:11–6:13      Ambassadors of Christ's Love

    6:14–7:1       A Warning against Relationships with Unbelievers

| | 7:2–4 | A Renewed Plea for the Corinthians' Love |
| E. | 7:5–16 | Continuation of Paul's Account of Recent Relations |
| F. | 8:1–24 | The Collection for the Saints in Judea |
| G. | 9:1–15 | The Matter of the Collection Addressed Once Again |
| H. | 10:1–13:10 | A Defense of Paul's Ministry as an Apostle |
| | 10:1–18 | Paul's Authority and Power |
| | 11:1–12:21 | Paul's Boasting |
| | 13:1–10 | Paul's Plans to Visit Corinth |
| I. | 13:11–13 | Closing Exhortations and Farewell |

## A. Greeting

1 ¹ Paul, an apostle of Christ Jesus by the will of God, and Timothy our brother to the church of God in Corinth, along with all the saints in all of Achaia. ² Grace and peace to you from God our Father and the Lord Jesus Christ.

## B. Statement of the Letter's Theme: Paul's Record Is of Selfless Service in God's Grace

³ Blessed be the God and Father of our Lord Jesus Christ, the compassionate Father and ever encouraging God! ⁴ He encourages us in all our afflictions so that we'll be able to encourage others who are in affliction by means of the encouragement we ourselves have received from God. ⁵ For just as Christ's sufferings overflow and include us, so too through Christ our encouragement is also unbounded. ⁶ If we suffer, it's for your encouragement and salvation; if we receive encouragement, it's so you'll be encouraged and enabled to endure the same sufferings we suffer. ⁷ Our hope in you is firm, for we know that if you share the suffering, you also share the encouragement.

8 For we want you to know, brothers, about our afflictions in Asia. We were so utterly weighted down, beyond our strength, that we doubted whether we could go on living. 9 We were convinced that we had received the death sentence, but that was so that instead of trusting in ourselves we would place our trust in God, Who raises the dead. 10 He delivered us from these terrible dangers of death, and He'll continue to deliver us. In Him we have placed our hope and God will rescue us again. 11 You must help us by praying for us, so that many people will give thanks for the gift we received through the prayers of many people.

12 For this is our boast — that our conscience can testify that we have conducted ourselves in the world, and especially toward you, with the single hearted simplicity and sincerity of God, not by worldly wisdom but by the grace of God. 13 For we write to you only what you can read and understand. I hope you'll fully understand, 14 as indeed you've partially understood us, that we are your boast just as you'll be our boast on the day of the Lord Jesus.

## C. A Review of Recent Troubled Relations Between Paul and the Corinthians

15 Because I was sure of all this I originally planned to come to you so you'd have a double gift. 16 *a* I was going to

---

*a* Ac 19:21.

1:8–10  The Roman province of "Asia" had its capital at Ephesus, from which city much of Paul's Corinthian correspondence was written. What the afflictions he experienced there were we cannot be sure, but their serious nature is also alluded to at 1 Cor 15:32.

visit you on my way to Macedonia and come to you again when I returned from Macedonia — and then be sent on my way to Judea by you. 17 In making this plan did I show myself to be fickle? Do I make my plans according to the way of the world, saying "Yes, yes" and "No, no" in one breath? 18 As God is faithful, we have not been saying both yes and no to you. 19 For Jesus Christ the Son of God who was proclaimed among you by us — by Silas, Timothy, and myself — was not both "Yes" and "No"; instead, the "Yes" was in him. 20 For all God's promises find their "Yes" in him, which is why it's through Jesus that we say "Amen" to the glory of God. 21 It's God Who establishes us in Christ with you and Who has anointed us, 22 Who has placed His seal on us and given our hearts the Spirit as a down payment.

23 I call on God as my witness, upon my life, that it was to spare you that I decided not to go to Corinth. 24 Not that we lord it over your faith — on the contrary, we're working *together* for your joy, for you stand firm in the faith.

2 1 The fact is I made up my mind not to go to you again if that would pain you, 2 for if I were to cause you pain who would there be to cheer me up except those whom I had pained? 3 I wrote what I did so that when I came I wouldn't receive pain from those who should have given me joy, for I was confident that as far as you were concerned my joy would be your joy. 4 I was in tears when I wrote to you, and what I wrote came from my troubled

---

1:22    The reference to being "sealed" is probably a reference to baptism.

and anguished heart. My intent was not to cause you pain but to let you know how great my love for you is.

5 But if anyone caused pain, it wasn't just me that he pained; not to exaggerate, but to some degree the pain was caused to all of you. 6 This punishment by the majority of you is sufficient for such a person, 7 so you should forgive and encourage him now, lest he be swallowed up in his overwhelming grief. 8 Therefore, I urge you to assure him of your love, 9 because the reason I wrote was to test you and find out if you're obedient in everything. 10 Anyone you forgive, I do too. Whatever I've forgiven, if there *was* anything for me to forgive, has been forgiven for your sake in the presence of Christ 11 to keep Satan from gaining an advantage over us — for we're well aware of his plans.

12 When I came to Troas to proclaim the good news of Christ a door of opportunity was opened for me in the Lord, 13 but I had no peace of mind because I didn't find my brother Titus there, so I bade them farewell and left for Macedonia.

## D. THE NATURE OF APOSTLESHIP
### THE SOURCE OF PAUL'S CONFIDENCE

14 But thanks be to God Who continually leads us in triumph in Christ and through us makes known the

---

2:5–11  While certainty is not possible, many believe the offense was a personal attack on Paul, probably a questioning of his authority.

2:14–16  A Roman "triumph" was a military victory parade which included, among other things, the procession of captives and the burning of incense. As many scholars have

fragrance of the knowledge of God in every place, 15 for we are the aroma Christ offers to God among those being saved and among those who are perishing. 16 For some it is a deadly fragrance which leads to death, for others it is a lifegiving fragrance which leads to life. Who is worthy of these things? 17 For we're not like so many other people who peddle the word of God for profit; we proclaim the word sincerely, having received it from God; we proclaim it in the sight of God and in Christ.

3 1 Are we beginning to commend ourselves again? Or do we, like some others, need letters of recommendation to you or from you? 2 *You* are our letter, written on our hearts, for all to know and read. 3 Yes, you're clearly a letter from Christ delivered by us, written not with ink but with the Spirit of the living God, not on stone tablets but on tablets of human hearts.

---

pointed out, however, the "aroma" and "fragrance" alluded to in vv. 15–16 probably owe more to Old Testament sacrificial imagery, in which God is said to be pleased by the odor of the sacrifice. Paul, of course, is referring to his own sacrifices in his ministry, sacrifices he gladly makes for the spiritual welfare of his converts.

3:1ff.    Here for the first time in the letter Paul contrasts himself with other teachers. They appear to have come to Corinth bearing letters of recommendation. At this point Paul's criticism is restrained, although it seems apparent that Paul's opponents must have placed greater emphasis on Jewishness and observance of at least some of the Torah. Later, when it became clear that these teachers were denigrating both Paul's person and his ministry in pointedly personal terms, Paul reacted vigorously in defense of his person, his ministry, and his authority (Chapters 10–13).

3:3    Jr 31:33.

# The Superiority of the New Covenant of the Spirit

⁴ This confidence we have is in God through Christ. ⁵ Not that we can take credit for anything ourselves, as if we had accomplished it on our own — our adequacy to the task comes from God. ⁶ He it is Who made us qualified to become ministers of a new covenant, a covenant not based on a written code but on the Spirit; for the letter kills, but the Spirit gives life.

⁷ Now if the ministry of death which was carved in letters on stone was so glorious that the Israelites were unable to gaze upon Moses' face because his face was illuminated by this transitory brightness, ⁸ won't the ministry of the Spirit be much more glorious? ⁹ For if the ministry that brought condemnation was glorious, then the ministry that brings restoration to fellowship with God will far exceed it in glory. ¹⁰ Indeed, in this respect, what was once glorious is now without glory because its glory has been surpassed,

---

3:4–18   The old covenant was a covenant of the letter, the Torah, while the new covenant is a covenant of the spirit. Therefore, since "the Lord is the Spirit," the very person of Christ becomes the focal point of the new covenant. Rather than obeying commandments written in stone the Christian becomes an imitator of Christ, the New Torah. The Torah, according to rabbinic theology, was the revelation of God, but, says Paul, it had a glory which was destined to fade. Christ is a far more perfect revelation of God and his glory will never fade. As we gaze upon the revealed glory of the Lord and become imitators of Christ we are transformed into His image.

3:6      Paul, of course, is not denying the Torah's essential and glorious role in salvation history. However, when opposed to the new covenant it leads to death. Paul deals with this problem at greater length in Romans.

3:7      This passage is a midrashic interpretation of Ex 34:29–30. Paul is intent on showing the superiority of the new covenant to the old covenant and how this superiority explains his ministry.

11 for if the Torah which was transitory had glory, then what's permanent will be far more glorious.

12 Since we have this hope we act with great boldness, 13 unlike Moses who placed a veil over his face so the Israelites wouldn't see the end of what was fading away. 14 But their minds were hardened, for to this day that same veil remains in place when they read the old covenant, because the veil is set aside only for those who are in Christ. 15 Instead, to this day whenever Moses is read a veil lays over their hearts, 16 *but whenever you turn to the Lord the veil is taken away.* 17 Now the Lord is the Spirit, and where the Spirit of the Lord is, there is freedom. 18 So all of us who gaze with uncovered faces at the glory of the Lord are being transformed into his image, from one level of glory to the next, and this comes from the Lord, who is the Spirit.

4 1 Therefore, since we received this ministry through God's mercy, we do not lose heart. 2 We have renounced shameful deeds done in secret, refusing to employ deceit or to water down the word of God. Instead, by openly proclaiming the truth we commend ourselves to the conscience of all men in the sight of God. 3 And even if our good news is veiled, it is veiled only from those who

---

3:13      Ex 34:33.

3:16      Ex 34:34.

4:1ff.      The surpassing glory of the new covenant accounts for their boldness, knowing as they do that they are God's appointed heralds. Thus their confidence is in God, not in themselves.

4:3–6      The gospel is veiled only to those who are spiritually blind because they follow the "god of this age." Worship of what is not God in whatever form is idolatry and leads to spiritual blindness. God's revelation in Christ exposes these intramundane powers for what they are.

are perishing. [4] The god of this age has blinded the minds of the unbelievers so they won't see the light of the good news of Christ's glory, who is the image of God. [5] For we don't proclaim ourselves — we proclaim Jesus Christ as Lord and ourselves as your servants for Jesus' sake. [6] For the God Who said, "Out of the dark a light will shine," has caused His light to shine in our hearts to reveal the knowledge of God's glory in Christ's face.

## Sharing in Jesus' Death and Life

[7] But we keep this treasure in clay vessels so that this extraordinary power will be seen to be from God and not from us. [8] We're afflicted in every way, but we're not crushed, uncertain but not in despair; [9] although we're persecuted we're not abandoned, knocked down but not dead — [10] we always bear the death of Jesus in our bodies so the life of Jesus may *also* be revealed in our bodies. [11] For in our lives we're constantly being delivered to death for Jesus' sake so that Jesus' life may also be revealed in our mortal flesh. [12] Therefore death is at work in us, but life is at work in you. [13] But since we have the same spirit of faith which is in accordance with these words of Scripture — *I*

---

4:6 Gn 1:3.

4:7–5:10 Paul now returns to the theme of suffering. For the Christian, suffering has value and meaning because in it we share in Christ's redemptive death so as to rise with him and share his life. All Christians are called to share in Christ's life in this way, but the apostles live out Christ's suffering most graphically.

4:13 Ps 116:10 (Septuagint).

*believed, and therefore I spoke* — we too believe and therefore we also speak out, 14 because we know that God Who raised the Lord Jesus will also raise us and bring us with you into His presence. 15 All this is for your sake so that as grace extends to more and more people it may lead to an increase of thanksgiving to the glory of God.

16 This is why we don't lose heart, for although our outer self is wasting away our inner self is being renewed, day by day. 17 Our slight, momentary affliction is producing for us an eternal fullness of glory which is beyond all comparison, 18 and so we keep our eyes on what is unseen rather than on what can be seen, for what can be seen is transitory but what is unseen is eternal.

5 1 For we know that if the tent which is our earthly dwelling should be destroyed we have a building from God, an eternal house not made by human hands. 2 Here we groan, because we long to put on our heavenly dwelling, 3 and if we *are* clothed with it we won't be found to be naked. 4 For while we live in this tent we groan in our troubled state of mind; we don't want to remove our clothing — we want to have clothing put over it so that what's mortal will be swallowed up by life. 5 God is the One Who has prepared us for this, and He has given us the Spirit as a down payment.

---

5:1–10   This passage is dense and complicated and is made more so by the way Paul shifts between images of building and clothing. Our earthly bodies ("tents") are alive, but in comparison to the heavenly bodies we long for they are dead. It's not that we long for death — after all these bodies were made by God and are good — rather, we long to have our living deaths swallowed up and transformed in the heavenly life. Our courage is a result of faith, for through faith we know that even as our earthly lives are dying we are coming to life in Jesus, a life that will not end with bodily death.

⁶ So we're always full of courage, even though we know that while we're at home in the body we're away from the Lord, ⁷ for we walk through faith, not by sight. ⁸ We're full of courage and we'd prefer to leave our bodies and be at home with the Lord. ⁹ Therefore our ambition is to please the Lord, whether we're at home or away. ¹⁰ ᵇ For all of us will have to appear before the judgment seat of Christ where each will receive either good or evil, depending on what we did while in the body.

## Ambassadors of Christ's Love

¹¹ Therefore, knowing as we do the fear of the Lord, we try to persuade others, but God knows us for what we are, and I hope that we're also well known to your consciences. ¹² We're not commending ourselves to you again — we're giving you an opportunity to boast about us, so you'll have something to say to those who boast about appearances rather than what's in the heart. ¹³ For if we've lost our minds, it's for God; if we're of sound mind, it's for you. ¹⁴ The love of Christ urges us on, since we're convinced that one man died for all and that as a result all have died. ¹⁵ He died for all so that those who live might no longer live for themselves but instead might live for the one who died and rose for them.

---

ᵇ *Rm 14:10.*

---

5:11–21 Paul appeals to the Corinthians to accept him as God's ambassador and to understand how this status affects all that he does, inspired as he is by the vision of Christ's love for all.

¹⁶ Therefore, from now on we regard no one as the world does. If at one time we looked upon Christ as the world does, we no longer do. ¹⁷ Therefore, anyone who's in Christ is a new creation — the old has passed away, behold the new has come! ¹⁸ All this is from God, Who reconciled us to Himself through Christ and has given us this ministry of reconciliation. ¹⁹ That is, in Christ God was reconciling the world to Himself, not counting their transgressions against them and entrusting us with the message of reconciliation. ²⁰ That makes us ambassadors for Christ, just as if God Himself were making His appeal through us. We beg you on behalf of Christ — be reconciled to God! ²¹ For our sake God had Christ become sin, even though he was without sin, so that in Christ we might become the righteousness of God.

6 ¹ We are sharing in God's work and we urge you not to accept God's grace in vain — ² for He says,
*At the acceptable time I heard you,*
*   on the day of salvation I came to your aid.*

Behold, now is the acceptable time; behold, now is the day of salvation! ³ We give no one any cause to take offense, so that no fault may be found with our ministry, ⁴ but as servants of God we commend ourselves in every way possible with

---

5:17    "A new creation." The Greek translates rabbinic terminology and thought, according to which a person who was brought to true knowledge of God was considered "a new creation."

6:1–7:4 Paul makes a final impassioned plea for the Corinthians to accept his love and return it, as well as to live lives worthy of God's promise.

6:2    Is 49:8.

great steadfastness — in afflictions, in dire need, in distress, [5] when beaten, in prison, subjected to mob violence, in hard work, in sleepless nights, in fasting, [6] in purity, in knowledge, in patience, in kindness, in the Holy Spirit, in sincere love, [7] in truthful words, in the power of God, with weapons of righteousness for both attack and defense, [8] in honor and dishonor, in ill repute and good repute, whether regarded as impostors or truthful, [9] as unknown or well known, as dying and yet we're alive, as subjected to punishment but not killed, [10] as sorrowful yet always rejoicing, as poor yet enriching many, as having nothing yet possessing everything.

[11] We have spoken openly to you, Corinthians; our hearts are open wide! [12] You're not constrained by *us*; you're constrained by your own affections! [13] In return — I speak now as if I were speaking to my own children — open wide your hearts to us!

## A Warning Against Relationships with Unbelievers

[14] Don't enter into relationships with unbelievers! After all, what partnership can there be between righteousness and wickedness? What do light and darkness have to share? [15] What agreement can there be between Christ and Belial? What is there in common between a believer and an unbeliever? [16] What accommodation can there be between the

---

Temple of God and idols? *We* are the Temple of the Living
God; as God has said,

> *"I will dwell and move about among them,*
> *I will be their God, and they shall be My people.*
> 17 *Therefore, come out of their midst*
> *and separate yourselves from them,"*
> *says the Lord;*
> *"Touch nothing that's unclean*
> *and I will take you in.*
> 18 *I will be your Father,*
> *and you will be My sons and daughters,"*
> *Says the Lord God Almighty.*

7 ¹ Since we have these promises, beloved, let us
cleanse ourselves from every defilement of flesh and
spirit and come to perfect holiness in the fear of God.


## A Renewed Plea for the Corinthians' Love

² Make room for us in your hearts! We've wronged
no one, we've corrupted no one, we've taken advantage
of no one! ³ I'm not saying this to condemn you — as I've
already said, you're in our hearts and we'll die together and
live together. ⁴ I have great confidence in you, I have great
pride in you. I'm wonderfully encouraged and despite all
our afflictions I'm brimming over with joy.

---

6:17    Is 52:11.
6:18    2 S 7:14; 1 Ch 17:13.

# E. CONTINUATION OF PAUL'S
## ACCOUNT OF RECENT RELATIONS

5 Even when we came to Macedonia our bodies had no rest. We were afflicted in every way — conflicts without, fear within. 6 But God, Who encourages the downhearted, encouraged us with the arrival of Titus. 7 It wasn't just his arrival that encouraged us, however, but the news of how you had encouraged Titus, for he told us of your longing for me and your sorrow, and of your zeal on my behalf. As a result, I rejoiced all the more! 8 For even if my letter caused you pain, I don't regret it now. Even if I regretted it at the time — for I can see the letter did hurt you, if only for a little while — 9 I rejoice in it now, not because it caused you pain but because your sorrow led you to repent. For your sorrow was directed toward God, and so you lost nothing through us. 10 For grief which is directed toward God produces a repentance that leads to salvation and is not to be regretted, whereas sorrow in a purely human sense brings death. 11 Just look at how much earnestness was produced by this sorrow which was directed toward God — you were filled with a desire to defend yourselves, with indignation, fear, longing, zeal, and with eagerness to see just punishment administered. In every respect you've proved your innocence in this matter. 12 So even though I wrote to you, it wasn't because of the one who did wrong or because of the one who received the injury — it was so you'd be able to clearly see in the sight of God how eager you are in our behalf. 13 For this reason we're encouraged.

And although we rejoiced because of our own encouragement, we rejoiced even more at Titus' joy, because his mind has been set to rest by you. ¹⁴ I may have been somewhat boastful about you to him, but I haven't been put to shame. Just as everything we told you was true, so too did our boasts to Titus prove true. ¹⁵ And his affection for you grows all the stronger when he recalls how you received him in fear and trembling. ¹⁶ I rejoice because I have every confidence in you.

## F. The Collection for the Saints in Judea

**8** ¹ We want you to know, brothers, about the grace God has given to the churches in Macedonia, ² for although they've been sorely tried with afflictions their abundant joy and extreme poverty have overflowed in a wealth of generosity. ³ I bear them witness — of their own accord they gave according to their means and even beyond their means, ⁴ earnestly begging us to allow them a share in helping the saints. ⁵ It was beyond what we'd hoped for, but first they gave themselves to the Lord and then to us by God's will. ⁶ As a result we've urged Titus to complete among you this work of love, which he previously began. ⁷ Just as you excel in every other respect — in faith, speech, knowledge, earnestness, and in your love for us — so too may you excel in this work of love.

---

8:7     Some manuscripts read "our love for you."

⁸ I'm not issuing any orders; instead, by telling you how eager others are to help I'm testing the genuineness of your love. ⁹ For you know the grace of our Lord Jesus Christ; although he was rich he became poor for your sake so that you might become rich through his poverty. ¹⁰ I'll give you my opinion in this matter — this is in your own interest. A year ago you began to desire to do this, ¹¹ and now you should complete what you began, so that your ready desire to undertake this work may be matched by your completion of it from what you have. ¹² For if you're willing to give, your giving will be acceptable to God based on what you have, not based on what you don't have. ¹³ My intent is not that others should rest while you are burdened, but that as a matter of equality ¹⁴ your current surplus should make up for what they lack. Later, their surplus may make up for what *you* lack, so that everything will be equal. ¹⁵ As it is written,

> *The one who had much didn't have an excessive amount,*
> *and the one who had little was not in need.*

¹⁶ Thanks be to God, Who put the same earnest concern for you into Titus' heart. ¹⁷ Not only did he agree to the course of action we urged upon him, but he's so very eager that he's going to you of his own accord. ¹⁸ We're sending with him the brother who is praised in all the churches for his proclamation of the good news — ¹⁹ not only that,

---

8:9     This is a reference to Christ's pre–existence. Cf. Ph 2:6–11.
8:15    Ex 16:18.
8:18    Or "for his gospel."

but he's been chosen by the churches to be our travelling companion in this service of love we're performing for the glory of God and to show our willingness to help. 20 We're trying to avoid being blamed by anyone for our handling of this generous gift, 21 for *our concern is to do what's right,* not only *in God's sight* but *also* in the eyes *of men.* 22 With them we're sending our brother whom we've tested many times and have found to be eager, but now he's even more eager because of the tremendous confidence he has in you. 23 As for Titus, he's my partner and co-worker for you; as for our brothers, they're messengers from the churches, the glory of Christ. 24 So show the churches your love and the reason we boast about you to them.

## G. The Matter of the Collection Addressed Once Again

9 1 It's superfluous for me to write to you about the help we're sending to the saints. 2 I know how eager you are and I boast about you to the Macedonians, saying that Achaia has been prepared since last year. As a result, your eagerness has stirred most of them up. 3 I'm sending the brothers so our boasting about you won't come to naught in this matter, so you'll be ready just as I said you would. 4 Otherwise, if some Macedonians come with me and find

---

8:20–21 Paul is quite aware of the precarious state of his relations with the Corinthians and is determined to leave no opening for misunderstanding.

8:21   Pr 3:4 (Septuagint).

you unprepared we'll be humiliated for being so confident — not to mention you! [5] Therefore I thought it was necessary to urge the brothers to go on ahead to you and arrange for the generous gift you've promised, so it will be ready as a gift and not as an exaction.

[6] Keep in mind that whoever sows sparingly will also reap sparingly, and whoever sows bountifully will also reap bountifully. [7] Each should give from the heart, not reluctantly or under compulsion, for *God* loves *a cheerful giver.* [8] Moreover, God is able to provide you with every gift so that you'll always have enough of everything and will have more than enough for every good work, [9] as it is written,

> *He's generous, He gives to the needy,*
> *His righteousness lasts forever.*

[10] He Who supplies seed to the sower and bread for food will also provide your seed, cause it to multiply, and increase the yield of your righteousness. [11] You'll be enriched in every way for your generosity, which will produce a thanksgiving to God through us. [12] For your contribution to this service not only supplies what the saints lack, it's also producing an outpouring of thanksgiving to God. [13] This test of your willingness to help will lead people to glorify God for your obedience to your profession of the good news of Christ and for your generosity in sharing with them and with everyone. [14] Then, as they pray for you, they'll long

---

9:7     Pr 22:8 (Septuagint).
9:9     Ps 112:9.
9:10    Is 55:10.

for you because of the immeasurable grace God has given you. ¹⁵ Thanks be to God for His inexpressible gift to you!

## H. A Defense of Paul's Ministry as an Apostle

**Paul's Authority and Power**

10 ¹ I, Paul, myself appeal to you by the humility and gentleness of Christ — I who am meek and mild with you when we're face to face, but bold with you when I'm away. ² I beg that when I come I won't have to act boldly with the confidence I intend to display toward those who think we behave in a worldly way. ³ For though we live in the world we don't wage war in a worldly way. ⁴ The weapons we use in our campaign aren't worldly weapons, they're God's powerful weapons for destroying strongholds. We destroy sophistry ⁵ and every proud obstacle to the knowledge of God and we capture every thought to bring it into obedience to Christ. ⁶ We stand ready to punish all acts of disobedience, once your obedience is complete.

⁷ Look the facts in the face. If anyone is confident that they belong to Christ they should think again, because we belong to Christ as much as they do. ⁸ I may boast a little too much about our authority, which the Lord gave us to build you up and not to destroy you, but I won't be put to shame. ⁹ I don't want it to look like I'm frightening you with letters. ¹⁰ Then they'll say, "His letters are severe and powerful, but his personal presence is weak and his speaking ability isn't worth mentioning." ¹¹ Those who think

that way had better understand that our actions when we come will be the same as what we say in our letters when we're away.

12 Not that we dare put ourselves in the same class or compare ourselves with those who think so highly of themselves, but when they measure themselves against one another and compare themselves to one another they show no understanding at all. 13 Our boasting won't exceed the limits of our ministry; it will stay within the bounds of the commission God assigned to us, which includes you. 14 When we came to you with the good news of Christ it wasn't as if our commission didn't include you and we were overreaching our authority, 15 so we're not going beyond the limits of our ministry and boasting about the work of others. Our hope is that as your faith increases the scope of our activity will be greatly enlarged, 16 so that we'll be able to proclaim the good news to lands beyond you and won't have to boast of work already done in someone else's area. 17 But *whoever boasts should boast in the Lord,* 18 for the one whom the Lord commends is the one who's approved, not the one who commends himself.

## Paul's Boasting

11 1 I wish you'd bear with me in a little foolishness — please bear with me! 2 For I'm jealous for you with the jealousy of God, because I betrothed you like a pure

---

10:17   Jr 9:24.

virgin to be presented to one husband — to Christ —
3 but I'm afraid that just as the serpent deceived Eve with
his cunning, your minds will somehow be led away from
a sincere devotion to Christ. 4 For if someone comes and
proclaims a different Jesus than we proclaimed, or if you
receive a different spirit than the one you received from us,
or if you receive a different gospel than the one you received
from us, you bear with it quite readily! 5 I don't consider
myself to be in any way inferior to these "super apostles"!
6 Maybe I lack something in speaking ability, but not in
knowledge! We made this clear to you repeatedly and in
every possible way.

7 Did I commit a sin by humbling myself so you could
be exalted, because I proclaimed God's good news to you
without any charge? 8 I robbed other churches by accepting money from them so I could serve you, 9 and when
I was among you and was in need I didn't burden any
of you — the brothers who came from Macedonia took
care of my needs. In every possible way I avoided being
a burden to you, and I'll continue to do so. 10 As Christ's
truth is in me, this boast of mine will not be silenced in
the districts of Achaia! 11 Why? Because I don't love you?
God knows I do!

12 What I'm doing I'll continue to do, to eliminate
any chance that those pretenders might find some pretext
under which they might claim to be regarded as our equals
in the ministry they boast of. 13 Such men are false apostles,

---

11:3    Gn 3:1–13.

dishonest workers who disguise themselves as apostles of Christ. 14 There's nothing remarkable in this; after all, even Satan disguises himself as an angel of light, 15 so it should come as no surprise if Satan's servants disguise themselves as servants of righteousness. Their end will be in accordance with their works!

16 I repeat, no one should think I'm a fool, but if you do, accept me as a fool just so I'll have a little something to boast about. 17 What I'm going to say is not the way the Lord would have me speak; I'm speaking foolishly, in boastful confidence. 18 Since many others boast of their human merits, I'll boast too! 19 ʿ After all, you gladly put up with fools, since you're so wise, 20 for if someone imposes upon you, preys upon you, takes advantage of you, puts on airs, or slaps you in the face, you bear with it. 21 To my shame, I have to admit that we were too weak to do that, but if anyone dares to boast — I'm speaking like a fool, now — I can be just as daring!

22 Are they Hebrews? So am I! Are they Israelites? So am I! Are they descended from Abraham? So am I! 23 Are they servants of Christ? Now I'm speaking like a madman — I'm even *more* so! I've worked harder, spent more time in prison, been beaten more severely, and have often been in danger of death. 24 Five times I received forty lashes less one from the Jews, 25 three times I was beaten with rods, once I was stoned, three times I was shipwrecked — a day

---

ʿ Ph 4:15–18.

---

11:24   Dt 25:3.

and a night I spent out on the deep! 26 In my many journeys I've been in danger from rivers, from robbers, from my own race, from Gentiles; I've been in danger in the city and in the wild, on the sea and from false brothers. 27 I've toiled and been through hardships, spent many sleepless nights, been hungry and thirsty; I've often gone without food, been cold and without sufficient clothing. 28 Apart from these external things, I experience daily cares and anxiety for all the churches. 29 If anyone is weak, I too am weak! If anyone is led into sin, I too am ablaze with indignation!

30 If I must boast, I'll boast of my weakness. 31 The God and Father of the Lord Jesus, Who is blessed forever, knows that I'm not lying. 32 *d* In Damascus the ethnarch, King Aretas, kept watch over the city of the Damascenes in order to arrest me, 33 but I was lowered in a basket from a window in the city wall and escaped his clutches.

12 1 I must boast. It may serve no purpose, but I'll go on and talk about visions and revelations from the Lord. 2 I know a man in Christ who fourteen years ago was caught up to the Third Heaven — whether in the body or out of the body I don't know, God knows. 3 And I know that this man — whether in the body or out of the body I don't know, God knows — 4 I know that he was caught up to Paradise where he heard things too sacred to be put into words, things which no man may utter. 5 I'll boast about this man, but as for myself I'll boast only of my weaknesses. 6 If I'm going to boast, I won't be a fool — I'll

---

*d* Ac 9:23–25.

tell the truth! But I'll spare you, so no one will think more of me than what they can see and hear of me. 7 But to keep me from getting puffed up as a result of these extraordinary revelations I was given a thorn in the flesh, an angel of Satan, to beat me so I wouldn't get puffed up. 8 Three times I begged the Lord to take it away from me, 9 but he told me, "My grace is enough for you, for my power is made perfect in your weakness." Therefore I'm all the more pleased to boast of my weaknesses, so that Christ's power may dwell with me. 10 For this reason I delight in weakness, insults, hardships, persecution, and difficulties for Christ's sake, for when I'm weak, that's when I'm strong.

11 I've been a fool, but you forced me to be one! I ought to be commended by *you* rather than by myself! I'm not one bit inferior to those super apostles, even if I *am* nothing. 12 I patiently performed signs among you which proved that I'm an apostle — signs, wonders, and miracles. 13 In what way were you treated worse than the other churches, except that I wasn't a burden to you? Forgive me for this injustice! 14 This is the third time now that I've prepared to come to you. I don't want your possessions, I want *you*! After all, children shouldn't be saving up for their parents, it's the parents who should be saving up for their children. 15 I'd gladly spend all my money and utterly exhaust myself for your souls. If I love you so much, will you love me less? 16 Let it be agreed, then, that I wasn't a burden to you, but could it be that I was crafty and took advantage of you by deceit? 17 Well, I didn't take advantage of you through anyone I sent to you, did I? 18 I urged Titus

to visit you and sent a brother with him. Titus didn't take advantage of you, did he? Didn't we follow in the same spirit? Didn't we leave the same footprints?

19 Have you been thinking all this time that we've been defending ourselves to you? We've been speaking in Christ in God's presence, and it's all been for your edification, my beloved! 20 My fear is that I'll come and find that all is not as I would like it to be with you, and you'll find me to be other than *you'd* like *me* to be. I'm afraid that I'll find strife, jealousy, anger, selfishness, slander, gossip, pride, and unholiness. 21 I'm afraid that I'll come again and God will humble me before you — I'll have to weep for many of those who sinned before and haven't repented of the impurity, immorality, and licentiousness they practiced.

## Paul's Plans to Visit Corinth

13 1 This is the third time I'm coming to you. *Any charge must stand on the testimony of two or three witnesses.* 2 On my second visit I warned those who sinned before and now I'm warning the rest of you again, that if I come again I won't spare you, 3 since you want proof that Christ is speaking in me. He's not weak in dealing with you — he's powerful among you! 4 He was crucified in weakness, but he lives by the power of God. We're weak in him, but in dealing with you we'll live with him by God's power.

---

13:1    Dt 19:15.

5 Test yourselves, see if you're living in faith, examine yourselves! Don't you realize that Christ Jesus is in you? Or have you failed the test? 6 I hope you'll find out that *we* haven't failed the test! 7 We pray to God that you won't do anything wrong — not so we'll appear to be successes, but so you'll do what's right, even though we may seem to be failures. 8 After all, we can't oppose the truth, we can only work *for* the truth. 9 We rejoice when we're weak and you're strong; our prayer is for your perfection. 10 The reason I'm writing this while away from you is so that when I come I won't have to be severe and use the authority the Lord has given me, that I'll be able to build you up, not tear you down.

# I. CLOSING EXHORTATIONS AND FAREWELL

11 Finally, brothers, rejoice! Mend your ways, encourage one another, live in harmony and peace, and the God of love and peace will be with you. 12 Greet one another with a holy kiss. All the saints greet you.

13 The grace of the Lord Jesus Christ, the love of God, and the fellowship of the Holy Spirit be with you all.

# THE LETTER TO THE

# GALATIANS

❧ ✠ ❧

Galatians takes us to the heart of several issues which are
central to an understanding of Saint Paul and his gospel.
The letter was written in response to a serious threat to the
"truth of the gospel" among the churches of Galatia, a region located in what is now central Turkey. Apparently Paul
had had to stop over among the Galatians as the result of a
serious illness and had taken the occasion to proclaim the
good news. At the time of writing, however, problems had
arisen among the predominantly Gentile converts. Jewish
Christian missionaries had appeared among them and had
raised doubts among the Galatians regarding Paul and the
gospel he had preached. These missionaries discounted
Paul's claim to apostolic authority and asserted that he
had taught the Galatians an abbreviated version of the
good news. Paul had proclaimed the good news that Jesus
is Messiah but, they maintained, he had failed to inform
them about the need to be circumcised and to observe the
Torah in order to be saved.

In the face of this fundamental challenge Paul responded with a passionate defense of both himself and of the gospel he preached. He adamantly maintained that his claim to be an apostle was based upon the personal call of Jesus himself, whom God had revealed to him. He also vigorously proclaimed the basic Christian truth that our relationship with God can never be restored by legal observance but only through accepting God's call to faith in Jesus. Included in this proclamation was the assurance that both Jews and Gentiles have equal access to salvation and a ringing call to the Christian life of freedom in the Spirit.

Because of the vigor of Paul's polemic, Galatians has sometimes been misunderstood. "Justification by faith" (what is here translated as being "restored to fellowship with God" through faith) is, indeed, central to the letter, but that was because of the requirements of the particular problem with which Paul found himself confronted. True, Christ's person had replaced the Torah, but since Christ had *replaced* the Torah rather than simply abolishing it, faith can never be placed in *opposition* to obedience. Thus Paul speaks of "the law of Christ" and insists that the fruit of life "in Christ" is ethical rectitude. In any discussion of Galatians it must be remembered that this new life in Christ is the true center of Paul's thought.

Galatians is also of great importance from an historical standpoint. In it we find Paul's own account of his conversion and his life prior to the missionary travels detailed in Acts, as well as his account of his relations with the "pillars" of the early Church, especially with Kephas (Peter) and James, "the brother of the Lord." To have the report of an actual eyewitness to these events is of extraordinary value, no matter how brief Paul's remarks may be in this regard.

Remarkably little can be definitely said about the time and place of composition for Galatians. It is variously dated as one of the very earliest of Paul's letters (several years prior to A.D. 50) or as falling into the middle years of his literary career, A.D. 55–57. Fortunately, there is no need to go into detail about the several theories which have been advanced concerning these matters, since they have no real bearing on the interpretation of the letter. Galatians may profitably be read immediately before Romans. The two letters share many important themes, and Galatians offers an excellent introduction to the more measured discussion of these common issues which we find in Romans.

### OUTLINE OF THE LETTER TO THE GALATIANS

A. 1:1–5        Greeting
B. 1:6–2:21     The Basis of the Gospel Paul Proclaimed
C. 3:1–4:7      The Meaning of Faith and Torah and Their Place in God's Plan
D. 4:8–5:12     Exhortation to Hold Fast to Freedom in Faith
E. 5:13–6:10    Christian Freedom in Daily Life
F. 6:11–18      Concluding Exhortation

## A. GREETING

1 ¹ Paul, an apostle not from men nor through a man but through Jesus Christ and God the Father, Who raised him from the dead, ² and all those brothers with me, to the churches of Galatia. ³ Grace and peace be with you from God our Father and the Lord Jesus Christ, ⁴ who gave himself for our sins to deliver us from the present evil age in accordance with the will of our God and Father, ⁵ to Whom be glory forever and ever, Amen!

## B. THE BASIS OF THE GOSPEL PAUL PROCLAIMED

⁶ I'm amazed that you're so quick to desert the One Who called you by the grace of Christ and are turning to a different gospel. ⁷ There is no other good news, of course, but there are some who are disturbing you and trying

---

1:1    "An apostle..." From the very beginning of the letter Paul signals that he will vigorously defend his authority and standing as an apostle against all challengers. The tone is quite uncharacteristic for Paul's greetings, normally so serene.

1:4    This verse also signals a theme for the letter, that salvation comes only through Jesus.

1:6    "I'm amazed..." marks an even more drastic departure from the usual epistolary format, for in place of the usual thanksgiving Paul gets right down to business, without any attempt to hide his concern. Some manuscripts read "by his grace" rather than "by the grace of Christ."

to distort the good news of Christ. ⁸ But even if we or an angel from Heaven should proclaim a gospel contrary to the good news we proclaimed to you, let them be accursed! ⁹ As we said before and now repeat, if anyone proclaims a gospel contrary to what you received from us, let him be accursed!

¹⁰ Who am I trying to gain favor with now, men or God? Am I seeking to please men? If I were still trying to please men, I wouldn't be a servant of Christ!

¹¹ I want you to know, brothers, that the good news I proclaimed is not a human gospel, ¹² for I didn't receive it from a man nor was I taught it — I received it through a revelation of Jesus Christ.

¹³ ᵃ You've heard what my life was like in Judaism, that I went to extraordinary lengths in persecuting the church of God and trying to destroy it, ¹⁴ ᵇ and that I advanced in Judaism beyond many contemporaries of my race, so much more zealous was I for the traditions of my fathers. ¹⁵ ᶜ But when the One Who set me apart from my mother's womb and called me through His grace was pleased ¹⁶ to reveal His Son to me so that I might proclaim his good news to the Gentiles, I didn't immediately consult with flesh and

---

ᵃ *Ac 8:3; 22:4–5; 26:13–18.*  ᵇ *Ac 22:3.*  ᶜ *Ac 9:3–6; 22:6–10; 26:13–18.*

1:10    Apparently Paul had been accused of trying to gain human favor by proclaiming a type of less rigorous, abbreviated gospel, in that he preached obedience to the Torah in the spirit, rather than according to the letter. Paul will vigorously assert that the new Christian freedom, far from being an abbreviation of the gospel, is of its very essence.

1:11–12ff. Paul now expands on the theme introduced at 1:1, that his calling as an apostle is not of human origin but is "through Jesus Christ and God the Father."

blood, [17] nor did I go up to Jerusalem to see those who were apostles before me. Instead, I went off to Arabia and later returned to Damascus.

[18] *d* Three years later I went up to Jerusalem to get to know Kephas, and I stayed with him for fifteen days. [19] I saw no other apostles except James, the Lord's brother. [20] Before God, what I'm writing to you is no lie! [21] Then I went to the regions of Syria and Cilicia. [22] The Judean churches in Christ had no personal knowledge of me — [23] they only heard that "the one who persecuted us is now proclaiming the faith he once tried to destroy," [24] and they glorified God because of me.

2 [1] *e* Fourteen years later I again went up to Jerusalem with Barnabas, taking Titus along also. [2] I went because of a revelation; I met privately with those held in repute and set out for them the gospel I proclaim among the Gentiles, lest I should somehow be running or have run in vain. [3] But not even Titus who was with me and is a Greek was required to be circumcised, [4] although it was urged by some false brothers who slipped in to spy on the freedom we have in Christ Jesus and wanted to enslave us.

---

*d* *Ac 9:26–30.*   *e* *Ac 11:30; 15:2.*

1:18    "Kephas." The Aramaic name for Peter, also derived from a word meaning "rock."

1:19    "James, the Lord's brother." In Semitic usage a relative was often referred to as a brother. In the Gospels it can be seen that James and Jesus had different mothers, cf. Mt 27:55; Mk 15:40–44; Lk 23:49; Jn 19:25.

2:4    Note the very strong language Paul uses — Jewish Christians who advocate obedience to the Torah are termed "false brothers" who want "to enslave us," so that a return to observance of the Torah would be slavery.

5 We didn't give in to them for a moment, so the truth of the gospel would be preserved for you. 6 Those who were held in repute — who they were makes no difference to me; God isn't influenced by such considerations — those who were held in repute added nothing. 7 On the contrary, when they saw that I had been entrusted with the gospel for the uncircumcised just as Peter had been entrusted with the gospel for the circumcised — 8 for the One Who worked through Peter for the apostleship of the circumcision also worked through me for the Gentiles — 9 and when they realized the grace that had been given to me, James and Kephas and John, who were considered the pillars, gave me and Barnabas the right hand of fellowship. We were to go to the Gentiles, and they to the circumcision. 10 Their one concern was that we should remember the poor, which was the very thing we were eager to do.

11 But when Kephas came to Antioch I opposed him to his face, because he was clearly wrong. 12 For before certain men came from James, Kephas ate with the Gentiles, but when they came he drew back and separated himself

---

2:5     While Paul constantly preaches respect for the consciences of others, he will not compromise on a matter of principle — to compromise "the truth of the gospel" is not true charity.

2:9     The use of the term "pillars" may derive from the image of the Church as the new Temple of God, and these disciples as the principal support for that Temple on earth.

2:10     "The poor." The Jerusalem church. Paul was eager for his Gentile converts to contribute to the Jerusalem church as a sign of the unity between Jew and Gentile which Christ had brought. 1 and 2 Corinthians and Romans contain numerous references to the collection Paul took up among his new churches.

2:12     For a Jew to eat with Gentiles was to become ritually impure, since Gentiles were considered "unclean."

because he was afraid of those who favored circumcision.
13 The rest of the Jews also joined in the hypocrisy — even
Barnabas was carried away by their hypocrisy. 14 But when
I saw that their actions were inconsistent with the truth of
the gospel I told Kephas in front of them all, "If you, a Jew,
live like a Gentile and not like a Jew, how can you force
the Gentiles to live like Jews?"

15 We're Jews by birth and aren't Gentile sinners, 16*f* but
we know that we can be restored to fellowship with God
only through faith in Jesus Christ, not by observance of the
Torah. We have believed in Jesus Christ so that we'll be
restored to fellowship with God through faith in Christ and
not by observance of the Torah, because no one *at all can
be restored to fellowship with God* by observance of the Torah.
17 But suppose, as we seek to be restored to fellowship with
God in Christ, we ourselves are found to be sinners? Does
Christ then serve the interests of sin? Not at all! 18 But if
I once again build up what I've torn down, I show that I
myself am a violator of God's law. 19 For through the Torah
I died to the Torah, so as to live for God. I've been crucified
with Christ! 20 It's no longer *I* who live, it's Christ who lives

---

*f* Rm 3:20–22.

---

2:16   Ps 143:2.

2:17–18 If in their new life in Christ, Jewish Christians are led to violate Torah rules
of purity, can it be said that Christ has led them into sin? On the contrary, the purpose of
the Torah was to prepare us to receive God's grace in Christ. To return to Torah observance
is to reject that grace and to be exposed as a true sinner.

2:19     The true purpose of the Torah was to lead to the realization that reconciliation
is necessary and that this cannot be effected by legal observance. This realization leads to
death with Christ to the Torah, but also to resurrection with him to life in the Spirit.

in me! And this life I live now in the flesh, I live through faith in the Son of God, who loved me and gave himself up for me. 21 I won't reject God's grace, for if righteousness came through the Torah then Christ died in vain.

## C. The Meaning of Faith and Torah and Their Place in God's Plan

**3** 1 You foolish Galatians! Who has cast a spell over you? Before your eyes Jesus Christ was publicly portrayed as crucified! 2 All I want to know from you is this — did you receive the Spirit as a result of observing the Torah or from listening and believing? 3 How can you be so foolish? Having begun with the Spirit will you now finish with the flesh? 4 Has your experience of all this been for nothing, if it truly was for nothing? 5 Does God give you the Spirit and work miracles among you because you observe the Torah or because you listen and believe? 6 *g* Thus, Abraham *believed God, and it was credited to him as righteousness.*

---

*g* Rm 4:3.

3:1–6    Paul begins his exposition with an appeal to the Galatians' own experience: without having been circumcised, they received the Spirit as witness of Christ's redemptive death and resurrection. Since this occurred through faith rather than observance of the Torah this means that faith, not legal observance, is the operative principle. To now turn to legal observance would be a retreat from the truth of the gospel. Abraham's experience foreshadows their own.

3:6      Gn 15:6.

⁷ ʰ You can see, then, that those who *believe* are the sons of Abraham. ⁸ Scripture foresaw that God would restore the Gentiles to fellowship with Him through faith and so it proclaimed the good news to Abraham beforehand, *Through you God will bless all the nations.* ⁹ Therefore, those who believe are blessed with Abraham, who had faith. ¹⁰ For everyone who relies on observance of the Torah is under a curse, as it is written, *Whoever fails to observe everything in the book of the Torah is cursed!* ¹¹ Now, that no one is restored to fellowship with God by observance of the Torah is evident, because *The righteous man shall live by faith.* ¹² But the Torah is not based on faith; instead, *Whoever does these things will live by them.* ¹³ Christ set us free from the Torah's curse by becoming a curse for us, as it is written, *Whoever hangs on a tree is cursed.* ¹⁴ So it is that in Christ Jesus the blessing of Abraham is able to come to the Gentiles, so that through faith we may receive the promise of the Spirit.

¹⁵ My brothers, let me give you an example. No one can set aside someone's will or modify it once it's been

---

ʰ *Rm 4:16.*

---

3:7–14   Paul next appeals to Scripture to underscore that only through faith and not through observance of the Torah is it possible to be restored to fellowship with God.

3:8       Gn 12:3.

3:10      Dt 27:26 (Septuagint).

3:11      Hab 2:4.

3:12      Lv 18:5.

3:13      Dt 21:23.

3:15–18   Having shown in the preceding verses that the call of the Gentiles to faith had been promised through Abraham, Paul now appeals to the example of a will to show that the promise takes precedence over the Torah.

ratified. ¹⁶ Now the promises were made to Abraham and his descendant. It doesn't say, "And his descendants," as if it were referring to many people; rather, it refers to one person, *And your descendant,* which is to say, Christ. ¹⁷ This is what I'm getting at; the Torah, which came four hundred and thirty years after the covenant had already been ratified by God, cannot invalidate the covenant so as to set aside the promise. ¹⁸ ⁱ For if the inheritance were dependent upon the Torah, it would no longer come from the promise, whereas God *did* give it to Abraham by a promise. ¹⁹ What, then, was the purpose of the Torah? It was added so that transgressions would be seen for what they are, to be in effect until the descendant to whom the promise was made came, and was promulgated by angels through an intermediary. ²⁰ Now there's no need for an intermediary when one party acts alone, and God is one.

²¹ So then, is the Torah contrary to God's promises? Not at all! Only if the Torah were able to give life would fellowship with God come from the Torah. ²² But Scripture confined everything under the power of sin so that what was promised might be given to those who believe, based on faith in Jesus Christ.

---

ⁱ *Rm 4:14.*

---

3:16      Gn 12:7.

3:19–22  Paul maintains that the Torah was of a lower order than the promise because the Torah was promulgated by angels and only as a temporary measure. The belief that God used intermediaries in his dealings with humans was common in Judaism. Verse 20 has been variously translated, but the general thrust is that the Torah is ancillary and subordinate to God's original promise to Abraham. The fact that intermediaries promulgated the Torah diminishes its significance when compared with God's direct promise to Abraham.

23 Before faith came we were imprisoned under the Torah, confined until such time as this faith was to be revealed. 24 So the Torah had custody of us until Christ came to restore us to fellowship with God through faith. 25 Now that faith has come we're no longer in its custody.

26 Through faith you're all sons of God in Christ Jesus, 27 for all of you who were baptized into Christ have clothed yourselves with Christ. 28 There's neither Jew nor Greek, there's neither slave nor free, there's neither male nor female — you're all one in Christ Jesus. 29 *j* And if you belong to Christ then you're Abraham's descendants, heirs in accordance with the promise.

4 1 Here's what I mean; as long as the heir is a minor, he's no different than a slave, even though he owns everything — 2 he's subject to guardians and trustees until the day that was set by his father. 3 It's the same with us — when we were minors we were enslaved by the elemental powers of the world. 4 But when the fullness of time had come, God sent forth His Son, born of a woman, born under the Torah, 5 *k* to redeem those who were under the Torah, so we could be adopted as God's sons. 6 And proof that you're His sons can be seen from the fact that God has sent the Spirit of His Son into our hearts, to cry, "Abba, Father!"

---

*j* *Rm 4:13.*   *k* *Rm 8:15–17.*

---

3:23–4:7 Paul concludes this section with several more metaphors — of imprisonment, sonship, and tutelage — to drive home the point that Christians are heirs of the promise and have been freed by Christ from the Torah.

4:3   "Elemental powers" were spiritual beings which were thought to control human life on earth. They were sometimes identified with angels, demons, or pagan gods.

[7] Therefore you're no longer a slave — you're a son, and if you're a son you're also an heir.

## D. Exhortation to Hold Fast to Freedom in Faith

[8] Back then when you didn't know God you were slaves to beings which by nature are not gods. [9] Now that you know God — or, rather, are known by God — how can you turn back once again to those poor, weak, elemental powers? Do you want to be their slaves again? [10] You observe days and months and seasons and years. [11] I'm afraid that all my work for you may somehow have been in vain.

[12] My brothers, I beg you, become like me as I have become like you! You did me no wrong — [13] you know that it was due to an illness of the flesh that I first proclaimed the good news to you, [14] and although my condition was a trial for you, you didn't despise or disdain me; instead, you received me like an angel of God, like Jesus Christ. [15] What has become of your blessed joy? For I bear you witness, if it had been possible you would have torn your eyes out and given them to me! [16] Have I become your enemy, then, by telling you the truth? [17] They court your

---

4:8–11   The "elemental powers" in this passage are probably to be identified with the angels by whom the Torah was promulgated. By adopting Jewish observances the Galatians would be putting themselves under the power of beings which were not God, just as they had been when they were still pagan Gentiles.

favor, but they don't mean you well — they want to have you for themselves so you'll court *their* favor. 18 Now it's always good to be made much of for a good purpose, and not just when I'm present with you. 19 My children, once again I'm suffering birth pains until Christ takes form in you. 20 I wish I were with you now and could change my tone, because now I'm at a loss to understand you.

21 Tell me, you who wish to be subject to the Torah, don't you understand what the Torah says? 22 For it's written that Abraham had two sons, one born of a slave woman and the other born of a free woman. 23 The one who was born of the slave woman was born according to the flesh, but the one who was born of the free woman was born through a promise. 24 This is an allegory — these women are two covenants. One covenant is from Mount Sinai and bears children into slavery — this is Hagar. 25 Now Hagar is Mount Sinai in Arabia and corresponds to the present Jerusalem, which is in slavery with her children. 26 The Jerusalem above, on the other hand, is free, and she is our mother, 27 for it is written,

> *Rejoice, barren woman, who have not given birth,*
> *break out and shout you who have not*
> *been in labor,*
> *Because the abandoned woman will have*
> *more children*
> *than the woman who has a husband.*

---

4:21–31  This allegory is noteworthy for its strongly negative polemic against the Torah, which is likened to a power which enslaves.

4:27  Is 54:1.

28 Now brothers, you, like Isaac, are children of the promise. 29 But just as at that time the son who was born according to the flesh persecuted the son born according to the Spirit, so it is even now. 30 But what does Scripture say? *Send the slave woman and her son away, for the slave woman's son shall not share the inheritance with the son* of the free woman. 31 So then, my brothers, we're not children of the slave woman but of the free woman.

5 1 Christ freed us for freedom, so stand firm and don't submit once again to the yoke of slavery.

2 Listen now! I, Paul, tell you that if you have yourselves circumcised, Christ will not be able to do you any good. 3 I bear witness once again to every man who has himself circumcised that he must observe the whole Torah. 4 Those of you who seek to be restored to fellowship with God through the Torah have separated yourselves from Christ, you've fallen away from grace. 5 For through the Spirit, by faith, we eagerly await the hope of fellowship with God. 6 For in Christ Jesus neither circumcision nor uncircumcision have any meaning — what matters is faith working through love.

7 You were running well; who has deflected you from following the truth? 8 Whoever persuaded you, it wasn't the One Who calls you! 9 *1* A little yeast can leaven the whole lump of dough. 10 I'm confident in the Lord that you'll take the same view, and the person who's disturbing you,

---

*1* 1 Cor 5:6.

4:30      Gn 21:10.

whoever he is, will be punished. 11 My brothers, if I am still preaching circumcision, why am I still being persecuted? In that case, the scandal of the cross has been abolished! 12 I wish those who are disturbing you by preaching circumcision would go on and castrate themselves!

## E. CHRISTIAN FREEDOM IN DAILY LIFE

13 You've been called to freedom, brothers — just don't let your freedom become an opportunity for the flesh. Serve one another through love. 14 For the whole Torah can be summed up in one command — *Love your neighbor as yourself!* 15 But if you bite and devour one another, watch out that you don't destroy each other!

16 But I tell you, walk according to the Spirit, and don't carry out the desires of the flesh. 17 *m* For the flesh's desires are opposed to the Spirit, and the Spirit is opposed to the flesh. They're opposed to each other so you won't just do whatever you want. 18 If you're led by the Spirit, you're not subject to the Torah. 19 Now it's evident what the works of the flesh are — fornication, impurity, and indecent acts, 20 idolatry, sorcery, hatred, strife, jealousy,

---

*m* Rm 7:15–23.

5:12 Traditional translations often moderate the coarseness of this passage with such euphemisms as "make eunuchs of themselves" or "mutilate themselves," but the Greek means quite literally to "cut away." The words "by preaching circumcision" are not in the original.

5:14 Lv 19:18.

5:20 The Greek word for "sorcery" is *pharmakeia*, from which such English words as "pharmacy" and "pharmacology" are derived. As can be deduced from the etymology, the first-

anger, selfishness, dissension, factionalism, 21 drunkenness, carousing, and similar things. I warn you now as I warned you before, that those who do these things will not inherit the Kingdom of God.

22 The Spirit's fruit is love, joy, peace, patience, kindness, goodness, faith, 23 gentleness, self-control. There is no law against these things! 24 Those who belong to Christ have crucified the flesh with its passions and desires. 25 If we live in the Spirit, let us also follow the Spirit. 26 Let's not be conceited, provocative, or envious toward one another.

6 1 My brothers, if anyone is caught in some kind of transgression, those of you who are spiritual should set him right in a spirit of gentleness. Watch out for yourself, so you won't be tempted too! 2 Bear one another's burdens, and in this way you'll fulfill Christ's law. 3 For if anyone thinks he's something even though he's nothing, he's only fooling himself. 4 Each of you should examine your own conduct and then you'll be able to boast of yourself, without worrying about anyone else, 5 for you will be bearing your own burden. 6 Whoever is taught the word should share all that's good with the one who teaches. 7 Don't be deceived; God cannot be outwitted. Whatever you sow, you'll also reap, 8 because whoever sows for his flesh will reap corruption

---

century sorcerer's stock in trade included a variety of drugs for different purposes. It is believed that some of these concoctions purported to be abortifacient and contraceptive.

5:22ff.    Paul now summarizes the preceding verses. He has already noted (v. 14) that the Torah can be summed up in the commandment to love. Those who would live "in Christ" must live "by the Spirit" (v. 16), and the life of the Spirit is expressed preeminently in love. Not only is the Torah not opposed to this (v. 23), but this fulfills the law of Christ, the New Torah.

from his flesh, whereas whoever sows for the Spirit will reap eternal life from the Spirit. 9 Let's not grow tired of doing good, for in due time we'll also reap a harvest if we don't give up. 10 So then, let's continue to do good to everyone as long as we have time, but especially to members of the household of the faith.

## F. CONCLUDING EXHORTATION

11 Look how large the letters are that I'm writing to you with my own hand! 12 Those who want to put on a good show in the flesh are the ones who are trying to force you to be circumcised, just so they won't be persecuted for the cross of Christ, 13 for these proponents of circumcision don't observe the Torah themselves — they only want you to be circumcised so they'll be able to boast about your flesh! 14 Far be it from me to boast of anything but the cross of Christ, through which the world is crucified to me and I to the world. 15 Neither circumcision nor uncircumcision is of any significance — a new creation is all that matters. 16 May peace and mercy be upon those who follow this rule, and upon God's Israel!

17 In the future, let no one cause me trouble, for I bear the marks of Jesus in my body!

18 The grace of our Lord Jesus Christ be with your spirit, my brothers. Amen!

---

6:15   In rabbinic thought a convert who was brought to a knowledge of God was said to be a "new creation."

# THE LETTER TO THE

# EPHESIANS

Ironically, one of the areas in which there is widespread agreement regarding Ephesians is that the letter was almost certainly not written directly to the church at Ephesus. Paul had used Ephesus as the base for his ministry in the Roman province of Asia (western Asia Minor) for over two years, and it is inconceivable from the example of his other letters that any letter to a church with which he had been associated for so long could be so devoid of personal references. In addition, many of the best textual witnesses omit the phrase "in Ephesus" from the first verse of the letter. In light of these facts, therefore, Ephesians is generally considered to be a type of encyclical letter, written for all the churches in the province of Asia at about the same time as the letters to Philemon and the Colossian church.

Unlike so many of his other letters, Paul had no particular crisis in mind when he wrote Ephesians — no urgent moral concerns, no dangerous doctrinal deviations.

Rather, the letter is an attempt to encourage the recipients to maintain unity in the truth of the gospel they have received. Paul's method of doing this is to review the plan of God which was revealed in Christ. By doing so Paul shows how great is God's power and glory and how great is the glory which we are called to share in, in Christ. This "in Christ" is important, for Ephesians is written from the standpoint of the Church's universal role, and the universal scope of salvation is also stressed. Not only are Jews and Gentiles to be united in Christ, but Christ is to be the head of "all things."

The review of God's plan for our salvation is contained in the first three chapters. Of note is Paul's deviation from his usual epistolary format, for a blessing precedes the thanksgiving section and in it Paul details the blessings we have received from God, our reasons for singing His praises. This not only sets the theme of the letter, it also sets the tone, for on several more occasions Paul will break out into prayer as he contemplates the sublimity of God's plan and the place in His plan which has been assigned to the human race.

The second half of the letter is a detailed discussion of various issues regarding life in Christ, including some of the most sublime words that have been written on marriage. Life in Christ is the fruit of faith and is our response to our call. Of urgent importance to Paul is that the unity of the Christian in Christ should be manifested in unity of spirit in Christ's body, the Church.

## OUTLINE OF THE LETTER TO THE EPHESIANS

| | | |
|---|---|---|
| A. | 1:1–2 | Greeting |
| B. | 1:3–14 | Blessing |
| C. | 1:15–23 | Thanksgiving |
| D. | 2:1–21 | In Christ Both Jews and Gentiles Are Reconciled and Are United in the Church |
| E. | 3:1–21 | Paul's Role in the Church as Apostle to the Gentiles |
| F. | 4:1–6:20 | Exhortation to Growth in the Life of Christ |
| G. | 6:21–24 | Conclusion |

## A. Greeting

1 ¹ Paul, an apostle of Christ Jesus by the will of God, to the saints [in Ephesus] who are faithful in Christ Jesus — ² grace and peace be with you from God our Father and the Lord Jesus Christ.

## B. Blessing

³ Blessed be the God and Father of our Lord Jesus Christ Who has blessed us in Christ with every spiritual blessing in the heavens. ⁴ He chose us in Christ before the foundation of the world to be holy and blameless before Him. In His love ⁵ He destined us beforehand to be His adopted sons through Jesus Christ, according to the purpose and desire of His will, ⁶ to the praise of the glorious grace He bestowed

---

1:3    "In the heavens." This introduces a prominent theme in Ephesians, in which Paul will refer frequently to "things in the heavens" (v. 10), "elemental spirits," and heavenly "powers." Both Jewish and pagan thought at the time held that human affairs — governmental, social, religious, etc. — were under the power or influence of spiritual beings, whether they were called angels, demons, or gods. Entire nations were thought to be under the tutelage of these beings. Paul may also have used this language of "powers" to refer to spiritual or demonic influences at work within human affairs without necessarily intending to specify spiritual existents as their source. Christ's mastery over this spiritual realm will thus be a source of "spiritual blessing," as, in Christ, we extend the effects of his redemption to all aspects of our individual and corporate lives as human beings.

upon us in His Beloved. 7 [a] Through Christ's blood we are redeemed and our sins are forgiven — such is the wealth of His grace 8 which He poured out upon us! With every manner of wisdom and understanding 9 He made known to us the mystery of His will, according to the purpose He displayed in Christ 10 as a plan for the fullness of time — to bring all things together in Christ, things in the heavens and things on earth. 11 God accomplishes all things in accordance with the purpose He has decided upon, and in Christ He chose and selected us in accordance with His plan 12 by which we who were the first to hope in Christ might exist to praise His glory. 13 In Christ you who heard the word of truth — the good news of your salvation — and believed it were sealed by the promised Holy Spirit, 14 which is the pledge that we shall gain our inheritance when God redeems what is His, to the praise of His glory!

## C. THANKSGIVING

15 And so, having heard of your faith in the Lord Jesus and your love for all the saints, 16 I give unceasing thanks and mention you in my prayers 17 that the God of our Lord Jesus Christ, the glorious Father, may give you a spirit of

---

[a] *Col 1:14.*

1:7     According to Judaic sacrificial theology "The life of the flesh is in the blood... it is the blood that makes an atonement for the soul" (Lv 17:11). Thus the reference to "blood" is properly understood within a sacrificial context, whereby the shedding of blood brings life. Cf. also 2:13.

wisdom and revelation by which you'll come to a knowledge of Him. ¹⁸ May the eyes of your hearts be enlightened so you'll come to know what the hope is to which He calls you, how rich is His glorious heritage which will be shared among the saints, ¹⁹ and how extraordinary is His great power for us who believe. The might of His power can be seen in the work ²⁰ He accomplished in Christ when He raised him from the dead and had him sit at His right hand in the heavenly realms, ²¹ far above every ruler, authority, power, and dominion, and above any name that can be named, not only in this age but also in the age to come. ²² *ᵇ He has put all things under his feet* and has given him as head over all things to the Church, ²³ which is his body, the fullness of the One Who fills all things in their totality.

## D. In Christ Both Jews and Gentiles Are Reconciled and Are United in the Church

2 ¹ ᶜ You used to be dead in the sins and transgressions
2 by which you followed this world's way of life, fol-

---

ᵇ Col 1:18.    ᶜ Col 2:13.

1:21    "Every ruler, authority, power, and domination." In this phrase Paul is referring to the "things in the heavens" (v. 10), those spiritual beings or influences which rule man in his corporate life. This reflects Paul's conviction that our redemption is not worked out in some "otherworldly" manner, but that man is to be saved within the context of his complete personality, with all its relationships and dynamics, both social and personal.

1:22    Ps 8:6.

2:1–3    "The ruler of the power of the air" is believed to be a reference to Satan. "Children of wrath" is a characterization of the entire human race as liable to divine punishment

lowing the ruler of the power of the air, the spirit that is currently at work in those who are disobedient. ³ We all once lived among them in the desires of the flesh; we did what the flesh and our imagination wanted and were, by nature, children of wrath, like the rest of them. ⁴ But God is rich in mercy and because of the great love He had for us, ⁵ even when we were dead in our transgressions, He brought us to life together with Christ — you've been saved by grace — ⁶ He raised us with him and had us sit together with Christ in the heavenly realms ⁷ so that in the coming ages He could show the extraordinary riches of His grace in His kindness toward us in Christ Jesus. ⁸ For by grace you have been saved through faith; and this was God's gift, it didn't come from you, ⁹ not from your own efforts, so that no one would be able to boast. ¹⁰ For we are His handiwork, created in Christ Jesus for the purpose of carrying out those good works for which God prepared us beforehand, so that we might lead our lives in the performance of good works.

¹¹ Therefore, remember that formerly you who are Gentiles by birth, you who are called the "uncircumcision" by what is called the "circumcision" (made in the flesh by human hands), ¹² remember that at that time you were

---

because of their sins. It is important to note that "desires of the flesh" includes desires of the mind — such as greed, pride, and envy — as well as desires of the body. In this context the word "flesh" refers to man in a fundamentally self-centered attitude in which God is ignored.

2:4–7    Here we find the familiar Pauline stress on the gratuitousness of God's redemption, which has come to us even though we were dead in sin and without any merit on our part.

separated from Christ, alienated from the community of Israel and strangers to the covenants made pursuant to the promise. You had no hope and were without God in the world, 13 but now you who were once far away have been drawn near through the blood of Christ.

14 For he is our peace. He has made the two — Jews and Gentiles — one, and in his flesh has torn down the dividing wall, the protective hedge, of enmity. 15 *d* He did this by setting aside the Torah with its commandments and regulations, making peace by creating one new man in himself out of the two 16 *e* and reconciling them both to God in one body by the cross, putting enmity to death by it. 17 He came and *proclaimed the good news of peace* to you *who were far off, and peace to those who were near,* 18 for through him we both have access in the one Spirit to the Father. 19 So then you're no longer strangers and aliens but fellow citizens with the saints and members of God's household. 20 You were built upon a foundation of apostles and prophets, and Christ Jesus was its cornerstone. 21 In him the whole building is joined together and grows into a holy Temple in the Lord, 22 and in him you are being built together into God's dwelling place in the Spirit.

---

*d* Col 2:14.  *e* Col 1:20.

---

2:14–15 "The dividing wall..." The rabbis spoke of the Torah as a barrier which maintained Israel's separateness and purity by isolating them from the Gentiles.

2:17    Is 57:19.

# E. PAUL'S ROLE IN THE CHURCH
## AS APOSTLE TO THE GENTILES

**3** [1] Because of this I, Paul, a prisoner for Christ [ Jesus] on behalf of you Gentiles — [2] for I'm sure you've heard of the stewardship of God's grace that was given to me for you, [3] how the mystery was made known to me in a revelation, as I've already written briefly. [4] *f* When you read this you'll be able to understand my insight into the mystery of Christ, [5] which wasn't made known to other generations of the sons of men as it has now been revealed to His holy apostles and prophets by the Spirit — [6] that the Gentiles are to be co-heirs, members of the same body, sharers in the promise in Christ Jesus through the good news. [7] I became a minister of the good news by a free gift of God's grace given me through the working of His power. [8] To me, the least of all the saints, was given the grace of proclaiming to the Gentiles the unfathomable riches of Christ [9] and to reveal for all the plan of the mystery that was hidden for ages in God, the creator of all things, [10] so that the multi-faceted wisdom of God might now be made known through the church to the rulers and powers in the heavens, [11] in accordance with the eternal plan He carried out in Christ Jesus our Lord. [12] In Christ we have free and confident access to God through our faith in him. [13] Therefore I ask you not to lose heart because of the afflictions I'm suffering on your behalf — this is your glory.

---

*f* Col 1:26–27.

[14] Because of this I bend my knees to the Father. [15] From Him every family in the heavens and on earth is named, [16] so that from the riches of His glory He may grant you inner strength and power through His Spirit. [17] May Christ dwell in your hearts through faith, firmly rooted and established in love, [18] so that with all the saints you may be able to understand the breadth, the length, the height, and the depth, [19] and know Christ's love which surpasses all knowledge so that you may be filled with all God's fullness.

[20] Now to Him Who is able to do so much more than all we can ask for or imagine, by the power at work in us, [21] to Him be glory in the church in Christ Jesus for all generations, forever and ever. Amen.

## F. EXHORTATION TO GROWTH IN THE LIFE IN CHRIST

4 [1] So I urge you — I, a prisoner in the Lord — to conduct yourselves in a manner worthy of the calling to which you've been called, [2] [g] with humility, gentleness, and patience. Bear with one another in love, [3] make every effort to maintain

---

[g] Col 3:12–13.

---

4:1ff.    Having painted a breathtaking picture of God's plan of salvation, Paul turns to the individual life of Christians. Even in his most exalted moments Paul maintains a firm grasp of reality. He reminds the Ephesians that no matter how awe inspiring the mystery of God may be, each individual Christian must work out their salvation in their daily life, no longer alone, however, but as a part of Christ's body, the Church.

unity of spirit in the bond of peace. ⁴ There is one body and one Spirit, just as you were called to the one hope of your calling. ⁵ One Lord, one faith, one baptism, ⁶ one God and Father of us all, Who is above all, through all, and in all.

⁷ Grace has been given to each of us according to the extent of Christ's gift. ⁸ Therefore Scripture says,

> *When he ascended on high he led*
> *    prisoners into captivity,*
> *he gave gifts to men.*

⁹ (Now what can "he ascended" mean except that he also descended, into the lower regions of the earth? ¹⁰ The one who descended is also the one who ascended far above all the heavens in order to fill all things.) ¹¹ To some the gift he gave was to be apostles, to others it was to be prophets, to others it was to be evangelists, pastors, or teachers. ¹² This was to equip the saints for the work of ministry, the building up of the body of Christ, ¹³ until we all attain to unity of faith and knowledge of the Son of God — to mature manhood, to the extent of Christ's full stature. ¹⁴ Thus we'll no longer be infants, tossed and carried here and there by every wind of teaching coming from human cunning, from their craftiness in developing deceitful schemes. ¹⁵ Instead, by speaking the truth in love we'll grow in every way into him — Christ — who is the head ¹⁶ ʰ upon whom the whole body depends.

---

ʰ Col 2:19.

4:7–11  Some have argued that the descent referred to was Christ's return on Pentecost to bestow the gifts of the Spirit. Among other factors we may note that Ps 68:18 (quoted) was used at the Jewish feast of Pentecost to commemorate the lawgiving at Sinai, the quintessential gift–giving of the Old Testament.

Joined together and united by all the supporting ligaments, when each part is working as it should the head causes the body to grow and build itself up in love.

17 Therefore I say this and bear witness in the Lord — you must no longer live as the Gentiles do, with their futile reasoning. 18 Their understanding is clouded and they're alienated from God's life because of their ignorance, which is caused by the hardening of their hearts. 19 They've grown callous and have given themselves over to licentiousness, greedily pursuing every sort of impurity. 20 That's not how you learned Christ, 21 not if you heard about him and were taught the truth as it is in Jesus. 22 *i* Put off the old man, your former way of life which is corrupted by deceitful desires! 23 Be renewed in your mind and spirit 24 *j* and put on the new man created in accordance with God's design in true righteousness and holiness.

25 Therefore, put away falsehood and *let everyone speak the truth to his neighbor,* because we're parts of one another. 26 *Be angry, but don't sin.* Don't let the sun set on your anger, 27 and don't give the Devil an opening. 28 The thief must no longer steal; instead, he must labor and do honest work with his own hands so he'll have enough to give to those in need. 29 Let no bad word come from your mouths; instead, say only what is necessary and will serve to edify, so that those who hear may receive grace. 30 Don't grieve the Holy

---

*i* Col 3:9. *j* Col 3:10.

4:25    Zc 8:16.
4:26    Ps 4:4 (Septuagint).

Spirit, with Whom you were sealed for the day of redemption. [31] Let all bitterness, anger, wrath, angry shouting, and slander be put away from you, along with all malice. [32] [k] Be kind to one another, compassionate, forgiving each other just as God forgave you in Christ.

5 [1] Be imitators of God as beloved children. [2] Walk in love, just as Christ loved us and gave himself up for us to God as an offering and sacrifice with a pleasing fragrance. [3] Don't even mention any sort of fornication, impurity, or greed among you, as is fitting among saints, [4] nor indecent behavior, foolish talk, or coarse joking. These things are improper; it's better to give thanks. [5] For you should know that no fornicator, or impure or greedy person — that is, no idolater — will have any share in the Kingdom of Christ and God.

[6] Let no one deceive you with empty words — it's through these things I've mentioned that God's wrath comes upon the disobedient. [7] Therefore, don't associate with them, [8] for once you were darkness, but now you're light in the Lord. Walk like children of light — [9] for the fruit of light is to be found in every sort of goodness, righteousness, and truth — [10] and examine everything to see what's pleasing to the Lord. [11] Don't participate in the unfruitful deeds of darkness; instead, show them up for what they are, [12] for it's disgraceful to even mention the things they do in secret. [13] But everything brought into the open by the light is

---

[k] Col 3:13.

5:3–5     The mention of "greed" among a list of sins related to sexuality seems puzzling at first, but the unifying idea is found in v. 5: such persons are idolaters — they make what they desire, rather than God, the center of their lives.

clearly revealed, [14] and everything thus revealed is light. Therefore it says,

> "Sleeper awake, and rise from the dead,
> And Christ will be your light."

[15] Be sure to walk carefully, wisely rather than foolishly. [16] [l] Make good use of your time, for the days are evil. [17] Therefore, don't be foolish — understand what God's will is. [18] Don't get drunk on wine, which is dissipation; instead, be filled with the Spirit. [19] [m] Speak to each other in psalms, hymns, and spiritual songs; sing praise to the Lord in your hearts, [20] giving thanks always and for everything to God the Father in the name of our Lord Jesus Christ.

[21] Be subject to one another out of reverence for Christ. [22] [n] Wives should be subject to their husbands as they are to the Lord, [23] for the husband is his wife's head just as Christ is the head of the church, and is himself the Savior of the body. [24] But just as the church is subject to Christ, so too wives should be subject to their husbands in everything. [25] [o] Husbands, love your wives, just as Christ loved the church and gave himself up for her, [26] to sanctify her by cleansing her with the bath of water and the word. [27] In this way he'll be able to present the church to himself in its glory, having neither stain nor wrinkle nor anything of that sort, but instead holy and unblemished. [28] In the same way

---

[l] Col 4:5.　[m] Col 3:16–17.　[n] Col 3:18; 1 P 3:1.　[o] Col 3:19; 1 P 3:7.

---

5:14　It is generally believed that this verse is a fragment of an early Christian hymn, probably used during the baptismal liturgy.

5:21–33　Paul, in this beautiful passage, places great emphasis on the mutuality of love and respect which should characterize the marriage union.

husbands should love their wives just as they love their own bodies. The man who loves his wife loves himself, [29] for no one ever hates his own flesh. On the contrary, he nourishes and cares for it just as Christ does for the church, [30] because we're parts of his body.

> [31]   *For this reason a man shall leave his father*
> *and mother*
> *and be joined to his wife,*
> *And the two shall be one flesh.*

[32] This is a tremendous mystery. I'm applying it to Christ and the church, [33] but each one of you should in the same way love his wife as he loves himself, and the wife should respect her husband.

**6** [1] [p] Children, obey your parents [in the Lord], because it's the right thing to do. [2] *Honor your father and mother!* This is the first commandment that comes with a promise — [3] *that all may be well with you and you may have a long life on earth.* [4] [q] And fathers, don't cause your children to resent you; instead, raise them by instructing and admonishing them as the Lord would.

[5] Slaves, obey your earthly masters with fear and trembling and with single-hearted devotion, just as you obey

---

[p] Col 3:20.   [q] Col 3:21–4:1.

5:31       Gn 2:24.
6:2–3     Ex 20:12; Dt 15:16.
6:5–9     Without fanfare Paul introduces a new element into the master/slave relationship, for he points out that slaves, too, have God–given rights and that masters will answer to God for their treatment of servants. This principle may also be applied in complete faithfulness to Paul's thought to all relationships involving subordination.

Christ, 6 and don't just try to impress them and curry favor. Instead, as servants of Christ who do God's will from the heart, 7 serve your masters enthusiastically as if you were serving the Lord and not a man. 8 For you know that if anyone does something good he'll receive the same thing from the Lord, whether that person is a slave or free. 9 And you masters, do the same for them. Stop threatening your slaves, because you know that the Lord in Heaven is both your Lord and their Lord, and he doesn't play favorites.

10 Finally, become strong through the Lord's power and might. 11 Put on God's armor so you'll be able to stand up against the schemes of the Devil, 12 for we're not engaged in a struggle with mere flesh and blood — we're fighting against the rulers and powers, against the cosmic powers of this dark world, against the spiritual forces of evil in the heavens. 13 Therefore, take up God's armor so you'll be able to oppose them on the day of evil and, by doing everything in your power, to remain standing. 14 So stand firm! *Gird your loins with truth and put on the breastplate of righteousness!* 15 *Put on your feet the boots of preparedness for the good news of peace!* 16 And along with all this take up the shield of the faith, with which you'll be able to extinguish all the flaming arrows of the Evil One. 17 Take *the helmet of salvation* and *the sword of the Spirit,* which is *the word of God*. 18 Pray at all times in the Spirit with every

6:14    Is 11:5; 59:17.

6:15    Is 52:7.

6:17    Is 59:17.

manner of prayer and supplication. To this end stay alert and persevere in supplication on behalf of all the saints, [19] and on my behalf, that when I open my mouth God will give me the words to boldly make known the mystery of the good news, [20] for which I'm an ambassador in chains. Pray that I'll speak out boldly as I should.

# G. Conclusion

[21] *ʳ* Tychicus, my beloved brother and faithful servant in the Lord, will tell you everything, so you'll know about my situation, what I'm doing. [22] *ˢ* I've sent him to you for that very reason, so you'll know how we are and so he'll be able to give your hearts encouragement.

[23] Peace and love be to the brothers, with faith from God the Father and the Lord Jesus Christ. [24] Grace be with all who love our Lord Jesus Christ with an undying love.

---

*ʳ* Ac 20:4; 2 Tm 4:12.   *ˢ* Col 4:7–8.

# THE LETTER TO THE

# PHILIPPIANS

Paul's ministry at Philippi is recounted in Acts (16:11–40; 20:6) but we can be sure that Acts' narrative is far from being the whole story, for it is clear from this letter that Paul's relations with the Philippians were particularly close and cordial. In fact, the Philippians had eagerly supported Paul in his missionary activities after he moved on, demonstrating a zeal for which Paul was especially grateful.

The city of Philippi was a Roman colony. It was established after the Roman conquest of Macedonia at a strategic commercial crossroads and was also situated near valuable mining sites. From Acts we learn that the Jewish community at Philippi was rather small, too small to even support a synagogue. Based upon the extent of the support they provided to Paul it would be fair to suppose, therefore, that the church at Philippi was largely composed of Gentile converts.

Philippians is generally considered apart from the other Captivity Letters, the rest of which appear to be more closely interrelated both stylistically and theologically, as well as from the standpoint of the persons who are mentioned in the letters. As a result, attempts have often been made to separate Philippians from the other Captivity Letters with regard to its date and place of composition. A date early in Paul's Caesarean imprisonment (perhaps A.D. 57 or 58) is an attractive theory for several reasons. First, Paul appears to be quite optimistic that he will be released soon, and he is confident that his imprisonment will be for the good of the gospel. Presumably his mood would have changed as his imprisonment dragged on. Second, Paul indicates that he is being held in the praetorium, which could very well refer to the governor's residence at Caesarea (although it could also have referred to such an establishment in Ephesus). Third, Paul's bitter polemic against the Jews fits in naturally with the dangerous position he found himself in at Caesarea, as compared with the more relaxed situation during his Roman captivity, as we know it from Acts.

In any event, the letter was written to thank the Philippians for the assistance they had sent as soon as they heard about Paul's imprisonment. The letter is to be carried by Epaphroditus, the Philippian who had brought the aid to Paul. Epaphroditus had had to remain with Paul for some time due to illness.

The letter itself finds Paul in a relatively exalted frame of mind, almost hoping that he will meet a martyr's end. Far from being in any way depressed, he repeatedly speaks of his own joy and urges the Philippians to rejoice as well. The intent of the letter is basically to encourage and exhort the Philippians to continue their already outstanding efforts to advance the gospel. With this purpose in mind, he emphasizes the need for them to conduct themselves in a manner worthy of the good news, to hold fast to the faith, and to maintain an unselfish unity in Christ. Throughout the letter Paul expresses himself with great personal warmth, leaving a beautiful testimony to the sincere Christian love he and the Philippians shared.

### OUTLINE OF THE LETTER TO THE PHILIPPIANS

| A. | 1:1–2 | Greeting |
| B. | 1:3–11 | Thanksgiving |
| C. | 1:12–30 | The Gospel Is Being Advanced Despite Paul's Imprisonment |
| D. | 2:1–18 | Exhortation to Unity in Christ |
| E. | 2:19–3:1 | News of Timothy and Epaphroditus |
| F. | 3:2–4:1 | A Warning Against Christ's Enemies and an Exhortation to Stand Firm in the Faith |
| G. | 4:2–9 | Concluding Admonitions |
| H. | 4:10–20 | Paul's Thanks for the Philippians' Generosity |
| I. | 4:21–23 | Farewell |

## A. GREETING

**1** ¹ Paul and Timothy, servants of Christ Jesus, to all the saints in Christ Jesus at Philippi, along with the bishops and deacons — ² the grace and peace of God our Father and the Lord Jesus Christ be with you.

## B. THANKSGIVING

³ I give thanks to my God every time I think of you. ⁴ Whenever I pray for you I offer my prayer joyfully, ⁵ because of your partnership in the good news from the first day up to the present. ⁶ Of this I'm convinced, that the One Who began the good work in you will bring it to completion on the Day of Jesus Christ. ⁷ It's right that I should feel this way about you because I have you in my heart, and because you all share my grace, both in my imprisonment and in the defense and confirmation of the good news. ⁸ For God is my witness that I long for all of you with the affection of Jesus Christ. ⁹ My prayer is that your love will increase more and more with knowledge and every manner of insight ¹⁰ so that you'll be able to discover what's best and may be pure and blameless for the Day of Christ, ¹¹ filled with the fruit of the righteousness that comes through Jesus Christ, to the glory and praise of God.

## C. The Gospel Is Being Advanced Despite Paul's Imprisonment

¹² I want you to know, my brothers, that the things that have happened to me have actually had the effect of advancing the gospel. ¹³ As a result it's become known throughout the praetorium and to everyone else that I'm in chains for Christ, ¹⁴ and my chains have given the majority of the brothers in the Lord the confidence to proclaim the word even more fearlessly.

¹⁵ Some proclaim Christ out of jealousy and contentiousness, but others proclaim him out of good will, ¹⁶ and these do it out of love, because they know I'm here for having defended the gospel. ¹⁷ Those who proclaim Christ out of jealousy do so insincerely in the hope of causing me trouble while I'm in prison. ¹⁸ What does it matter? The important thing is that one way or another Christ is proclaimed, whether from false or sincere motives, and for that I rejoice. And I *will* rejoice, ¹⁹ for I know that it will lead to my deliverance, through your prayers and the support of the Spirit of Jesus Christ. ²⁰ It is my eager expectation and hope that I won't be ashamed, but that now as always Christ will be boldly honored in my person whether I live or die. ²¹ For me, to live is Christ and to die is gain. ²² If I continue to live in the flesh that means I'll have fruitful labor, yet I

---

1:13 "Praetorium" could either mean the headquarters of the Praetorian Guard in Rome or the residence of a provincial governor, such as in Caesarea.

1:19 "It will lead to my deliverance." This probably refers to vindication before the heavenly court rather than before a human court. Jb 13:16 (Septuagint).

don't know which to prefer. 23 I'm torn between the two alternatives — I wish to depart and be with Christ, for that is far better, 24 but for your sake it's more necessary to remain in the flesh. 25 Since I'm convinced of this, I know I'll stay and remain with you all to further your progress and joy in the faith, 26 so that when I'm once more with you your pride in me may overflow in Christ Jesus.

27 The main thing is to conduct yourselves in a manner worthy of Christ's good news, so that whether I come and see you or whether I'm away I'll hear that you're standing firm in one spirit, working together with one mind for the faith of the gospel 28 and not frightened in any way by your enemies. This will be a sign to them of their coming destruction, but of your salvation which will come from God. 29 For God has graciously allowed you not only to believe in Christ but also to suffer for him. 30 You're engaged in the same struggle which you saw me engaged in, and now hear that I'm still engaged in.

## D. Exhortation to Unity in Christ

2 1 If life in Christ provides any ecouragement, any comfort in love, any sharing in the Spirit, any affection and compassion, 2 then complete my joy by being of one mind, sharing the same love, being united in spirit, and thinking as one. 3 Do nothing out of selfishness or a desire to boast; instead, in a spirit of humility toward one another, regard others as better than yourselves. 4 Each of you should

look out for the rights of others, rather than looking after your own rights. 5 Have the same outlook among you that Christ Jesus had,

> 6 Who, though he was in the form of God,
>> did not consider equality with God
>>> something to hold on to.
> 7 Instead, he emptied himself and took on
>> the form of a slave,
>> born in human likeness,
>>> and to all appearances a man.
> 8 He humbled himself and became obedient,
>> even unto death, death on a cross.
> 9 For this reason God exalted him
>> and gave him a name above every
>>> other name,
> 10 So that at the name of Jesus every knee shall bend,
>> in the heavens, on earth, and below the earth,
> 11 And every tongue will proclaim to the glory
>> of God the Father,
>> that Jesus Christ is Lord.

---

2:6–11 Whether this passage was written by Paul or was a pre–Pauline hymn, as many scholars believe, it is agreed that this passage refers to Christ as pre–existing and represents some of the "highest" Christology in the New Testament. There are numerous allusions to Isaiah's Suffering Servant, in which the importance of Christ's obedience is stressed. This obedience was congenial to the rabbinic concept of complete loyalty to the Torah.

2:6    Is 53:12.

2:7    "The form of a slave," i.e., Jesus appeared to be a normal human being, a slave of sin.

2:8    Is 53:7–8, "Even to death on the cross." Christ's obedience was truly extraordinary, for it embraced a shameful death which bore the Torah's curse: "Cursed be everyone who hangs on a tree" (Dt 21:33).

2:9    Is 52:13.

2:10–11    Is 45:23 (Septuagint).

12 So then, my beloved, be obedient as you always have been; not just as you were when I was present — in my absence now you must be even more so. Set about accomplishing your salvation with fear and trembling, 13 for God is the One Who is leading you both to desire and to work for His chosen plan. 14 Do everything without grumbling or arguing 15 so that you'll be blameless and pure, unblemished children of God amidst a twisted and perverted generation, among whom you'll shine like stars in the world. 16 Hold fast to the word of life, so that on the Day of Christ I'll be able to boast that I didn't work or toil in vain. 17 *a* But even if I'm poured out like a libation upon the sacrificial offering of your faith, I'll rejoice and be glad with all of you, 18 and likewise you too should rejoice and be glad with me.

## E. NEWS OF TIMOTHY AND EPAPHRODITUS

19 I hope in the Lord that I'll soon be able to send Timothy to you, so that I'll be cheered by finding out about you. 20 I have no one else like him who is so sincerely concerned about you, 21 for they all look out for their own interests, not those of Christ Jesus. 22 But you know Timothy's worth, and that he served with me in advancing the gospel like a child serves his father. 23 Therefore I hope to

---

*a* 2 Tim 4:6.

2:17     A "libation" was a sacrificial offering of a liquid, performed by pouring it out or, as here, by pouring it over another sacrificial offering. The pouring served to destroy the offering by rendering it unrecoverable, as burning did with a solid offering.

send him as soon as I see how things stand with me, 24 and I trust in the Lord that I too will soon be able to come.

25 I've thought it necessary to send you Epaphroditus, my brother, co-worker, and fellow soldier, whom you sent to minister to me in my need, 26 since he was longing for all of you and was distressed that you had heard that he was ill. 27 He *was* ill, in fact, and was close to death, but God had mercy on him, and not only on him but on me as well, so that I wouldn't have grief upon grief. 28 So I'm all the more eager to send him so that when you see him again you'll rejoice, and I'll be free from anxiety. 29 Receive him in the Lord, then, with joy, and honor people like him, 30 because for the sake of Christ's work he came close to death, risking his own life to perform those services you yourselves were unable to perform for me.

3 1 And so, my brothers, rejoice in the Lord. To write the same things to you is no trouble for me and makes you more secure.

## F. A WARNING AGAINST CHRIST'S ENEMIES AND AN EXHORTATION TO STAND FIRM IN THE FAITH

2 Beware of those dogs, beware of the evil-doers, beware of the mutilation. 3 We are the *true* circumcision, who

---

3:2–3    This passage refers to Jews or Jewish Christians who wished to impose observance of the Torah on Gentile converts. "Dogs" was a term commonly used by Jews to refer to Gentiles, and now Paul tosses it back at his bitter opponents; "evildoers" may refer ironically to the harm they do while claiming to rely upon deeds done in observance of the Torah;

worship God in spirit and put our trust in Christ Jesus rather than in the flesh, <sup>4</sup> although I have reason for confidence in the flesh, as well. If anyone else thinks they have reason for confidence in the flesh, I have better reasons! <sup>5</sup> <sup>*b*</sup> I was circumcised on the eighth day, from the people of Israel, the tribe of Benjamin, a Hebrew from Hebrews, a Pharisee with regard to the Torah, <sup>6</sup> <sup>*c*</sup> a zealous persecutor of the church, blameless as to righteousness under the Torah. <sup>7</sup> But whatever I had gained from all this, I have come to consider it loss for the sake of Christ. <sup>8</sup> In fact, I consider everything to be loss for the sake of the surpassing greatness of knowing Christ Jesus my Lord. For his sake I've cast everything aside and regard it as so much rubbish so that I'll gain Christ <sup>9</sup> and be found in him, having no righteousness of my own based on observance of the Torah but only that righteousness which comes through faith in Christ, the righteousness that comes from God and which is based on faith. <sup>10</sup> My goal is to know him and the power of his resurrection, to understand the fellowship of his sufferings and become conformed to his death <sup>11</sup> in the hope of somehow attaining resurrection from the dead.

<sup>12</sup> Not that I've already achieved this or that I'm already perfect! But I continue to strive in the hope of making

---

*b* Rm 11:1; Ac 23:6; 26:5.   *c* Ac 8:3; 22:4; 26:9–11.

---

"mutilation" was, in Greek, a derisively punning reference to circumcision and may also refer to the ban on mutilated persons belonging to the Jewish priesthood (Lv 21:5, 20; Dt 23:1).

3:10      Paul wishes to understand the process by which, through suffering, we come closer to Christ.

it my own, because Christ [Jesus] has made *me* his own.
13 My brothers, I don't consider that I've won yet, and
for this reason I forget what's behind me and reach out
for what's in front of me. 14 I strain toward the goal to
win the prize — of God's heavenward call in Christ Jesus.
15 So let us who are mature adopt this attitude, and if your
attitude is otherwise, God will reveal this to you as well.
16 But let's conduct ourselves in the light of what we've
already attained.

17 My brothers, be imitators of me. Watch those who
behave in accordance with the example we've given you.
18 I've told you many times and now I tell you with tears
in my eyes, there are many who behave like enemies of
Christ's cross. 19 They'll end up being destroyed; their god
is their own desires — they glory in their shame, their concern is for earthly things. 20 But we are citizens of Heaven,
and we eagerly await a savior from Heaven, the Lord Jesus
Christ. 21 He'll transform our lowly bodies so that they'll
have the same form as his glorious body, by means of the
power that enables him to subject everything to himself.

4 1 Therefore, my beloved brothers whom I long for,
my joy and my crown, be steadfast in the Lord.

---

3:18    Most commentators are in agreement that the "enemies of Christ's cross" are
heterodox Christians, rather than the Jews.

3:19    The reference to "their own desires (lit., "belly")" is probably meant to apply
in a broad sense to a life spent focused on oneself.

## G. Concluding Admonitions

2 I urge Euodia and Syntyche to think as one in the Lord. 3 And I ask you, my true comrade, to help these women who joined me in the struggle for the gospel, along with Clement and the rest of my co-workers — their names are in the Book of Life. 4 Rejoice in the Lord, always; again I say, rejoice! 5 Let all know how considerate you are. The Lord is near. 6 Don't be anxious; instead, give thanks in all your prayers and petitions and make your requests known to God. 7 And God's peace which is beyond all understanding will keep your hearts and minds in Christ Jesus.

8 And so, my brothers, whatever is true, whatever is honorable, whatever is just, whatever is pure, whatever is pleasing, whatever is gracious, if there is any excellence or anything praiseworthy, think of *these* things. 9 What you have received from me, what you have learned, what you have heard, what you have seen in me, do these things, and the God of peace will be with you.

## H. Paul's Thanks for the Philippians' Generosity

10 It's a great joy to me in the Lord that now at last your concern for me has been revived — you *were* concerned but you had no opportunity to show it. 11 Not that I suffered any want — I've learned to be content with what I have.

---

4:2    Euodia and Syntyche are women's names.

12 I know how to live in straitened circumstances, and I know how to live amid plenty. I've learned this secret under every conceivable circumstance, whether full or hungry, well provided for or suffering want. 13 I'm able to do everything through the One Who strengthens me. 14 Nevertheless, you did well to share in my affliction.

15 *d* You Philippians also know that in the beginning of my proclamation of the good news, when I left Macedonia, not one church extended a partnership to share in giving and receiving, except for you alone. 16 Even in Thessalonica you once and then again sent me help. 17 Not that I'm interested in receiving gifts — rather, I want to see the credits to your account keep increasing. 18 I have everything I need; in fact, I have *more* than enough. I've received what Epaphroditus brought on your behalf, and I'm fully supplied. It was a fragrant aroma, an acceptable sacrifice that was pleasing to God. 19 My God will fill all your needs by means of His glorious riches in Christ Jesus. 20 Glory be to our God and Father for ever and ever, amen.

# I. Farewell

21 Greet each saint in Christ Jesus. The brothers with me greet you. 22 All the saints greet you, especially those who belong to Caesar's household. 23 May the grace of the Lord Jesus Christ be with your spirit.

---

*d* 2 Cor 11:9.

# THE LETTER TO THE

# COLOSSIANS

Colossians is a companion letter to the Letter to Philemon. Both were written to the city of Colossae in Asia Minor, but whereas Philemon was written to a specific person, Colossians was written to the congregation there at large. Both letters were to be delivered by Tychicus.

Colossae was a relatively small town in the region of Phrygia, and Paul had never personally been there. Instead, the Colossians had received the good news from a fellow Colossian named Epaphras. The letter itself was in response to a report Epaphras had brought to Paul in prison to the effect that the congregation was being unsettled by certain persons who were advocating doctrines which were at variance with what Epaphras had taught them. Probably at Epaphras' request, Paul wrote this letter to put the Colossians on guard against the new teaching and to urge them to hold fast to the faith they had received through Epaphras. The result is a marvel of tact, considering that Paul could claim no particular authority with respect to the Colossians.

The teaching which was troubling the church at Colossae appears to have been an amalgam of both Hellenistic and Jewish elements. A special reverence for the "elemental spirits" or angels was prominent in this teaching, as well as an insistence upon adherence to Jewish customs and rituals. The teachers of these doctrines claimed great wisdom for themselves and, based upon what we can tell from Paul's letter, assigned great importance to human reason and speculation in formulating their positions.

Paul's exhortation to the Colossians rests firmly upon the person of Jesus Christ and the truth of the gospel. Jesus is superior to everything, both in the heavens and on earth, and has subjected all the powers and authorities. In Christ we share in God's fullness, for Christ is the fullness of God, and so it makes no sense for the Colossians to follow the rules and regulations of these inferior powers rather than the gospel of Christ. Moreover, Christ is the source of true wisdom and spiritual strength, and no human "philosophizing" can compare with the wisdom and strength we receive through the gospel.

These concerns occupy the first two chapters of the letter. The remainder is a moral exhortation to lead the true life in Christ. The latter portion is notable for raising the issues of household relations — husband/wife, parents/children, and master/servant — which are developed at somewhat greater length in Ephesians. However, what Paul has to say here applies not only to the family but also touches on the transformation of all human relationships in Christ.

### Outline of the Letter to the Colossians

A.  1:1–2        Greeting

B.  1:3–14       Thanksgiving

C.  1:15–2:5     Christ in Us, the Mystery of God

D.  2:6–23       Exhortation to Be Firm in the Faith and to Resist Judaizing Tendencies

E.  3:1–4:6      Practical Counsels to the True Life in Christ

F.  4:7–18       Personal News and Conclusions

## A. Greeting

1 ¹ Paul, an apostle of Christ Jesus by God's will, and our brother Timothy ² to the holy and faithful brothers in Christ at Colossae — grace and peace be with you from God our Father.

## B. Thanksgiving

³ When we pray for you we always give thanks to God, the Father of our Lord Jesus Christ, ⁴ because we've heard of your faith in Christ Jesus and your love for all the saints ⁵ which comes from the hope stored up for you in Heaven. You first heard of this hope in the word of truth, the good news ⁶ that has come to you. This good news has been increasing and producing fruit in the whole world, just as it has among you from the day you heard and came to know the grace of God in truth. ⁷ ᵃ You learned the good news from our beloved fellow servant Epaphras, who is a faithful minister of Christ on our behalf, ⁸ and he informed us of your love in the Spirit.

---

ᵃ *Phm 23.*

---

1:6     As always, Paul stresses that the good news is a free gift ("grace") from God, unmerited by any actions on the part of those who have received it.

1:7     Some manuscripts read "on your behalf."

⁹ Therefore, from the day we heard of you we haven't ceased praying for you. May God fill you with the knowledge of His will through wisdom and all manner of spiritual understanding, ¹⁰ that you may conduct yourselves in a manner worthy of the Lord and fully pleasing to him — fruitful in every type of good work and increasing in knowledge of God. ¹¹ We pray that you will be strengthened with all the power of His glorious might so that your steadfastness and patience will be perfected and you may joyfully ¹² give thanks to the Father Who made you worthy to share in the portion of the saints in light. ¹³ He has rescued us from the power of darkness and has brought us into the Kingdom of His beloved Son, ¹⁴ ᵇ by whom we are redeemed and our sins are forgiven.

## C. CHRIST IN US, THE MYSTERY OF GOD

¹⁵ He is the image of the unseen God,
      the firstborn of all creation,

---

ᵇ *Eph 1:7.*

1:11    "His glorious might" refers to the power by which God raised Jesus. Cf. also Rm 6:4.

1:12    The Greek word translated "portion" was the same word used in the Septuagint which referred to the "portions" of Palestine which were allocated to the twelve tribes of Israel.

1:13–14  The idea of a New Exodus is a favorite Pauline theme and a metaphor which he often applies to the Christian life.

1:15–20  The background for this hymn–like passage is to be found in the Old Testament Wisdom literature, in which Wisdom becomes a personified attribute of God. The rabbis identified Wisdom with the Torah, whereas Paul applies these passages to Christ.

1:15ff.   This passage is considered to be a reference to Pr 8:22, in which Wisdom is described as begotten by God at the beginning. As the image of God Jesus is thus also the

<sup>16</sup> For in him all things in the heavens and on earth
  were created,
   both the seen and the unseen,
  Whether thrones, dominions, rulers, or powers;
   all things were created through him and for him.
<sup>17</sup> He is before all things
  and in him all things hold together.
<sup>18</sup> <sup>c</sup> He is the head of the body,
  of the church,
  He is the beginning, the firstborn from the dead,
   so that he might be above all else,
<sup>19</sup> For in him all the Fullness was pleased to dwell
<sup>20</sup> <sup>d</sup> and through him reconciled all things to
   Himself,
  Making peace by the blood of his cross,
   reconciling everything on earth or in the
   heavens.

<sup>21</sup> You were once alienated from God and were His
enemies both in intent and in your evil deeds, <sup>22</sup> but now
God has reconciled you through Christ's body of flesh — by
means of his death — so God will be able to bring you before Himself, holy, unblemished, and blameless, <sup>23</sup> as long as

---

<sup>c</sup> *Eph 1:22–23.* <sup>d</sup> *Eph 2:16.*

image of the Wisdom of God and is the New Torah, for the rabbis had come to equate
the Torah with the Divine and Creative Wisdom.

 1:16 This verse can be seen as a rejection of those dualist systems which maintained
that God did not create all things but that a principle of evil was responsible for some
aspects of creation. The "unseen" things probably refer to the "elemental spirits" (2:8)
which were believed to have power over man's "corporate life," as manifested in religion
and politics, for example.

you remain firmly established in the faith and aren't shifted from the hope of the gospel you heard — the gospel which has been proclaimed to every creature under Heaven, and of which I, Paul, am a minister.

24 I rejoice in what I'm suffering for you now; in my flesh I'm completing what is lacking in Christ's afflictions on behalf of his body, that is, the church. 25 I am a minister of the church in accordance with the responsibility God gave me with regard to you — to fully proclaim the word of God, 26 the mystery which was hidden for ages and generations. But now it has been revealed to His saints, 27 to whom God chose to make known the richness of this glorious mystery among the Gentiles — this mystery is Christ in you, the hope of glory. 28 It is Christ whom we proclaim, and we admonish and instruct everyone in all wisdom so that we'll be able to present each of them as perfect in Christ. 29 To this end I toil and strive, and Christ's mighty energy is at work in me.

2 1 For I want you to know how great my labor is on your behalf, as well as on behalf of those in Laodicea and all those who haven't seen me in person. 2 My goal is to encourage their hearts as they are drawn together in love so that they may have the full wealth of conviction that comes from understanding and leads to knowledge of God's mystery — of Christ — 3 in whom all the treasures of wisdom and knowledge are hidden. 4 I say this so no one will deceive you with a plausible sounding line of argumen-

---

2:1        Laodicea was the major city of the region in which Colossae was located.

tation. 5 For although I may not be present, I am with you in spirit, and I rejoice to see how you maintain good order and how firm your faith in Christ is.

## D. Exhortation to Be Firm in the Faith and to Resist Judaizing Tendencies

6 Therefore, since you've received Christ Jesus the Lord, live your lives in him; 7 be rooted and built up in him and firmly established in the faith just as it was taught to you; be filled with thanksgiving. 8 See that no one leads you into captivity by means of "philosophy" or the empty deceptions of human traditions, which follow the elemental spirits of the world rather than Christ. 9 For in Christ the fullness of divinity dwells in bodily form 10 and in him you reach completion; he is the head of every ruler and power. 11 In him you also received a circumcision, one which was not performed by hand; with Christ's circumcision you put off the body of flesh — 12 *e* you were buried with him in baptism and in baptism you also rose with him through faith in the power of God, Who raised Christ from the dead. 13 *f* Although you were dead because of your transgressions and because your flesh was uncircumcised, God brought you to life with Christ by forgiving all our transgressions

---

*e* Rm 6:4.  *f* Eph 2:1–5.

2:8–9    The "elemental spirits" were the angelic beings which were thought to influence human rulers. As we have seen (1:16), these angelic "rulers and powers" are subordinate to Christ, who has saved us from subjection to them.

14 *g* and canceling our commitment to obey the decrees of the Torah, which stood as an accusation against us. He set it aside and nailed it to the cross; 15 He stripped the rulers and powers and, in Christ, held a public triumph over them.

16 *h* So let no one judge you in matters concerning food and drink, or regarding festivals, new moons, or the Sabbath. 17 These things are a foreshadowing of what is to come, but the reality is Christ's. 18 You are not to be disqualified by those who insist on self-mortification and worship of angels, based upon things they've seen in visions. Such people have become puffed up without reason by relying on their own world-centered minds 19 *i* rather than holding fast to the Head, from which the whole body, with its joints and ligaments, receives what it needs and is held together, deriving its growth from God. 20 If you have died with Christ to the elemental spirits of the world, why do you observe rules and regulations as if you were still living in the world? 21 "Don't touch this! Don't taste that! Don't handle this!" 22 Don't all these rules concern things

---

*g Eph 2:15.    h Rm 14:1–6.    i Eph 4:16.*

2:14    The words "of the Torah" are not in the original.

2:16–23   Having addressed the true basis for our salvation in the preceding verses, Paul now proceeds to warn the Colossians against the practices which some in the community have adopted. These practices appear to have combined asceticism and ritualism based on Jewish influences.

2:18–20   Paul held to the common Jewish view that the Torah was given to Moses by angelic intermediaries rather than directly from God. Thus he may be indulging in sarcasm at the expense of those who were introducing practices from the Jewish law when he refers to "angel worship." Paul has no problem with curbing sensuality, but he is troubled by the fascination with intermediaries, who are subordinate to Christ.

2:21–22   These verses refer to dietary and purification regulations, probably of Jewish origin.

which are destined to be destroyed through use, and aren't they simply human precepts and teachings? 23 These rules *appear* to be wise from the standpoint of piety, humility, and discipline of the body, but they're of no use in controlling self-indulgence.

## E. PRACTICAL COUNSELS
## TO THE TRUE LIFE IN CHRIST

3 1 If you've been raised with Christ, seek the things that are above, where Christ is seated at God's right hand; 2 think about the things that are above, not about things on earth, 3 for you've died and your life is hidden with Christ in God. 4 When Christ, your life, appears, then you too will appear with him in glory.

5 Put to death those parts of you which are earthly — fornication, impurity, passion, evil desires, and that greed which is idolatry. 6 It's because of these things that God's wrath is coming [upon the disobedient]; 7 you too used to do these things when you lived for them. 8 But now you must cast them all aside — wrath, anger, malice, slander, obscene language from your mouths. 9 *j* Don't lie to one another, now that you've stripped off the old man with his

---

*j* *Eph 4:22.*

2:23    Lit., "indulgence of the flesh." "Self–indulgence" has been preferred because "the flesh" referred not only to sensual passions but also to other sins which derive from a selfish, self–centered attitude.

deeds [10] [k] and put on the new one, which is being renewed according to the image of its Creator for the knowledge of God. [11] Here there is no Greek or Jew, circumcised or uncircumcised, barbarian or Scythian, slave or free, but Christ is all and in all.

[12] [l] So then, as God's chosen ones, holy and beloved, clothe yourselves with true compassion, kindness, humility, gentleness, patience; [13] [m] bear with one another and forgive each other if anyone has a grievance against someone else. Just as the Lord forgave you, you too should do the same. [14] But over all these things put on love, which perfects and binds the whole. [15] Let the peace of Christ rule in your hearts, the peace to which you were called in one body, and be thankful. [16] [n] Let the word of Christ dwell in you richly; teach and admonish each other with all wisdom; sing psalms, hymns, and spiritual songs to God with thanks in your hearts. [17] Whatever you do whether in word or deed, do it all in the name of Jesus the Lord, and give thanks to God the Father through him.

[18] [o] Wives, be subject to your husbands, as is fitting in the Lord. [19] [p] Husbands, love your wives and don't be harsh with them.

[20] [q] Children, obey your parents in all things, for that is pleasing to the Lord. [21] [r] Fathers, don't cause your children to be resentful, so they won't become discouraged.

---

[k] *Eph 4:24.*  [l] *Eph 4:2.*  [m] *Eph 4:32.*  [n] *Eph 5:19–20.*  [o] *Eph 5:22.*  [p] *Eph 5:25.*
[q] *Eph 6:1.*  [r] *Eph 6:4.*

3:18–19  As always when Paul discusses family relations he stresses mutuality of obligations: the husband's duties are no less binding than those of the wife.

22 ⁵ Slaves, obey your earthly masters in all things, not just to impress them and curry favor but with single-hearted devotion, in fear of the Lord. 23 Whatever you do, let it be from the heart, as if you were working for the Lord rather than for men, 24 in the knowledge that as your reward you'll receive an inheritance from the Lord. Serve Christ the Lord, 25 ᵗ for the wrong-doer will be repaid for the wrong he has done, and God will not play favorites.

4 1 ᵘ Masters, do what's just and fair for your slaves, for you know that you too have a Lord in Heaven.

2 Persevere in prayer, stay awake while you pray and be thankful. 3 At the same time, pray for us, that God may open for us a door of opportunity to proclaim the mystery of Christ, for the sake of whom I'm in prison. 4 Pray that I'll be able to make this mystery clear, since I must speak of it. 5 ᵛ Conduct yourselves wisely toward outsiders, make good use of your opportunities. 6 Always be pleasant in your speech but season it with salt, so you'll always be able to answer everyone.

## F. PERSONAL NEWS AND CONCLUSION

7 ʷ Our beloved brother Tychicus will tell you every-thing concerning my situation — he's a faithful minister

---

ˢ *Eph 6:5–8.*   ᵗ *Eph 6:9.*   ᵘ *Eph 6:9.*   ᵛ *Eph 5:16.*   ʷ *2 Tm 4:12.*

3:22–23 "In fear of the Lord." This phrase in v. 22 is best explained by v. 23. Duties in life should be performed in order to please the Lord.

and fellow servant in the Lord. [8] [x] I'm sending him to you so you'll know how things stand with us and to encourage your hearts, [9] [y] along with our faithful and beloved brother Onesimus, who is one of you. They'll let you know about everything that's going on here.

[10] [z] My fellow prisoner Aristarchus greets you, as well as Barnabas' cousin Mark (concerning whom you've received instructions — if he comes to you, receive him), [11] and Jesus who is called Justus. Of those who are Jewish these are the only ones who are co-workers for the Kingdom of God, and they've been a comfort to me. [12] Epaphras, one of you and a servant of Christ [Jesus], greets you — he continually strives on your behalf in his prayers, that you may be perfect and fully convinced of all God's will. [13] I bear him witness that he's worked hard for you and for those in Laodicea and Hierapolis. [14] [a] Demas and my beloved Luke, the physician, greet you. [15] Greet the brothers at Laodicea as well as Nympha and the church at her house. [16] And when you've read this letter, have it read to the Laodicean church as well, and you should also read the letter from Laodicea. [17] [b] Tell Archippus, "See that you fulfill the ministry you received in the Lord."

[18] The greeting is in my own hand — Paul's. Remember my chains! Grace be with you!

---

[x] *Eph 6:21–22.*   [y] *Phm 10–12.*   [z] *Ac 27:2; Phm 24.*   [a] *2 Tm 4:10–11; Phm 24.*   [b] *Phm 2.*

4:10     "Mark"; believed to be Mark the Evangelist.

4:13     Hierapolis was a city near Colossae.

4:15     It is equally possible, based on manuscript evidence and linguistic probabilities, that this phrase should read, "Nymphas and the church at his house."

# THE FIRST LETTER TO THE

# THESSALONIANS

Paul's first letter to the church in Thessalonica is also one of the earliest of his letters which has been preserved and, thus, one of the earliest Christian writings. It is usually dated around A.D. 50–51. Of all Paul's letters its background is the most thoroughly described in Acts, stretching from 16:6 to 18:5. Briefly, Paul had had great initial success in Thessalonica (the capital of Macedonia) but was forced to leave because of the determined hostility of a part of the Jewish community there. Paul proceeded on through Greece, eventually winding up in Athens where he waited for his companions Silas and Timothy, who had stayed behind in Thessalonica to continue instructing the young community. After he was joined by Timothy, he became anxious for the spiritual welfare of the Thessalonian church and sent Timothy back to check on matters. Timothy's return with a positive report was the occasion for this letter.

In structure this letter follows the usual format, except that the thanksgiving section is quite extended and is interwoven with relatively detailed accounts of Paul's previous relations with the Thessalonians. In addition to being thankful, Paul is also anxious to distinguish his mission from that of other itinerant preachers, who were common in the Hellenistic world at that time. He then goes on to deliver a brief moral exhortation as well as additional instruction regarding the *parousia*, the return of the Lord. Although the instruction regarding Christ's coming is not lengthy, the entire letter is pervaded by a concern with eschatology. This is shown, for example, in the choice of words with apocalyptic overtones such as "affliction" and "wrath," which when applied to the suffering of the Thessalonians may have heightened their expectations of an imminent *parousia*.

While Acts, as it usually does, gives more prominence to Jewish converts, there are indications — at 2:14 and in the general tone of the letter — that the great majority of the Thessalonian church was composed of Gentile converts.

## OUTLINE OF THE FIRST LETTER TO THE THESSALONIANS

| A. | 1:1 | Greeting |
|----|-----|----------|
| B. | 1:2–3:13 | Thanksgiving |
| C. | 4:1–12 | Moral Counsels |
| D. | 4:13–5:11 | Doctrinal Instruction: Resurrection from the Dead and the Coming of Jesus |
| E. | 5:12–25 | Concluding Counsels on Leading the Life in Christ |
| F. | 5:26–28 | Greetings and Farewell |

## A. Greeting

**1** <sup>1</sup> Paul, Silvanus, and Timothy to the church of the Thessalonians in God the Father and the Lord Jesus Christ — grace and peace be with you!

## B. Thanksgiving

<sup>2</sup> We always give thanks to God for all of you and mention you in our prayers, constantly <sup>3</sup> calling to mind before our God and Father your active faith, your loving labors, and your steadfast hope in our Lord Jesus Christ. <sup>4</sup> For we know, brothers beloved by God, that you have indeed been chosen, <sup>5</sup> because our proclamation of the good news didn't come to you in words alone but also with power, with the Holy Spirit, and with complete certainty. You know what we were like for your sake while we were among you, <sup>6</sup> <sup>a</sup> and you became imitators of us and of the Lord, for although your acceptance of the word caused you considerable affliction, you received it with joy inspired by the Holy Spirit. <sup>7</sup> As a result, you became an example for all the believers in Macedonia and Achaia. <sup>8</sup> For the word

---

<sup>a</sup> Ac 17:5–9.

1:7    "Achaia," i.e., Greece proper.

of the Lord has gone forth from you not only in Macedonia and Achaia — news of your faith in God has reached every place, so that we have no need to say anything! ⁹ Those people themselves recount what sort of reception we had among you, and how you turned to God from idols to serve the living and true God ¹⁰ and to await His Son from Heaven — Jesus, whom He raised from the dead and who delivers us from the coming wrath.

2 ¹ For you yourselves know, my brothers, that our reception by you was not in vain. ² ᵇ Although we had previously suffered and been mistreated in Philippi, as you know, God gave us the courage to proclaim God's good news to you in spite of considerable opposition. ³ For the appeal we make is not based upon deceit or impure motives or deception. ⁴ On the contrary, since God has judged us worthy to be entrusted with the good news, we proclaim it with that in mind — not in order to please men but to please God, Who is able to discern what's in our hearts. ⁵ We never resorted to flattery, as you know, nor did our words serve as a cover for greed — God is our witness! — ⁶ and we didn't seek human honors, whether from you or from others, ⁷ although as apostles of Christ we could have made demands upon you. Instead we were gentle with you, like a nursing mother comforting her child. ⁸ Such was our affection for you that we were prepared to share with you not only God's good news but even our very selves, so dear had you become to us. ⁹ For you remember, brothers, how

---

ᵇ Ac 16:19–24.

we labored and toiled — we worked night and day so we wouldn't be a burden to any of you while we proclaimed God's good news. 10 You and God are witnesses to how devoutly, uprightly, and blamelessly we behaved toward you believers, 11 and you also know how, like a father with his own children, 12 we exhorted you, encouraged you, and urged you to conduct yourselves in a manner worthy of God, Who calls you to the glory of His Kingdom.

13 A further reason that we constantly give thanks to God is that when you received the word of God that you heard from us you didn't accept it as mere human words but for what it truly is, the word of God which is at work in you believers. 14 You became imitators, brothers, of the churches of God in Christ Jesus which are in Judea — you suffered the same things at the hands of your fellow countrymen as they did from the Jews, 15 who killed both the Lord Jesus and the prophets and drove us out. They displease God and show their hostility to all men 16 by trying to prevent us from proclaiming to the Gentiles that they can be saved. In this they constantly complete the full measure of their sins. But God's wrath has come upon them at last!

17 So, brothers, when we were separated from you for a little while you were absent from our sight but not from our hearts, and we became all the more eager to see your faces — our desire to see you was strong, indeed! 18 We wanted to come to you — I, Paul, tried to do so

---

2:14    "Fellow countrymen." This phrase tends to indicate that it is Gentiles rather than Jews who are persecuting the Thessalonians, and leads to the conclusion that the majority of converts were also of Gentile, rather than Jewish, origin.

more than once — but Satan thwarted our desires. ¹⁹ For
what is our hope, our joy, our crowning boast before our
Lord Jesus Christ when he comes, if not you? ²⁰ *You* are
our glory and our joy!

3 ¹ᶜ Therefore, when we could no longer bear it, we
decided to remain alone in Athens ² and sent Timothy, our brother and co-worker for God in the good news
of Christ, to strengthen and encourage you in your faith
³ so that no one would be disturbed by these afflictions. You
yourselves know that we are destined for this, ⁴ for when we
were with you we warned you that we would have to suffer
affliction precisely as it has come to pass, as you know. ⁵ This
is why when I could no longer bear it I sent to find out the
state of your faith, lest the Tempter had somehow tempted
you and all our work might be for naught.

⁶ ᵈ But Timothy has just now come to us from you
and has given us the good news about your faith and love,
and that you hold our memory dear, longing to see us just
as we long to see you. ⁷ Therefore, brothers, in all our distress and affliction your faith has encouraged us, ⁸ because
now we can live if you stand firm in the Lord. ⁹ For what
thanksgiving can we render to God for all the joy we feel
before our God for your sake? ¹⁰ More than ever we pray
night and day to see your faces and complete what's lacking in your faith.

¹¹ May God our Father and our Lord Jesus make
straight our road to you! ¹² May the Lord cause you to

ᶜ Ac 17:15.   ᵈ Ac 18:5.

increase and overflow with love for one another and for everyone, just as we do for you, 13 so as to strengthen your hearts to be blameless in holiness before our God and Father when our Lord Jesus comes with all his saints.

## C. Moral Counsels

4 1 And so, brothers, we beg you and exhort you in the Lord Jesus that, just as you learned from us how you should live if you are to please God, as you are now living, you should do so more and more. 2 For you know the instructions we gave you through the Lord Jesus. 3 Your sanctification is what God wills for you — you should avoid fornication; 4 you should learn to exercise control over your body in holiness and honor, 5 and not in lustful passion as the Gentiles do, who don't know God; 6 let no man sin and take advantage of his brother in this matter, for the Lord will avenge all these things, just as we warned you before. 7 For God called us to holiness, not to impurity. 8 *e* Therefore, whoever rejects this instruction rejects not man but God, Who gives His Holy Spirit to you.

9 There's no need for us to write to you about brotherly love, for you yourselves have been taught by God to love

---

*e* Lk 10:16.

4:3     The Greek word *porneia*, here translated "fornication," was sometimes used in a technical sense in rabbinic theology with the meaning of "marriage within forbidden degrees of consanguinity." That meaning is also possible in this context.

one another [10] and you do this with regard to all the brothers in Macedonia. But we exhort you, brothers, to do even more. [11] Aspire to live a quiet life; mind your own affairs and work with your hands, as we instructed you, [12] so you'll have the respect of outsiders and will lack for nothing.


## D. Doctrinal Instruction:
## Resurrection from the Dead
## and the Coming of Jesus


[13] Brothers, we want you to understand how it is with those who have fallen asleep, so you won't grieve like others do, who have no hope. [14] For if we believe that Jesus died and rose again, then through Jesus God will also bring with him those who have fallen asleep.

[15] [f] Indeed, we can tell you, based on the Lord's teaching, that we who are alive, who remain until the Lord's coming, will not precede those who have fallen asleep. [16] The Lord himself will come down from Heaven and

---

[f] 1 Cor 15:51–52.

---

4:11    "Work with your hands." Some of the Thessalonians may already have been neglecting their work because of expectations of an imminent *parousia*, an issue which is dealt with explicitly and forcefully in 2 Thessalonians. Cf. also 5:14.

4:13–18  The expectation that the Lord would return soon to bring about the "end of the world" was widespread in the early Church. Since many converts had a poorly developed understanding of the afterlife this sometimes led to concern for the fate of those who died before the Lord's *parousia* or coming. Paul undoubtedly shared this expectation but was careful to avoid speculation on specific dates and times, cf. 5:1ff.

issue a command, with an archangel's voice and a blast from God's trumpet. Those who died in Christ will rise first, <sup>17</sup> then we who are living, who remain, will be caught up into the clouds with them to meet the Lord in the air, and so we'll always be with the Lord. <sup>18</sup> Encourage one another with these words.

5 <sup>1</sup> But as for the specific time or occasion, brothers, there's no need for us to write to you, <sup>2 g</sup> for you yourselves are well aware that the day of the Lord will come like a thief in the night. <sup>3</sup> Just when people are saying, "We have peace and security!" sudden destruction will come upon them, the way labor pains come to a pregnant woman, and there will be no way for them to escape. <sup>4</sup> But brothers, you aren't in the dark, so the day of the Lord can't take you by surprise like a thief, <sup>5</sup> for you're all sons of the light and sons of the day. We don't belong to the night or to darkness, <sup>6 h</sup> so let's not sleep like others do — let's stay awake and be sober! <sup>7</sup> For those who sleep sleep at night, and those who get drunk get drunk at night, <sup>8</sup> whereas we who belong to the day should remain sober, *clothed in the breastplate* of faith and love and the *helmet* of hope *in salvation*. <sup>9</sup> God has not destined us for His wrath — He has destined us to gain salvation through our Lord Jesus Christ, <sup>10</sup> who died for us so that whether we are awake or sleeping we will live with him. <sup>11</sup> So encourage and strengthen one another, as you are doing.

---

*g* Mt 24:43; Lk 12:39–40; 2 P 3:10.    *h* Mk 13:35–37; Eph 6:13–17.

5:8    Is 59:17.

## E. Concluding Counsels
## on Leading the Life in Christ

12 We beg you, brothers, to respect those who labor among you and direct and admonish you in the Lord. 13 *i* Have the utmost respect for them and love them for the sake of their work. Be at peace with one another. 14 We urge you, brothers, to admonish those who are lazy, encourage the fainthearted, help the weak, and be patient with everyone. 15 *j* See that no one pays back evil for evil; instead, always seek to do good to one another and to everyone.

16 Rejoice always, 17 pray constantly, 18 give thanks no matter what happens, for this is God's will for you in Christ Jesus. 19 Don't stifle the Spirit 20 or despise prophecy — 21 test everything and keep what's good. 22 Avoid every kind of evil.

23 May the God of peace Himself sanctify you completely, and may your spirit, soul, and body be kept sound and blameless for the coming of our Lord Jesus Christ. 24 He Who calls you is faithful, and He will do it!

25 Brothers, pray for us, too!

## F. Greetings and Farewell

26 Greet all the brothers with a holy kiss. 27 I adjure you by the Lord to read this letter to all the brothers.

28 The grace of our Lord Jesus Christ be with you!

---

*i* Mk 9:50.   *j* Mt 5:39ff.

# THE SECOND LETTER TO THE

# THESSALONIANS

This letter is believed to have been written shortly after 1 Thessalonians, in about A.D. 50–51. Apparently the first letter had not had the desired effect and the community continued to be disturbed by apocalyptic speculations and other disorders. New Christians were beginning to neglect work and their everyday responsibilities (3:6–15) as a result of their belief that the day of the Lord had already come (2:2). There may even have been attempts to capitalize on Paul's authority by using letters purporting to have been from him or by misrepresenting his oral teaching (2:2).

Paul's reply, delivered in forceful terms, has been the Church's ever since: nobody knows when the day of the Lord will come. The process is a mystery under the ultimate control of God. As they wait for the end, Paul's instruction to Christians is: "Don't grow weary of doing good" (3:13). In other words, Christians are not to turn from the world in favor of millennial speculation but instead are to continue in the world, but transformed "in Christ," to use a phrase which will feature prominently in Paul's future letters.

Paul's prescription for those who fail to follow this advice is simple and stern: "Anyone who refuses to work should not be allowed to eat" (3:10). Nevertheless, as always with Paul, the bitter medicine is not to be administered in a vindictive or malicious spirit but is intended to shame the perpetrator and lead him to mend his ways (3:14–15).

While numerous scholars have questioned the authenticity of 2 Thessalonians, the trend of recent scholarship is toward a greater openness to the letter's authenticity. The arguments for Pauline authorship maintain that the style is Paul's and that the teaching is in essentials the same as in 1 Thessalonians — any differences are only what might be expected as a result of the development of the situation in Thessalonica. Moreover, the letter clearly presupposes that the Temple in Jerusalem is still standing (2:4).

## OUTLINE OF THE SECOND LETTER TO THE THESSALONIANS

A. 1:1–2       Greeting
B. 1:3–12      Thanksgiving
C. 2:1–17      Warning Against False Teaching on the Coming of Jesus
D. 3:1–15      Concluding Exhortation to Pray and to Avoid Idle Living
E. 3:16–18     Greeting and Farewell

## A. Greeting

1 <sup>1</sup> Paul, Silvanus, and Timothy to the church of the Thessalonians in God our Father and the Lord Jesus Christ. <sup>2</sup> Grace and peace be with you from God the Father and the Lord Jesus Christ.

## B. Thanksgiving

<sup>3</sup> We're bound to give thanks to God for you always, brothers, as is proper, because your faith is growing wonderfully and the love each of you has for one another is increasing. <sup>4</sup> As a result we ourselves boast in the churches of God of your steadfastness and faith in all the persecutions and afflictions which you endure. <sup>5</sup> This is proof that God's judgment is just and it will lead to your being considered worthy of God's Kingdom, for which you're suffering. <sup>6</sup> It's right for God to pay back in suffering those who are causing you to suffer <sup>7</sup> and to give rest to you who are suffering as well as to us at the revelation of the Lord Jesus, when he comes from Heaven with his mighty angels, <sup>8</sup> *with a blazing fire, to wreak vengeance on those who don't know God* and don't

---

1:8     Ps 79:6; Is 66:15; Jr 10:25.

obey the good news of our Lord Jesus. ⁹ They'll undergo the punishment of eternal destruction and be shut off *from the face of the Lord and from his glorious might* ¹⁰ when he comes on that day to be glorified with his saints and to be marvelled at by all the believers, because you believed our witness. ¹¹ We pray always that this will come to pass for you, that God will consider you worthy of His call, and that by His power He will fulfill every desire for goodness and every work of faith, ¹² so that the name of our Lord Jesus will be glorified in you, and you in it, in accordance with the grace of our God and the Lord Jesus Christ.


## C. WARNING AGAINST FALSE TEACHING ON THE COMING OF JESUS

2 ¹ Now as for the coming of our Lord Jesus and our being gathered to him, we beg you, brothers, ² not to be too quickly shaken in mind or disturbed, whether by a spirit-inspired utterance, by preaching, or by a letter

---

1:9     Is 2:10, 19, 21. Note that "destruction" does not indicate annihilation — a complete cessation of existence — but is essentially synonymous with separation from Christ and God.

2:1–12     As in 1 Thessalonians, Paul refuses to speculate about dates or times for the day of the Lord. He reminds the Thessalonians that "the mystery of evil" is already at work, but the culmination of this process is being held in check for an indefinite length of time by a mysterious person or force called the "Restrainer." We are unfortunately unable to establish the identity of this "Restrainer," although there has been no lack of theories. The three leading candidates are the Roman Empire (or the Emperor himself), some supernatural force, or Satan. Ultimately, however, God is in control of this process (2:10–12), and it is God Who will determine the "proper time" (2:6).

purporting to be from us and claiming that the day of the Lord has come. 3 Let no one deceive you in any way. Unless the apostasy comes first and the man who embodies all wickedness is revealed, who is doomed to perdition 4 and opposes *and exalts himself against every* so-called *god* and object of worship so as *to seat himself in God's Temple* and proclaim that he's God — 5 Don't you remember that I told you all this while I was still with you? 6 And now you know what's restraining him, so that he'll be revealed at his proper time. 7 For the mystery of evil is already at work; only the Restrainer is holding it back for the present, until he's removed. 8 Then the wicked one will be revealed and the Lord *will slay him with the breath of his mouth* and destroy him when he appears at his coming. 9 *a* The wicked one's coming will be Satan's work and will be accompanied by power and false signs and wonders 10 and with all manner of wicked deception against those who are to perish, because they refused to love the truth and save themselves. 11 That's why God is sending the power of error to cause them to believe what's false, 12 so that all who delighted in wickedness instead of believing the truth will be condemned.

13 But we must always give thanks to God for you, brothers beloved of the Lord, because God has chosen you as first fruits to be saved through sanctification by the Spirit and belief in the truth. 14 It was for this that He called you

---

*a* Mt 24:2.

2:4      Dn 11:36.
2:8      Jb 4:9; Is 11:4.
2:13    Some manuscripts read "from the beginning" instead of "as first fruits."

through our good news to possess the glory of our Lord Jesus Christ. ¹⁵ So then, brothers, stand firm and hold fast to the tradition we taught you, whether by word of mouth or by a letter of ours. ¹⁶ May our Lord Jesus Christ himself and God our Father, Who loved us and through His grace gave us everlasting encouragement and good hope, ¹⁷ encourage and strengthen your hearts for every good work and word.

## D. Concluding Exhortation
## to Pray and to Avoid Idle Living

**3** ¹ Finally, pray for us, brothers, that the word of the Lord may spread quickly and be glorified as it was among you ² and that we may be delivered from perverse and evil men, for not all have the faith. ³ But the Lord is faithful and will strengthen you and protect you from evil. ⁴ We have every confidence in you in the Lord that you are doing and will do what we have commanded. ⁵ May the Lord guide your hearts to the love of God and the steadfastness of Christ.

⁶ Brothers, we command you in the name of the Lord Jesus Christ to avoid any brother who leads an idle life which is not in accord with the tradition you received from us. ⁷ You know how you should imitate us — we weren't lazy when we were among you, ⁸ nor did we eat anyone's bread without paying for it. Instead, we worked night and day, laboring and toiling so as not to burden any of you. ⁹ Not that we didn't have the right to be supported, but

because we wanted to give you ourselves as an example to imitate. 10 And indeed when we were among you we commanded that "anyone who refuses to work should not be allowed to eat." 11 We hear that some of you are leading idle lives and are behaving like busybodies instead of working. 12 We command and exhort such people in the Lord Jesus Christ to work quietly and eat their own bread. 13 And you, brothers, don't grow weary of doing good. 14 If anyone doesn't obey our instructions in this letter, take note of him and don't associate with him, so as to put him to shame. 15 Yet don't regard him as an enemy; instead, admonish him as a brother.

## E. GREETING AND FAREWELL

16 May the Lord of peace himself grant you peace at all times and in all ways. The Lord be with all of you.

17 This greeting is written with my own hand — Paul's. This is my sign in every letter, this is how I write. 18 The grace of our Lord Jesus Christ be with all of you.

---

3:17    It appears to have been Paul's usual practice to dictate his letters to a secretary, actually writing only the last few lines himself. It is possible that in some letters the scribe also had a hand in composing the letter. Here, Paul writes the last few words in his own hand, and states that this is his handwriting, as a means of authenticating the letter and guarding against forgers attempting to claim his authority for their own purposes.

# THE FIRST LETTER TO

# TIMOTHY

Of all the Pastoral Letters, 1 Timothy diverges the most markedly from what is usually considered to be Pauline. All scholars agree that its style is the most consistently different from what we have come to expect from Paul. But its differences are not confined to stylistic matters only — they extend to the subject matter as well. The letter is largely devoted to matters of church organization: the qualifications of bishops and deacons; the treatment of various groups within the church, notably widows and elders, and behavioral guidelines for women, the rich, and slaves; how to deal with doctrinal deviations among the faithful; and practical advice on how Timothy is to comport himself while he is in charge of the church at Ephesus in Paul's absence.

There are also subtle differences of emphasis and outlook. "Faith" is regularly used in the unusual (for Paul) sense of a body of religious truths, rather than as our response to God's revelation in Christ. The attitudes expressed toward women and slaves appear to be somewhat strange when compared to the Paul we know from his other letters, even allowing for the different circumstances presupposed by this letter. In addition, no mention whatsoever is made of friends and co-workers, certainly a very unusual feature in a Pauline letter.

Those scholars (the overwhelming majority) who regard 1 Timothy as pseudonymous have more freedom in assigning a date and place to the letter. Scholars who support Pauline authorship usually place it late in Paul's life, precisely because so little is known about Paul's life after he reached Rome. Among those who support Pauline authorship, Robinson makes the interesting suggestion that the letter was written between the two Corinthian letters, while Paul was based in Ephesus but was traveling throughout the Aegean region. The strength of this suggestion is that it places the letter at a time when Timothy was still somewhat new to Paul's work. This would explain why Paul spells out in such detail exactly what Timothy is to do, an aspect of the letter which is difficult to explain if it is placed later in Paul's life.

## OUTLINE OF THE FIRST LETTER TO TIMOTHY

A. 1:1–2      Greeting

B. 1:3–20      Timothy Is Instructed to Oppose False Teachers

C. 2:1–3:16      The Roles and Qualities of Various Categories of Believers

     2:8–15      The Behavior of Men and, Especially, of Women

|       | 3:1–7     | The Qualities of a Bishop |
|       | 3:8–16    | The Qualities of Deacons |
| D.    | 4:1–16    | The Errors of the False Teachers and Instructions on How to Counter Them |
| E.    | 5:1–6:2   | Practical Guidance on How to Treat Certain Classes of the Faithful |
|       | 5:1–2     | In General |
|       | 5:3–16    | Widows |
|       | 5:17–25   | Elders |
|       | 6:1–2     | Slaves |
| F.    | 6:3–19    | Concluding Exhortations, Warnings, and Counsel |
| G.    | 6:20–21   | Farewell |

## A. Greeting

1 ¹ Paul, an apostle of Christ Jesus by command of God our Savior and Christ Jesus our hope, ² to Timothy, my true child in the faith: grace, mercy, and peace from God the Father and Christ Jesus our Lord.

## B. Timothy Is Instructed to Oppose False Teachers

³ As I urged you when I was leaving for Macedonia, remain at Ephesus and instruct certain persons to refrain from teaching false doctrines ⁴ and occupying themselves with myths and endless genealogies, which give rise to speculation rather than the working out of God's plan which is received through faith. ⁵ The purpose of this instruction is to foster that love which flows from a pure heart, a clean conscience, and sincere faith. ⁶ Certain persons have departed from these principles and have become sidetracked in fruitless discussions ⁷ out of a desire to be teachers of the Torah, but they don't understand the words they use or the matters about which they make confident assertions.

---

1:7     Here we learn, from the reference to the Torah, that the false doctrines have arisen from a Judaizing tendency.

⁸ Now we know that the Torah is good if it's used as a law, ⁹ in the realization that it's not intended for the righteous but for the lawless and disobedient, godless sinners, the unholy and profane, patricides and matricides, murderers, ¹⁰ fornicators, sodomites, kidnappers, liars, perjurers, and whatever else is opposed to sound teaching ¹¹ in accordance with the glorious good news of the blessed God with which I've been entrusted.

¹² I give thanks to Jesus Christ our Lord who has strengthened me, because by appointing me to his ministry he considered me trustworthy — ¹³ I who had previously been an insolent and blasphemous persecutor. But he had mercy on me because I acted ignorantly out of unbelief, ¹⁴ and the grace of our Lord Jesus was given to me in abundance, along with the faith and love which are in Christ Jesus. ¹⁵ This teaching may be trusted and is worthy of complete acceptance — Christ Jesus came into the world to save sinners, of whom I am the first. ¹⁶ The reason Christ Jesus had mercy on me, the first of all sinners, was to demonstrate all his patience, as an example for those who were to believe in him for everlasting life. ¹⁷ To the King of ages, to the one, immortal, invisible God, be honor and glory for ever and ever, amen.

¹⁸ I'm entrusting you with this instruction, Timothy my child, in accordance with the prophecies made about you long ago. May those words inspire you to fight the good fight ¹⁹ with faith and a good conscience. By reject-

---

1:17     This is believed to have been taken from an early liturgy.

ing conscience certain persons have made a shipwreck of their faith. 20 Among them are Hymenaeus and Alexander, whom I've handed over to Satan in the hope that they'll learn not to blaspheme.

## C. The Roles and Qualities of Various Categories of Believers

2 ¹ First of all, I urge that supplications, prayers, intercessions, and thanksgivings be made for all men — ² for kings and for all those in positions of authority — that we may lead a peaceful, quiet life, holy and respectable in every way. ³ Such a life is good and acceptable in the sight of God our Savior, ⁴ Whose wish is that all may be saved and may come to knowledge of the truth. ⁵ For there is one God and one mediator between God and men — the man Christ Jesus, ⁶ who gave himself as a ransom for all; this testimony was given at the time God had chosen. ⁷ [a] I was made a herald and apostle to give this testimony — I'm

---

[a] *2 Tm 1:11.*

1:20    Hymenaeus is mentioned at 2 Tm 2:17 in conjunction with a certain Philetus. They are described as claiming that the resurrection has already taken place. This probably means that they regarded resurrection of the dead as taking place symbolically in baptism, but denied an afterlife.

2:1ff.    The attitude expressed here toward civil authorities would be rather anachronistic if 1 Timothy had been written after the Neronian persecution of the middle to late 60s. It is instructive to compare these sentiments with the unrelenting hostility expressed in the Revelation to John.

2:6    "This testimony..." This obscure phrase may refer either to Jesus' death or his words.

speaking the truth, I'm not lying — a teacher of the Gentiles in faith and truth.

## The Behavior of Men and, Especially, of Women

8 Therefore my desire is that at every place the men should lift holy hands in prayer without anger or arguing. 9 [b] Likewise, the women should dress in a modest, respectable manner, decorating themselves sensibly, not with elaborate braids and gold, or pearls or expensive garments. 10 Instead, they should adorn themselves with good deeds, as is proper for women who claim to be religious. 11 A woman should learn in silence and complete submissiveness. 12 I don't permit a woman to teach, nor to have authority over a man; instead, she should be silent. 13 For Adam was formed first, and then Eve. 14 Moreover it wasn't Adam who was deceived, it was the woman who was deceived and sinned. 15 But women will be saved by childbearing, if they persevere in faith, love, and holiness, with modesty.

## The Qualities of a Bishop

3 1 This teaching is trustworthy — "if anyone aspires to be a bishop he desires to undertake an honorable task." 2 [c] Therefore a bishop must be above reproach, married only

---

[b] 1 P 3:3.   [c] Tt 1:6–9.

2:8    "At every place," i.e., where there is a church.
2:12   "A man" probably refers to a woman's husband.

once, temperate, sensible, respectable, hospitable, skillful in teaching, 3 not a drunkard, not a bully; instead he should be gentle, peaceable, and not greedy. 4 He should manage his own household well and raise his children to be obedient and honorable. 5 (If someone doesn't know how to manage his own household, how will he be able to care for the church of God?) 6 He must not be a recent convert, so he won't become self-important and incur the judgment that befell the Devil. 7 He must be well regarded by outsiders; otherwise, he may fall into disgrace and be trapped in the Devil's snare.

## The Qualities of Deacons

8 Likewise deacons must be honorable, not two-faced, not over-indulgers in wine, not greedy for material gain, 9 adhering to the mystery of the faith with a clear conscience. 10 Moreover they should first be tested and then, if they're found to be without fault, they may serve as deacons. 11 Their wives, too, must be honorable, not given to slander, temper-

---

3:8     "Two-faced." Lit., "double-tongued."

3:8–13     While some authors maintain that verse 11 refers to women deacons (the one Greek word in question can mean either "women" or "wives") the total context makes this unlikely, at least if "deacon" is understood as an ecclesiastical office. Verses 8–10 clearly view deacons as men, and verse 12 specifies that deacons are to be *males* (translated "men") who have had only one wife. In addition, 2:9–15 should be consulted regarding the letter's general attitude toward women; it is hard to visualize the author of those lines ordaining (in a technical sense) women as deacons. On the other hand, this passage probably envisions the wives of deacons assisting them in their ministry. Women were often deacons in the more general sense of the Greek word, as helpers. In Romans we have also seen Paul's patroness Phoebe referred to as a deacon or minister and engaged in helping Paul by delivering an important letter and establishing contact with the Roman church.

ate, and trustworthy in all things. 12 Deacons should be men who have had only one wife and who guide their children and their households correctly, 13 for those who serve well as deacons acquire for themselves a good standing as well as great confidence in their faith in Christ Jesus.

14 I hope to come to you soon, but I'm writing these things to you 15 in case I'm delayed, so you'll know how to behave in the household of God, which is the church of the living God, the pillar and foundation of the truth. 16 The mystery of our religion is undeniably great —

> He was manifested in the flesh,
>> vindicated in the spirit,
>>> seen by angels,
> Proclaimed among the Gentiles,
>> believed in throughout the world,
>>> taken up in glory.

## D. The Errors of the False Teachers and Instructions on How to Counter Them

4 1 Now the Spirit expressly states that in the end times there will be some who leave the faith. They'll follow deceitful spirits and the teaching of demons, 2 led by the hypocrisy of liars whose consciences have been deadened. 3 They forbid marriage and require abstinence from foods that God created

---

4:2    "Whose consciences have been deadened." Perhaps most literally, "whose consciences have been rendered insensible by cauterization." However, it is also possible that the Greek means that their consciences have been branded as a sign that they belong to the demons.

to be received with thanksgiving by believers who know the truth. 4 But everything created by God is good and nothing is to be rejected when it's received with thanksgiving, 5 for it's sanctified by the word of God and by prayer.

6 If you point this out to the brothers you'll be a good minister of Christ Jesus, nourished by the words of faith and the good teaching you've followed. 7 Have nothing to do with profane myths and old wives' tales. Train yourself in godliness, 8 for while physical training has a limited value godliness is valuable from every standpoint, since it holds promise both for this life and for the life to come. 9 This teaching is trustworthy and deserves full acceptance — 10 the reason we toil and strive is because we've placed our hope in the living God, Who is the Savior of all, especially of those who believe.

11 Command and teach these things. 12 Let no one look down on you because you're young; be an example for the faithful in word, conduct, love, faith, and purity. 13 Until I come, attend to reading, encouraging, and teaching. 14 Don't neglect the gift that was given to you when, guided by prophecy, the council of elders laid hands on you. 15 Cultivate these things, devote yourself to them, so your progress will be clear to all. 16 Keep a close watch over yourself and your teaching; persevere, for by doing this you'll save yourself as well as your listeners.

---

4:10     "Strive." Some manuscripts read "'are reviled."

4:13     "Reading," i.e., of Scripture in a public setting to his congregation.

4:14     This passage seems to envision prophetic speeches as a part of the ordination ceremony for church elders.

## E. Practical Guidance on How to Treat Certain Classes of the Faithful In General

**5** ¹ Don't reprimand an older man — encourage him as you would your father. Treat younger men as brothers, ² older women like mothers, and younger women like sisters, with the utmost purity.

### Widows

³ Treat as widows only those who are truly widows. ⁴ If a widow has children or grandchildren they should first learn to perform their religious duty toward their own household and repay their parents, for this is pleasing in the eyes of God. ⁵ A woman who is truly a widow and has been left alone sets her hope on God and continues both night and day in supplication and prayer, ⁶ but a widow who lives a life of self-indulgence is dead even though she's alive. ⁷ Issue these instructions as well, so that they'll be irreproachable. ⁸ But if anyone doesn't provide for their relatives, especially their own family, they've renounced their faith and are worse than an unbeliever. ⁹ A widow should be put on the roll only if she's over sixty years old and has been married once; ¹⁰ she should have a reputa-

---

5:9    "Put on the roll." This whole passage appears to presuppose that the local church will have an official list of widows — perhaps corresponding to a formal organizational grouping — by which the church will be enabled to decide how to allocate the community's resources.

tion for good deeds, such as having raised children, shown hospitality, washed the feet of the saints, aided those who were afflicted, or devoted herself to all sorts of good works. 11 Refuse to put younger women on the roll, for when their sensual urges are aroused they're drawn away from Christ and want to get married, 12 then they're condemned for having broken their first promise. 13 Besides, they learn to be lazy and go about from house to house, and they become not only lazy but gossips and busybodies, saying things that shouldn't be said. 14 So I want young widows to marry, have children, manage their household, and thus give the adversary no opportunity to slander us, 15 for some have already turned aside to follow Satan. 16 If any woman believer has relatives who are widows she must help them herself — the church should be free of such burdens, so it can help those who are *truly* widows.

## Elders

17 Elders who rule well should be considered worthy of double compensation, especially those who labor at preaching and teaching, 18 *d* for Scripture says, *Don't muzzle an ox while it's threshing,* and "The worker deserves his pay."

---

*d* Mt 10:10; Lk 10:7.

5:17    While some scholars claim to see a difference in function between "bishops" (3:1) and "elders," the distinction appears forced. It is more probable that the terms were used interchangeably, or as "functional equivalents."

5:18    Dt 25:4.

¹⁹ Don't consider any accusation against an elder unless it's *supported by two or three witnesses*. ²⁰ Those who *do* sin should be rebuked in front of everyone, so the others will be afraid. ²¹ I charge you before God, Jesus Christ, and the chosen angels to follow these rules impartially — do nothing based on favoritism. ²² Don't be too quick to lay your hands on anyone, and don't take part in anyone else's sins — keep yourself pure. ²³ Stop drinking only water — take a little wine to aid your digestion and because of your frequent illnesses.

²⁴ The sins of some men are so evident that they go before them to judgment, while the sins of others follow behind. ²⁵ Likewise, good works are evident, or even if they're not they can't be hidden.

## Slaves

6 ¹ All who are under the yoke of slavery should regard their masters as worthy of respect, so the name of God and our teaching won't be reviled. ² Those whose masters are believers should not be insolent to them just because they're brothers — on the contrary, they should be even better servants because those who benefit from their service are believers and are beloved.

---

5:19    Dt 19:15.
5:22    "Lay your hands on," i.e., ordain as an elder.

## F. CONCLUDING EXHORTATIONS,
## WARNINGS, AND COUNSEL

Teach and urge these things. 3 Whoever teaches differently and doesn't agree with our Lord Jesus Christ's sound words and with teaching which is in accord with true religion 4 is blinded by pride and doesn't understand anything. Instead he has a sick craving for controversy and verbal disputes. These produce envy, discord, slander, unfounded suspicion, 5 and constant irritation among men who have become depraved in mind and have been deprived of the truth — they think religion is a means of gain. 6 Religious sentiment is indeed a great gain when it is free of concern for material goods, 7 for we brought nothing into the world and can take nothing out of it. 8 If we have food and shelter we should be content with that. 9 Those who want to be rich fall into temptations and snares, into many foolish and harmful desires which plunge them into destruction and ruin. 10 For love of money is the root of all evil; in their desire for money, some have strayed from the faith and have been pierced with many sorrows.

11 But you, O man of God, flee these things! Strive for righteousness, true religion, faith, love, steadfastness, and gentleness. 12 Fight the good fight of faith, seize the eternal life to which you were called when you nobly professed your faith before many witnesses. 13 I command you before God Who gives life to all things and before Christ Jesus who made his noble profession when he testified before Pontius Pilate — 14 keep the commandment irreproachably and

without blemish until our Lord Jesus Christ appears. 15 His appearance will be made manifest at the proper time by the blessed and only Sovereign, the King of kings and Lord of lords, 16 Who alone is immortal and dwells in unapproachable light. No one has seen Him, nor can He be seen. To Him be honor and power forever, amen.

17 Command those who are rich in the present age not to be arrogant and not to place their hope in uncertain riches. Instead, we should place our hope in God, Who grants us all things in rich supply for our enjoyment. 18 The wealthy should do good and grow rich in good deeds, be generous and share, 19 and lay up for themselves a good foundation for the future so they'll be able to grasp the true life.

## G. Farewell

20 Timothy, guard what has been entrusted to your care! Avoid irreligious chatter, oppose that so-called knowledge which is false; 21 some who profess it have missed the mark as far as the faith is concerned.

Grace be with all of you.

# THE SECOND LETTER TO

# TIMOTHY

In contrast to 1 Timothy, 2 Timothy is the most Pauline of the Pastoral Letters. It purports to be a letter of encouragement to Timothy and generally conforms to what we would expect of Paul in this situation. If it is pseudonymous, it is certainly remarkable for its sensitivity in portraying Paul as aging and alone, in prison for Christ. Again in contrast to 1 Timothy there are many personal references to well-known companions of Paul, references which, if authentic, tend to group this letter with Colossians and Philemon.

The dominant theme is the need to be faithful and steadfast. Particularly noteworthy is the way in which Paul always has Christ in mind throughout the letter; never does the letter sink into self-pity, for Paul has complete faith in Christ. Paul's concern is not for himself but for the young churches which Timothy must oversee, lest they be led astray by false teachers.

## OUTLINE OF THE SECOND LETTER TO TIMOTHY

A.  1:1–2        Greeting

B.  1:3–14       Thanksgiving and Exhortation
                 to Timothy

C.  1:15–2:13    A Call to Timothy to Suffer with Paul
                 in Christ

D.  2:14–4:8     Be Faithful and Oppose False Teaching

E.  4:9–22       Personal News and Greetings

## A. Greeting

**1** <sup></sup> ¹ Paul, an apostle of Christ Jesus by the will of God in accordance with the promise of the life which is in Christ Jesus, ² to Timothy my beloved child — grace, mercy, and peace from God the Father and Christ Jesus our Lord.

## B. Thanksgiving and Exhortation to Timothy

³ I give thanks to God — Whom I serve with a clear conscience, as did my forefathers — when I mention you in my prayers, which I do unceasingly, night and day. ⁴ When I remember your tears I long to see you and be filled with joy. ⁵ ᵃ I remember your sincere faith — it dwelt first in your grandmother Lois and your mother Eunice and I'm certain it dwells in you as well. ⁶ For this reason I remind you to stir up the flame of God's gift, which is yours through the laying on of my hands, ⁷ for God didn't give us a spirit of cowardice — He gave us a spirit of power, love, and good judgment. ⁸ So don't be ashamed to bear witness to our Lord, nor to me, his prisoner; instead, join with me in suffering for the good news through the strength that comes from God. ⁹ He saved us and called us to a holy way of life,

---

ᵃ Ac 16:1.

not because of what we had done but in accordance with His plan and His grace which He granted us in Christ Jesus before the beginning of the ages. [10] It has now been made manifest through the appearance of our Savior Christ Jesus, who destroyed death and brought life and immortality to light through the good news, [11] [b] for which I have been appointed a preacher, an apostle, and a teacher. [12] This is the reason I'm suffering these things, but I'm not ashamed, for I know whom I've believed and I'm confident that he's able to guard what was entrusted to me until that day. [13] Hold fast to the example of sound teaching that you received from me, in the faith and love which are in Christ Jesus. [14] Guard the precious trust, through the Holy Spirit that dwells in us.

## C. A CALL TO TIMOTHY TO SUFFER WITH PAUL IN CHRIST

[15] As you know, all those in Asia have deserted me, including Phygelus and Hermogenes. [16] May the Lord grant mercy to the household of Onesiphorus, because he has revived me many times and has not been ashamed of my chains. [17] On the contrary, when he was in Rome he eagerly sought me out and found me — [18] may the Lord grant that he may find mercy from the Lord on that day!

---

[b] 1 Tm 2:7.

He also rendered many services for me at Ephesus, as you well know.

2 ¹ So, my child, be strong in the grace which is in Christ Jesus. ² The things you heard from me before many witnesses, entrust them to faithful men who will be capable of teaching others. ³ Share in my suffering like a good soldier of Christ Jesus. ⁴ No one serving as a soldier can get entangled in affairs of everyday life, because he wants to please the one who enlisted him. ⁵ And an athlete isn't awarded the crown unless he competes in accordance with the rules. ⁶ The farmer who works hard should be the first to receive a share of the harvest. ⁷ Think over what I'm saying, for the Lord will give you understanding in all things.

⁸ Remember Jesus Christ who was raised from the dead and was descended from David, in accordance with the good news I proclaimed. ⁹ It's for this that I'm suffering and in chains like a criminal, but the word of God cannot be chained. ¹⁰ The reason I'm willing to endure it all for the sake of those who were chosen, is so they'll be able to attain salvation in Christ Jesus, with eternal glory. ¹¹ This teaching can be trusted,

> If we've died with him we'll also live with him;
> ¹² ᶜ if we endure we'll also reign with him;
>     if we deny him, then he'll deny us too;

---

ᶜ *Mt 10:33; Lk 12:9.*

2:4      The idea behind the phrase "affairs of everyday life" is probably that the soldier should not moonlight in a second job. The lesson for the Christian is that of singleness of purpose.

<sup>13</sup> if we're unfaithful, he remains faithful,
    for he can't deny himself.


## D. BE FAITHFUL AND OPPOSE FALSE TEACHING


<sup>14</sup> Keep reminding people of these things, warn them before God not to engage in disputes over words — such disputes serve no purpose but the ruin of those who listen to them. <sup>15</sup> Make every effort to present yourself as acceptable to God, a laborer who need not be ashamed and correctly interprets the word of truth. <sup>16</sup> Avoid irreligious chatter, for it leads people to further wickedness <sup>17</sup> and their talk spreads like a cancer. Among them are Hymenaeus and Philetus. <sup>18</sup> They've departed from the truth by saying that the resurrection has already taken place, and they are upsetting the faith of some. <sup>19</sup> Nevertheless God's firm foundation stands and bears this seal: *The Lord knows those who are His,* and "Let everyone who calls on the name of the Lord keep away from evil." <sup>20</sup> In a great house there aren't just gold and silver vessels — there are also wooden and clay ones, some of which are for more honored use and some for less honored use. <sup>21</sup> So if someone purifies himself from these things he'll be a vessel that's destined for honored use, set apart and useful to the master, ready for every good work. <sup>22</sup> Flee youthful passions, strive for righteousness, faith,

---

2:18    Hymenaeus and Philetus appear to have regarded resurrection as taking place symbolically at baptism and to have denied an afterlife.

2:19    Nb 16:5

love, and peace, together with those who call upon the Lord from pure hearts. 23 Avoid foolish and stupid controversies, because you know that they lead to quarrels. 24 A servant of the Lord should not quarrel — he should be kind to everyone, skilled at teaching, tolerant, 25 able to correct opponents gently, in case God should grant them repentance and lead them to recognize the truth, 26 return to their senses, and escape the Devil's snares, by whom they had been held captive to do his will.

3 1 Understand this — in the final days there will be difficult times. 2 For men will be selfish, greedy, braggarts, arrogant, abusive, disobedient to their parents, ungrateful, unholy, 3 inhuman, merciless, slanderous, lacking in self-control, brutal, enemies of what's good, 4 treacherous, reckless, conceited, given over to pleasure rather than being lovers of God. 5 They'll have the outward appearance of piety but will deny the power of religion. Avoid them! 6 For included among them are those who worm their way into homes and mislead poor weak women who are burdened with sins and influenced by all kinds of passions. 7 These women are always trying to learn but are never able to arrive at a knowledge of the truth. 8 Just as Jannes and Jambres opposed Moses, so too these men oppose the truth. They're corrupt in mind and their faith is worthless, 9 but they won't get very far, for their folly will be apparent to all, just as was the folly of Jannes and Jambres.

---

3:8    In Jewish legend, Jannes and Jambres were said to have been the names of Pharaoh's magicians (cf. Ex 7:11; 8:18–19).

¹⁰ But you have followed my teaching, my way of life, my purpose, my faith, my patience, my love, my steadfastness, ¹¹ *d* my persecutions, my sufferings, everything that happened to me in Antioch, in Iconium, and in Lystra, all the persecutions I endured — and the Lord delivered me from them all. ¹² And in fact everyone who desires to live a holy life in Christ Jesus will be persecuted, ¹³ while evil men and impostors will grow ever worse, deceiving and being deceived. ¹⁴ But remain faithful to what you've learned and believed, remembering from whom you learned it. ¹⁵ Remember that from childhood you have been familiar with the holy Scriptures, which are able to instruct you and lead you to salvation through faith in Christ Jesus. ¹⁶ All Scripture is inspired by God and is useful for teaching, reproving, correcting, and training in righteousness, ¹⁷ so that the man of God may be fully capable of carrying out every good work.

4 ¹ I charge you before God and Christ Jesus, who is to judge the living and the dead, and by his appearance and his Kingdom — ² proclaim the word, insist upon it whether it's convenient or inconvenient, show error for what it is, reprove and encourage, but always display patience in your teaching. ³ The time will come when people will not tolerate sound teaching; instead, because their ears are itching, they'll follow their own desires and gather teachers for themselves. ⁴ They'll stop listening to the truth and will turn to myths. ⁵ But keep your self-control at all times,

---

*d* Ac 13:14–14:20.

endure suffering patiently, do the work of an evangelist, perform your ministry fully and completely.

6 *e* As for me, my life is already being poured out like a libation — the time of my departure is imminent. 7 I've fought the good fight, I've finished the race, I've kept the faith. 8 From here on the crown of righteousness is being laid aside for me, which the Lord, the just judge, will award me on that day, and not only me but all those who have longed for his appearance.

## E. Personal News and Greetings

9 Do your best to come to me quickly. 10 *f* Demas has abandoned me out of love for this present world and has gone to Thessalonica, Crescens has gone to Galatia, and Titus to Dalmatia — 11 *g* only Luke is with me. Get Mark and bring him with you, for he's useful to me in the ministry. 12 *h* Tychicus I sent to Ephesus. 13 When you come, bring the cloak I left at Troas with Carpus as well as the scrolls, especially the parchments. 14 *i* Alexander the coppersmith has done me considerable harm — the Lord will repay him in accordance with his deeds! 15 Be on your guard against him, for he strenuously opposed our teaching.

16 At my first hearing no one came to my aid — they all abandoned me, may it not be held against them! 17 But the

---

*e* Ph 2:17.  *f* Col 4:14; Phm 24; 2 Cor 8:23; Gal 2:3; Tt 1:4.  *g* Col 4:10, 14; Phm 24.
*h* Ac 20:4; Eph 6:21–22; Col 4:7–8.  *i* 1 Tm 1:20.

Lord came to my aid and strengthened me so that through me the proclamation of the good news might be fully accomplished and all the Gentiles might hear it, and I was delivered from the lion's mouth. [18] The Lord will deliver me from all evil and will save me for his heavenly Kingdom, to him be glory for ever and ever, amen.

[19] Greet Prisca and Aquila and the household of Onesiphorus. [20] *j* Erastus remained at Corinth and I left Trophimus ill at Miletus. [21] Do everything in your power to come before winter. Eubulus greets you, as well as Pudens, Linus, Claudia, and all the brothers. [22] The Lord be with your spirit. Grace be with all of you.

---

*j Ac 19:22; 20:4; 21:29; Rm 16:23.*

4:19     Prisca and Aquila were well known associates of Paul, mentioned not only in Acts but in 1 Corinthians and Romans as well.

4:21     "Linus." Possibly the same Linus who became the second pope. If so, this would be an argument for a Roman setting for the letter.

# The Letter to

# TITUS

Titus was Paul's companion and co-worker during some of Paul's most productive years, although he is known only from Paul's letters and is not mentioned in Acts. That Paul had great confidence in him can be seen from the fact that Paul used him for very sensitive missions, such as trips to the recalcitrant church in Corinth bearing letters from Paul (cf. 2 Corinthians). This letter itself, however, offers little of a personal nature; it is brisk and businesslike in tone and, like 1 Timothy, is concerned with church organization, the threat posed by false teachers, and the need for the faithful to lead orderly, respectable lives.

At the time of writing, Titus is in Crete, and Paul is writing to give him instructions on how to organize the new churches there. Among those who support Pauline authorship (the minority view), the suggestion is sometimes made that the letter was written while Paul was en route back to Jerusalem for his last visit.

## OUTLINE OF THE LETTER TO TITUS

A.  1:1–4            Greeting

B.  1:5–16           Instructions on Titus' Mission in Crete,
                     Especially with Regard to False Teachers

C.  2:1–3:11         Proper Behavior of the Faithful

D.  3:12–15          Closing Instructions and Greetings

---

## A. Greeting

1 <sup>1</sup> Paul, a servant of God and an apostle of Jesus Christ for the purpose of advancing the faith of God's chosen ones and their knowledge of religious truth, ² in hope of the eternal life which was promised before time began by God, Who never lies, and Who, ³ at the proper time, revealed His word in the proclamation with which I have been entrusted by the command of God our Savior — ⁴ ᵃ to Titus, my true child in our common faith; grace and peace from God the Father and our Savior Christ Jesus.

## B. Instructions on Titus' Ministry in Crete, Especially with Regard to False Teachers

⁵ The reason I left you in Crete was to correct any shortcomings and to appoint elders in every city in accordance with the instructions I gave you — ⁶ ᵇ if the man is blameless, married once, and has children who are believers and are not accused of profligacy or rebelliousness.

---

ᵃ  *2 Cor 8:23; Gal 2:3; 2 Tm 4:10.*   ᵇ  *1 Tm 3:2–7.*

---

1:5–7   Here we clearly see that "bishop" and "elder" are essentially equivalent terms in the Pastoral Letters.

7 For a bishop, as God's steward, must be above reproach, not arrogant, not quick-tempered, not a drunkard, not a bully, and not greedy. 8 Instead, he should be hospitable, he should love what's good, be prudent, upright, holy, and self-disciplined. 9 He must adhere to the true word as it was taught so he'll be able both to offer encouragement with sound teaching and to refute opponents.

10 For there are many who are rebellious, who are empty talkers and deceivers, especially those who support circumcision. 11 You must silence them, because they're upsetting entire households by teaching what they shouldn't for the sake of dishonest gain. 12 One of them, a prophet of their own, said:

> "Cretans have always been liars,
>     evil beasts, and lazy gluttons."

13 This testimony can be trusted. Therefore rebuke them sharply so they'll be sound in the faith 14 and won't give themselves over to Jewish myths and the commandments of men who reject the truth. 15 Everything is pure for those who are pure, but for those who are corrupt and unbelieving nothing is pure — both their minds and consciences are corrupt. 16 They claim to know God, but deny Him by their actions; they're detestable and disobedient and unfit for any good deed.

---

1:10    "Those who support circumcision," i.e., Jewish Christians who favored requiring Gentile converts to be circumcised.

1:12    Epimenides is probably the Cretan "prophet" referred to here.

## C. Proper Behavior of the Faithful

2 [1] You, however, must say what is in accord with sound teaching. [2] Urge older men to be temperate, serious, sensible, sound in faith, love, and steadfastness. [3] Likewise, urge older women to be reverent in their behavior, not slanderous nor slaves to wine; they should teach what's good [4] and encourage young women to love their husbands and children, [5] to be sensible, chaste, devoted homemakers, generous and submissive to their husbands so the word of God won't be blasphemed. [6] Likewise, encourage the young men to be sensible. [7] Be a model of good works in every respect; in your teaching demonstrate integrity, seriousness, [8] and sound speech which is beyond reproach so that whoever opposes us will be ashamed and will have nothing bad to say about us. [9] Slaves are to be submissive to their masters in everything, to give satisfaction and not be contentious; [10] they are not to pilfer but are to show complete good faith so that in every respect they will adorn the teaching of God our Savior.

[11] For the grace of God has appeared with salvation for all men, [12] teaching us to reject impiety and worldly passions and to live sober, upright, and godly lives in this present age [13] as we await our blessed hope — the appearance in glory of our great God and of our Savior Christ Jesus. [14] He gave himself for us to redeem us from all wickedness and to purify for himself a people eager for good works. [15] Say these things, encourage and reprove with authority — let no one disregard you.

3 ¹ Remind them to be submissive to rulers and authorities, to be obedient and ready for any good work; ² to slander no one, to be peaceable and gentle, to show consideration for everyone. ³ For we too were once foolish, disobedient, deceived, enslaved by various desires and passions, spending our lives in malice and envy — we were hateful, and we hated one another.

> ⁴ But when the goodness and loving kindness
>     of God our Savior appeared —
> ⁵ not because of righteous acts we had performed
>     but through His mercy —
> He saved us through the bath of rebirth
>     and renewal in the Holy Spirit,
> ⁶ which He poured out upon us so richly
>     through our Savior Jesus Christ
> ⁷ so that we might be restored to fellowship with
>     God by his grace
>         and become heirs in hope of eternal life.

⁸ This teaching can be trusted, and I want you to insist upon it so that those who have come to believe in God will be intent upon busying themselves with good deeds — these are good and are beneficial to others. ⁹ But avoid foolish controversies, genealogies, strife, and disputes about the Torah — these things are useless and futile. ¹⁰ Warn a heretic once or twice and then have nothing to do with him, ¹¹ in

---

3:1     The attitude expressed here toward civil authorities would be rather anachronistic if Titus had been written after the Neronian persecution of the middle to late 60s. The unremitting hostility exhibited in the Revelation makes an interesting contrast.

the realization that such people are perverted and sinful and stand self-condemned.

## D. Closing Instructions and Greetings

12 ᶜ When I send Artemas or Tychicus to you do everything in your power to come to me at Nicopolis, for I intend to spend the winter there. 13 ᵈ Do everything in your power to send Zenas the lawyer and Apollos on their way, and see that they lack nothing. 14 Our people should learn to be occupied with good deeds so as to provide for urgent needs and so they won't be unfruitful.

15 All those with me greet you. Greet those who love us in the faith. Grace be with all of you.

---

# THE LETTER TO

# PHILEMON

Philemon is a letter of extraordinary humanity and charm. While in prison Paul had come in contact with and converted a runaway slave named Onesimus. Onesimus' master, Philemon, was a prominent Christian in Colossae and Paul decided to send Onesimus back. In the letter he pleads with great tact and eloquence that Onesimus should be allowed to return to Paul to help him in his work.

In Galatians Paul had said that "in Christ" "there's neither slave nor free." Brave words, but words which had no legal authority in the Roman Empire. Powerless before the administrative apparatus of the Empire, Paul used his most powerful weapon, the moral authority of the gospel, to challenge Philemon to express his Christian faith in action.

Paul knew he was unable to revolutionize the social reality of his world by his efforts alone, but by his words and example he articulated the principles by which Christians of every age are called to transform their hearts and their daily lives, and in this way the world around them, by living the life of Christ and bringing the good news of this Way to all their brothers and sisters.

_____

¹ Paul, a prisoner for Christ Jesus, and our brother Timothy to our beloved fellow worker Philemon, ² ᵃ our sister Apphia, our fellow soldier Archippus, and the church at your house — ³ grace and peace be with you from God our Father and the Lord Jesus Christ!

⁴ I always give thanks to God when I mention you in my prayers, ⁵ for I hear of the faith and love you have for the Lord Jesus and all the saints, ⁶ and I pray that your fellowship in the faith may serve to lead you to a deeper understanding of all the good that we have in Christ. ⁷ Your love has been a great joy and comfort to me because the hearts of the saints have been refreshed through you, my brother.

⁸ Therefore, while I'm bold enough in Christ to order you to do what *should* be done, ⁹ I prefer to base my appeal on your love for me — I, Paul, an ambassador and now also a prisoner for Christ Jesus. ¹⁰ ᵇ I appeal to you on behalf of my child, Onesimus, whom I have begotten while in prison. ¹¹ He was formerly useless to you, but now is useful both to you and to me. ¹² I'm sending him back to

---

ᵃ Col 4:17. ᵇ Col 4:9.

2    "The church at your house." "Your" is in the singular and it is generally accepted that it refers to Philemon, a natural supposition since he appears to have been a man of some means.

9    "Ambassador." The Greek word (*presbutes*) literally means "old man" and is very closely related to the word for "ambassador" (*presbeutes*). Most commentators believe "ambassador" is the intended meaning.

11    "Useless... useful." This is a pun on the name Onesimus, which means "useful." It was a common name for slaves.

you, which is to say, I'm sending my heart. 13 I wanted to keep him with me so that he might serve me on your behalf while I'm imprisoned for the gospel, 14 but I preferred not to do anything without your knowledge because I wanted your good deed to be voluntary rather than compelled. 15 Perhaps the reason he was taken from you for a time was so you could have him back forever, 16 no longer as a slave but as more than a slave — as a beloved brother, especially beloved to me, but how much more to you as well, both in the flesh and in the Lord!

17 So if you regard me as a partner you'll receive him as you would me, 18 and if he has wronged you or owes you anything, charge it to my account. 19 I, Paul, am writing this with my own hand — I'll pay you back (not to mention that you owe me your very self)! 20 Yes, my brother, you can be of use to me in the Lord — refresh my heart in Christ!

21 I write to you with complete confidence in your obedience, for I know you'll do even more than I ask. 22 At the same time, prepare a guest room for me, for I hope to be granted to you through your prayers.

23 *c* My fellow prisoner Epaphras greets you in Christ Jesus, 24 *d* as do Mark, Aristarchus, Demas, and Luke, my fellow workers.

25 The grace of the Lord Jesus Christ be with your spirit!

---

*c* Col 1:7; 4:12.   *d* Col 4:10, 14; 2 Tm 4:10–11.

16        "In the flesh." This phrase refers to Onesimus under the aspect of his simple humanity, whereas "in the Lord" refers to his status as a Christian "brother."

23        Epaphras founded the church at Colossae.

# THE LETTER TO THE

# HEBREWS

The Letter to the Hebrews is unique among New Testament letters in that it provides no identification of the author — indeed, there is no salutation at all and the composition would probably never have been called a letter except for the addition of Chapter 13. Properly speaking, Hebrews is an address, an "exhortation" (13:22), forwarded to its audience because the author was unable to be present to deliver the address in person.

To whom was Hebrews written? Most scholars are in agreement that the recipients were a community, or a portion of a community, of Jewish Christians. They had not themselves heard the Lord, but had received the good news from persons who had personally heard and seen Jesus (2:3). After their initial devotion, however, these Jewish Christians were in danger of losing their faith and returning to Judaism. It appears that the author of Hebrews was well known, certainly by reputation, to the recipients of the letter, and was asked by third parties to write the letter in order to head off the impending crisis of faith. The letter is thus an extended polemic asserting the superiority of the New Covenant, the Christian faith, to the Old Covenant.

Many different locations have been suggested for this community — Alexandria, Corinth, Jerusalem, Colossae — but the one which enjoys the most favor at the present time is Rome. The Roman church had been established very early on, certainly in the 40s A.D., and had first taken root in the city's populous Jewish community. It had not been long before Gentile converts outnumbered Jewish Christians, but for many decades the Jewish Christians remained a distinctive presence in Rome. Relations between the Jewish Christians and the rest of the Jewish population in Rome became quite acrimonious — so much so that in A.D. 49, the Emperor Claudius expelled all Jews from the city as a result of riots caused by disagreements among the Jews about a certain "Chrestus." Paul's co-workers Priscilla and Aquila were among those expelled (Ac 18:2).

Scholars believe traces of this background can be found in Hebrews. At 13:24 the author writes: "Those from Italy send their greetings to you." Does this mean that the letter is being sent from outside Italy back to Italy, or that it is being sent from someplace in Italy to an unknown destination? Increasingly, scholars believe that the former alternative is the correct interpretation. There are other even more tempting possibilities. For example, at 10:32 and following, we learn that in the early days of their faith the recipients of the letter had had to endure public mistreatment and the seizure of their property. It is believed by many that this passage refers to the troubles of A.D. 49.

More controversially, some scholars believe that the letter may have been written just before or during the persecution of the Church by Nero. These scholars point to 13:7, which seems to indicate that the leaders of the community had been martyred — they are certainly dead — and 12:4, with its comment that the readers "haven't yet resisted to the point of shedding blood." Others, perhaps the "leaders," have already given their lives for the faith.

As for what precipitated the crisis of faith, there are also a variety of hypotheses. Those who argue strongly for a Roman setting speculate that this community of Jewish Christians may have been tempted, in the face of the Neronian persecution, to seek safety by reverting to Judaism. But while the pressures of persecution may have been a contributing factor to the crisis, they were probably not decisive. By the writer's own testimony, the community had, in the past, accepted seizure of their property with equanimity, even with joy. While the Neronian persecution was much more severe, genuine theological concerns must have been involved. Therefore, other scholars see an anxiety caused by the consciousness that the end had not yet come and that Christians were still imperfect and in need of forgiveness. In this situation, recollections of Jewish rituals of forgiveness tugged at the converts — they felt a need for greater assurance of forgiveness. If we are to judge from the author's emphasis, concern with the efficacy of Christ's sacrifice must, in fact, have been a major concern for the community. We are probably safe in assuming, therefore, that both external pressures as well as internal anxieties were contributing factors to the faith crisis which Hebrews addresses.

Who was the author? Early tradition, especially in the Eastern Church, testifies that Paul wrote the letter. Modern scholars almost universally reject this ascription, and ancient writers were aware of the difficulties involved as well. That there is a Pauline connection seems likely from the mention of Timothy being released from prison (13:23), unless a totally unrelated Timothy, otherwise unknown to us, is intended. On the other hand, the style and thought is quite distinct from that of Paul. The early Church Father Origen, writing from Egypt and reviewing the many hypotheses which had already arisen regarding the letter's authorship, gave it as his opinion that only God knew the truth of the matter, because the style was clearly not Paul's.

Interestingly, the Roman church, which was familiar with Hebrews from a very early date (it is quoted by *1 Clement* and *The Shepherd of Hermas*), resisted ascribing the letter to Saint Paul. Many scholars believe this was because, although the identity of the true author was no longer known to the Roman church, it *was* known that the author had not been Paul.

The most popular non-Pauline theories of authorship have been those of Apollos and Barnabas. Both of these men provide the Pauline link, and both were considered learned in Jewish theology prior to their conversions. Once again, however, attractive as these hypotheses may be, we are safer to side with Origen's opinion. There is simply no way of knowing for sure.

The reason so much energy has been expended in seeking an identity for the author is clear, of course, for the author was one of the theological giants of the New Testament. The letter is written in a fine Greek style, probably the overall best in the New Testament, and presents its thesis in a sustained argument from beginning to end, without digressions. The author was a man of powerful intellect who could deal with complex Christological issues with a sure hand, painting with broad, bold brush strokes but equally comfortable with detailed argumentation. He also possessed great tact and sensitivity. He had received a difficult commission in a crisis situation, but he resists the temptation to simply condemn the recipients. Instead, he carefully balances warnings and reprimands by providing encouragement and reasons for confidence. Central to the whole letter is the majestic picture of Jesus — Son of God through whom the universe was created, great high priest who can intercede with us before God, but also our brother who can sympathize with our weakness.

With regard to the date of Hebrews, there appears to be a clear trend favoring a date prior to the destruction of the Temple in Jerusalem in A.D. 70. While such a date is not required by references to Jewish sacrificial ritual — the letter deals with this subject in the abstract — there is widespread agreement that the letter's argument comes into much sharper focus when viewed against the background of the Temple.

An outline of the Letter to the Hebrews is provided below. Because of the compact, sustained nature of the letter's argument, however, a summary of the contents of each section follows the outline itself, to which the reader may conveniently refer as a supplement to the outline and notes.

## OUTLINE OF THE LETTER TO THE HEBREWS

A.  1:1–2:18       The Son of God Reveals the Greatness of God's Salvation and Its Superiority to Prior Revelations

B.  3:1–5:10       Christ the Trustworthy and Compassionate High Priest

C.  5:11–6:20      Exhortation to Greater Maturity

D.  7:1–28         Christ's Priesthood Superior to the Aaronic Priesthood

E.  8:1–10:18      Superiority of Christ's New Covenant

F.  10:19–12:29    Culminating Exhortation to Faithfulness

    10:19–39     A Call to Faith

    11:1–40      Examples of Faith from the Old Testament

    12:1–29      A Call to Perseverance

G.  13:1–25        Practical Counsels, Closing Exhortations, and Concluding Messages

## SUMMARY

A.   God's culminating revelation is through His Son and is as superior to prior revelations as His Son is superior to the angels. The Son's superiority is amply documented in Scripture. The Torah was revealed by angels, and transgressions of it were strictly punished — how much more strictly then will we be punished if we disregard so great a salvation as is offered by God! How great is that salvation? All things have been subjected to man and God's Son shared in flesh and blood to save us from fear of death. Thus, because he became like us, he is able to help us.

B.     Therefore, think of Jesus' faithfulness, and think of the fate of unbelievers. Those who were unbelieving in the desert, God did not allow to enter into His rest, and nothing can be hidden from God. But we have a great high priest who is merciful, who can sympathize with our weakness, and who represents us before God. Through what he suffered he was made perfect and God made him a high priest in the order of Melchizedek.

C.     We have much to say about those things which have been mentioned, but you've become hard of hearing. But let's leave behind the elementary teaching of Christ and move on to the mature teaching. We *must* move on, for to fall away after being baptized spells ruin — it's like crucifying the Son of God. But we feel sure you're destined for better things. Your hope is in the example of God's promise to Abraham, and even more in the promise to Jesus, a forerunner on our behalf — "you will be a priest forever in the line of Melchizedek!"

D.     The story of Abraham and Melchizedek shows that Melchizedek was the greater. Unlike the Levitical priests, our high priest, Jesus, is perfect, brings salvation, and his priesthood lasts forever — just the kind of high priest we needed. If the Levitical priesthood had been able to bring perfection, there would have been no need for a new priest in Melchizedek's line. But the Torah has been superseded, and that means that there must be a new priesthood.

E.   If the first covenant had been perfect, there would have been no need for a new covenant, but God found fault with Israel and decided upon a new covenant. Under the first covenant the high priest could enter the sanctuary only once a year, on the Day of Atonement. Year after year the high priest enters the sanctuary bearing the blood of animals for his sins and those of the people. These sacrifices could not take away sins. But under the new covenant Christ, the perfect high priest, entered a sanctuary not made by human hands bearing his *own* blood as an offering for sins once and for all, thus securing for us an eternal redemption.

F.   The blood of Jesus gives us the confidence to approach God with full assurance, so let's maintain our hope and render mutual encouragement. For to sin after receiving the truth would expose us to fearful punishment. Bolster your confidence by thinking back to how you bore up under suffering in the early days of your faith.

Faith is what gained approval for the patriarchs and prophets of old, and yet they didn't receive the promise — God has saved that for us!

Keep your eyes fixed on Jesus and think of all he

suffered. View your sufferings as discipline from God your Father. The call you are receiving is not coming from a mountain like Sinai but is the proclamation of Jesus, mediator of the new covenant. See that you don't reject that voice.

G.   Continue in brotherly love. Follow the example of faith of your leaders and share Jesus' sufferings, offering a sacrifice of praise to God.

## A. The Son of God Reveals the Greatness of God's Salvation and Its Superiority Over Previous Revelations

1 ¹ Of old God spoke to our fathers through the prophets many times and in various ways, ² but in these last days He has spoken to us through a Son, whom He designated heir of all things and through whom He created the universe. ³ He is the radiance of God's glory, the full expression of God's being, and he sustains the universe with his powerful word. When he had brought about purification from sins he took his seat at the right hand of the Majesty on high, ⁴ having become as much superior to the angels as the name he inherited is superior to theirs.

⁵ For to which of the angels did God ever say,

> *You are My son,*
> *this day have I begotten you.*

Or again,

> *I will be a Father to him*
> *and he will be a son to Me.*

---

1:1–4    The letter opens with a brief review of the *kerygma* of the early Church, the original proclamation of the good news. This summary strongly emphasizes the Son's glory and high dignity and combines two early approaches to Christology, that of pre–existence (for it was through the Son that the universe was created) and that of exaltation, which stresses Jesus' completion of God's plan of salvation.

1:3       Ws 7:26.

1:5       Ps 2:7; 2 S 7:14.

⁶ And again when He brings His firstborn into the world
He says,

> Let all God's angels worship him.

⁷ Of the angels He says,

> He makes His angels winds,
> and His servants flaming fire,

⁸ while of His Son He says,

> Your throne, O God, is forever and ever,
> the righteous scepter is the scepter of
> Your Kingdom.
>
> ⁹ You loved righteousness and hated wrongdoing,
> Therefore God, your God, has anointed you
> with the oil of gladness,
> far above your companions,

¹⁰ and,

> It was You at the beginning, Lord, who established
> the earth,
> and the heavens are the work of Your hands;
>
> ¹¹ They will perish, but You will remain,
> they'll all grow old like a cloak,
> ¹² Like a mantle You will roll them up,
> like a cloak they'll be changed.
> You are ever the same,
> and Your years will never end.

---

1:6     Dt 32:43 (Septuagint).

1:7     Ps 104:4 (Septuagint).

1:8–12   Ps 45:6–7; Ps 102:25–27 (Septuagint). Note that references to God in Scripture
are here explicitly applied to the Son.

13 And to which of the angels has He ever said,

> *Sit at My right hand,*
>> *till I make your enemies a stool*
>>> *for your feet.*

14 Aren't all the angels ministering spirits who are sent to serve, for the sake of those who are going to receive salvation?

2 1 Therefore we must pay more attention than ever to what we've heard so that we won't drift off course. 2 For if the word spoken through angels was reliably established, and every transgression and act of disobedience received just retribution, 3 how will we escape if we disregard so great a salvation? It was first proclaimed by the Lord, then was confirmed for us by those who had listened. 4 At the same time God bore witness through signs and wonders and all sorts of mighty deeds, and by distributing the gifts of the Holy Spirit according to His will.

5 For it wasn't to angels that God subjected the world

---

1:13    Ps 110:1.

2:1ff.    Chapter 2 is balanced at the beginning and end: at the beginning by a warning concerning the possibility of punishment (2:1–3) and at the end by reassurance that we will receive help from Jesus, the merciful and faithful high priest (2:17–18).

2:2–4    The true purpose in establishing Jesus' superiority to the angels now becomes apparent, for "the word spoken through angels" refers to the Torah, which was believed by Jews of that time to have been revealed through the intermediation of angels. The salvation proclaimed by Jesus is thus as superior to the Torah as Jesus himself is to the angels.

2:5–18    The author now turns to the humanity of Jesus, to establish Christ's solidarity with us in preparation for discussing his role as high priest. A priest must be one with those he represents. Jesus must be a *high* priest, however, because only the high priest could preside at the Day of Atonement rituals, and the author sees Jesus as fulfilling the Day of Atonement sacrifices.

to come, about which we are speaking. 6 Someone testified somewhere,

> *What is man, that You should think of him,*
> > *the son of man, that You should be concerned*
> > *for him?*
> 7 *You made him less than the angels for a while,*
> > *and crowned him with glory and honor,*
> 8 *You placed all things beneath his feet.*

In making all things subject to man, God left nothing beyond his control. Right now we're not yet able to see all things subjected to man, 9 but we do see Jesus, who *for a little while was made lower than the angels* so that he could taste death for all, now *crowned with glory and honor* because of the death he suffered.

10 It was fitting that God, for Whom and through Whom all things exist, should through suffering perfect the pioneer of their salvation so as to lead many sons to glory. 11 For the one who sanctifies and those who are sanctified have one and the same origin, for which reason Jesus is not ashamed to call them brothers, 12 for instance, when he says,

> *I will proclaim Your name to my brothers,*
> *I will praise You before the assembly;*

---

2:6–8    Ps 8:4–6.

2:9      "Jesus... was made lower than the angels," i.e., by becoming a human being Jesus was subject to the angels, like all other humans.

2:10     "Pioneer." The Greek word most commonly refers to the founder of a city. In this context it is applied to Jesus in the sense of one who goes ahead and leads the way. First used here in the introductory section of the letter, this word is repeated in the concluding exhortation (12:2).

2:12     Ps 22:22.

¹³ and again,

> *I will put my trust in Him;*

and again,

> *Here am I, with the children God has given me.*

¹⁴ Now since the "children" are all made of flesh and blood, he too shared in the same flesh and blood so that through his death he would destroy the one who has power over death, that is, the Devil, ¹⁵ and in this way would deliver those who all their lives were in bondage through fear of death. ¹⁶ For it's surely not with the angels that he's concerned; no, *He is concerned with the descendants of Abraham.* ¹⁷ Therefore he had to become like his brothers in every respect so he could become a merciful and trusted high priest before God and expiate the sins of the people. ¹⁸ For since he himself was tested through what he suffered, he's able to help those who are tempted.

## B. CHRIST THE TRUSTWORTHY AND COMPASSIONATE HIGH PRIEST

**3** ¹ Therefore, holy brothers, who share in a heavenly calling, think of Jesus, the apostle and high priest of the

---

2:13     Is 8:17–18 (Septuagint).

2:16     Is 41:8–9.

3:1ff.     In Chapters 3 and 4 we find similar balancing sections: 3:7–4:13 is an extended warning of the consequences of loss of faith, 4:14–16 provides reasons for being confident, to reassure the readers. For Jesus as "apostle" or "messenger," cf. Ml 2:7.

faith we profess, 2 for he is trusted by God Who appointed him, just as *Moses was trusted in God's household.* 3 But Jesus is worthy of far more glory than Moses, just as the founder of a household deserves more honor than the house itself. 4 Every house is founded by someone, but God is the founder of everything. 5 Now *Moses was trusted in all God's house* as *a servant*, bearing witness to the things that were to be spoken by God in the future, 6 but Christ is trusted as a son over God's house — and *we* are His house if we maintain our confidence and pride in our hope.

7 Therefore, as the Holy Spirit says,

> *Today if you hear His voice,*
> 8 *Harden not your hearts as in the rebellion,*
> > *on the day of temptation in the desert,*
> 9 *Where your ancestors put Me to the test*
> > *and knew My works*
> 10 *for forty years.*
> *Therefore I became provoked with that generation*
> > *and said, "Their hearts always stray,*
> > *they don't know My ways."*
> 11 *As I swore in My wrath,*
> > *"They shall never enter My rest!"*

12 Take care, brothers, that none of *you* have evil, unbelieving hearts in rebellion against the living God — 13 encourage one another every day, as long as there is a day to be

---

3:2, 5    Nb 12:7.

3:7–11    Ps 95:7–11 (Septuagint).

called "today," so that none of you will become hardened by the deceitfulness of sin. 14 After all, we have become partners with Christ, if only we maintain our original confidence firm to the end, 15 as it is said,

> *Today if you hear His voice,*
> *Harden not your hearts as in the rebellion.*

16 Who were those who heard God's voice yet rebelled? Wasn't it all those who came out of Egypt under Moses? 17 And with whom *was He provoked for forty years*? Wasn't it with those sinners whose *corpses fell in the desert*? 18 Who was it that *He swore wouldn't enter into His rest,* if not those who were disobedient? 19 And so we see that it was because of their unbelief that they were unable to enter.

4 1 Therefore, as long as God's promise to allow us into His rest remains open, we should fear lest any of you be considered to have fallen short. 2 For we, too, received the good news, just as those before us did, yet the word did them no good since it didn't meet with faith in those who heard it. 3 It is we who have believed who are entering into God's rest, as He said,

> *As I swore in My wrath,*
> *"They'll never enter into My rest!"*

---

3:15     Ps 95:7–8 (Septuagint).

3:17     Nb 14:29.

3:18     Nb 14:22–23; Ps 95:11.

4:1ff.     Chapter 4 develops the idea of God's "rest," which was introduced in Chapter 3. This term signifies salvation, the fulfillment of God's plan.

4:3     Ps 95:11.

And yet God's work was complete from the creation of the world, 4 for Scripture speaks somewhere about the seventh day in these words, *On the seventh day God rested from all His work.* 5 And again in the previous passage, *They'll never enter into My rest.* 6 It follows, therefore, that some will enter God's rest, but since those who received the good news in former times were barred because of their unbelief, 7 God once again set a day, "Today," saying much later in David's Psalms the words which have already been quoted,

> Today if you hear His voice,
> Harden not your hearts.

8 If Joshua had given them rest, God would not have later spoken about another day. 9 So then, there remains to God's people the Sabbath rest, 10 for whoever enters God's rest receives rest from his labors, just as God rested from *His* labors. 11 So let us zealously strive to enter that rest, for we don't want to fail by following this same example of unbelief.

12 For the word of God is living and active, sharper than any two-edged sword. It pierces to the dividing line between soul and spirit, joints and marrow, and it can discern the innermost thoughts and intentions of the heart. 13 No creature can hide from Him — everything is naked and laid bare to the eyes of Him, to Whom we must render an account.

14 Therefore, since we have a great high priest who has passed through the heavens — Jesus the Son of God — let

---

4:4     Gn 2:2.
4:5     Ps 95:11.
4:7     Ps 95:7–8 (Septuagint).

us hold fast to the faith we profess. <sup>15</sup> For our high priest isn't one who is unable to sympathize with our weaknesses; he was tempted in every way we are, yet never sinned. <sup>16</sup> Therefore, let us confidently approach the throne of grace to receive mercy and find grace to help us in time of need.

**5** <sup>1</sup> For every high priest is chosen from among men and appointed to represent them before God, to offer gifts and sacrifices for their sins. <sup>2</sup> Such a high priest is able to deal patiently with those who have gone astray through ignorance, since he himself is subject to human weakness; <sup>3</sup> and because he too is weak he must offer sacrifice for his own sins as well as for those of the people. <sup>4</sup> Moreover, no one can take the honor of the high priesthood for himself — he can only be chosen by God, as in the case of Aaron.

<sup>5</sup> And so it was with Christ: he did not assume the dignity of the high priesthood on his own but was chosen by the One Who said to him,

> *You are My son,*
> *this day have I begotten you,*

<sup>6</sup> or as He says in a different place,

> *You are a priest forever,*
> *in the line of Melchizedek.*

<sup>7</sup> <sup>a</sup> When Jesus was in the flesh he offered prayers and supplications to the One Who was able to save him from death,

---

<sup>a</sup> *Mt 26:36–46; Mk 14:32–42; Lk 22:39–46.*

5:3    Lv 9:7.
5:5    Ps 2:7.
5:6    Ps 110:4.

accompanied by loud cries and tears, and God heard him because of his devotion and reverence. 8 Son though he was, he learned obedience from what he suffered, 9 and when he was made perfect he became the source of eternal salvation for all who obey him, 10 and God declared him high priest *in the line of Melchizedek.*

## C. Exhortation to Greater Maturity

11 Concerning this we have much to say and it will be difficult to explain, since you've become hard of hearing. 12 *b* By this time you should be teachers, and yet once again you need someone to teach you the ABCs of God's word — you need milk instead of solid food. 13 Anyone who lives on milk is still a child and is inexperienced in the word of righteousness, 14 whereas solid food is for the mature, those who have practiced and trained themselves so that they can distinguish between good and evil.

6 1 Let us leave behind the elementary teaching of Christ, then, and move on to the mature teaching, instead of once again laying the foundation — repentance from dead works, reliance upon faith in God, 2 instruction about baptisms, the laying on of hands, resurrection of the dead, and eternal judgment. 3 And this we shall do, if God

---

*b* 1 Cor 3:2.

---

6:2    "Instructions about baptisms." This phrase probably contrasts various Jewish ritual ablutions and purification ceremonies to the rite of Christian initiation. The word "enlightenment" (6:4, 10:32) also is a probable reference to Baptism, based on early Christian terminology.

will allow it. 4 For it's impossible to restore to repentance those who have once been enlightened, who have tasted the heavenly gift and became sharers in the Holy Spirit, 5 who have tasted the goodness of God's word and the powers of the coming age, 6 and yet have fallen away and so are crucifying the Son of God of their own accord and are holding him up to contempt. 7 For earth which drinks the rain that repeatedly falls upon it and brings forth vegetation which is useful to those for whom it was cultivated receives a blessing from God, 8 but if *it produces thorns and thistles* it's worthless and is on the verge of being cursed — in the end it will be burned.

9 But even though we speak in this way, beloved, we feel sure that you are destined for better things — those that pertain to salvation. 10 For God is not so unjust as to overlook your deeds and the love you've shown for His name by serving the saints, as you continue to do. 11 Our desire is for each of you to show the same zeal for bringing about the fulfillment of your hope right to the end. 12 Don't be lazy! Imitate those who through faith and patience are inheriting the promises.

13 When God made His promise to Abraham He *swore by Himself,* since there was no one greater for Him to swear by, 14 saying, *Surely, I will bless you and make your descendants numerous!* 15 And so, after waiting patiently, Abraham obtained what God had promised. 16 Men swear in the

---

6:8    Gn 3:17–18.
6:14   Gn 22:16–17.

name of someone greater than themselves, and the oath serves as a guarantee to put an end to any dispute. 17 Likewise, when God wished to provide the heirs of the promise with an even more convincing demonstration of how unchangeable His will was, He confirmed it with an oath. 18 He did this so that, as a result of two unchangeable things about which it's impossible that God should play false, we who have fled to His protection would be provided a powerful encouragement to grasp the hope that lies before us. 19 This hope is our soul's anchor, firm and reliable; it leads behind the sanctuary curtain, 20 where Jesus has gone as a forerunner on our behalf — he has become a high priest *forever in the line of Melchizedek.*

## D. Christ's Priesthood Superior to the Aaronic Priesthood

7 1 This *Melchizedek, the king of Salem and a priest of the Most High God, met Abraham as Abraham was returning from his defeat of the kings. Melchizedek blessed him* 2 and *Abraham* apportioned to Melchizedek *a tenth of everything* he had

---

6:18    "Two unchangeable things." This phrase refers to the preceding verse (6:17); the "two... things" are the promise and the oath.

6:19–20  Lv 16:2; Ps 110:4. By entering the inner sanctuary Jesus secures access to God for us. This is possible because of the superiority of Jesus' priesthood, sacrifice, and covenant, the themes of the next sections of the letter. In Judaism, only the high priest entered the sanctuary, but now, in union with Jesus, our hope, we will be led into the heavenly Holy of Holies, into God's presence. The Temple liturgy is but a shadow of the reality that Jesus' sacrifice has gained for us.

7:1–2    Gn 14:17–20.

7:2      "Salem," later Jerusalem, is related to the Hebrew word for "peace."

captured. The name Melchizedek first of all means *king of righteousness,* but he was also *king of Salem,* that is, the king of peace. 3 He is without father, mother, or genealogy; there was no beginning or end to his life, and like the Son of God he remains a priest forever.

4 You can see how great he is, because the patriarch Abraham gave him a tenth of the spoils. 5 Those descendants of Levi who become priests have a commandment by which, in accordance with the Torah, they levy a tithe on the people, that is, they take a tenth from their brothers, even though they too are descended from Abraham. 6 Melchizedek could not trace his descent to them, and yet he collected tithes from Abraham and blessed Abraham who had received the promises. 7 Now there can be no dispute that the superior person is the one who blesses the inferior. 8 In one case the tithes are collected by mortal men, while in the other by one whom Scripture affirms is alive. 9 And in a manner of speaking Levi (who himself receives tithes) actually paid tithes *through Abraham,* 10 for he was still in his father's loins when *Melchizedek met Abraham.*

11 So then, if perfection had come through the Levitical priesthood — for the people received the Torah from the priesthood — what need would there have been for another priest to arise, *in the line of Melchizedek* rather than in the line

---

7:3     Scripture contains no reference to either the birth or the death of Melchizedek, and so the author says his life has not ended; cf. 7:8.

7:5     Nb 18:21.

7:9–10     "Levi." The author refers not only to the individual but also to the entire priestly tribe of his descendants. Their priesthood is thus seen to be inferior to that of Melchizedek.

of Aaron? <sup>12</sup> But when there's a change in the priesthood this must signify a change in the law, as well. <sup>13</sup> Now the one concerning whom these things were said belongs to a different tribe, and no one from that tribe has ever officiated at the altar. <sup>14</sup> For it's clear that our Lord arose from Judah, and Moses said nothing about priests with regard to that tribe. <sup>15</sup> The matter becomes even more obvious if another priest arises in the likeness of Melchizedek, <sup>16</sup> one who has become a priest by the power of an indestructible life rather than in accordance with a law concerning physical descent, <sup>17</sup> for it is testified,

> *You are a priest forever,*
> *in the line of Melchizedek.*

<sup>18</sup> On the one hand an earlier law is set aside because it has proved weak and ineffective — <sup>19</sup> for the Torah brought nothing to perfection — on the other hand a better hope is introduced by means of which we can draw near to God.

<sup>20</sup> Moreover, to the extent that this took place with an oath — for the others became priests without an oath being taken, <sup>21</sup> but in the case of this priest an oath was taken when God said to him,

> *The Lord has sworn*
> *and shall not change His mind,*
> *"You are a priest forever"* —

<sup>22</sup> to that same degree Jesus has become the guarantee of a better covenant. <sup>23</sup> There is an additional difference — those

---

7:17    Ps 110:4.
7:21    Ps 110:4.

priests were numerous because death cut their ministry short, 24 whereas Jesus' priesthood is permanent because he remains forever. 25 Thus he is able for all time to bring complete salvation to those who approach God through him, since he's always alive to intercede for them.

26 And it fit in with our needs to have such a high priest — holy, innocent, undefiled, set apart from sinners, and exalted above the heavens. 27 Unlike the high priests, he has no need to offer daily sacrifices first for his own sins and then for those of the people — he did that once and for all when he offered himself up. 28 The Torah appoints as high priests men who have their share of weaknesses, whereas God's oath, which came after the Torah, appoints His Son, who has been made perfect forever.

## E. SUPERIORITY OF CHRIST'S NEW COVENANT

8 1 Now this is the main point in what we've been saying: that is just the type of high priest we have. He has taken his seat at the right hand of the throne of Majesty in Heaven, 2 a minister in the sanctuary, the true tent that was set up by the Lord, not by man. 3 Every high priest is appointed to offer gifts and sacrifices, which means that this priest, too, must have something to offer. 4 Now if he were on earth he wouldn't be a priest at all, since there are already priests who

---

7:27     Lv 9:7.
8:1      Ps 110:1.

offer gifts in accordance with the Torah. 5 Those priests serve
in a copy and shadow of the heavenly sanctuary, as Moses
was warned when he was about to erect the tent, *See that
you make everything according to the pattern you were shown on
the mountain.* 6 But now Jesus has received a ministry which
is far superior to theirs; it's as superior as the covenant he
mediates is, and is based on better promises.

7 For if the first covenant had been perfect there would
have been no need for a second, 8 but God finds fault with
them, and says,

> *Behold the days will come, says the Lord,*
>> *when I'll make a new covenant with the house*
>>> *of Israel,*
>> *and with the house of Judah.*
> 9 *It won't be like the covenant I made with their*
>> *ancestors*
>>> *on the day I took their hand and led them*
>>>> *out of Egypt.*
> *For they didn't abide by My covenant*
>> *and so I rejected them, says the Lord,*
> 10 *This is the covenant I'll make with the house of Israel*
>> *after those days, says the Lord:*
> *I will put My laws in their minds*
>> *and write them on their hearts;*
> *I will be their God*
>> *and they shall be My people.*

---

8:5     Ex 25:40.
8:8–12  Jr 31:31–34 (Septuagint).

11 *They won't need to teach their fellow citizens*
          *or their brothers, saying, "Know the Lord!"*
      *Because they'll all know Me,*
          *from the least of them to the greatest.*
12 *For I'll have mercy on their unrighteousness*
          *and will no longer remember their sins.*

13 By speaking of a "new" covenant, God has declared the first one to be obsolete, and what has become old and obsolete will soon disappear.

9 ¹ The first covenant had regulations governing worship and an earthly sanctuary. ² A tent was erected — the outer one, which is called the Holy Place — and in it were the lampstand, the table, and the bread of offering. ³ Behind the second curtain was the tent called the Holy of Holies, ⁴ which contained the gold incense altar and the ark of the covenant which was completely covered with gold. In the ark was a gold jar containing manna, Aaron's staff which had sprouted, and the stone tablets of the covenant. ⁵ Above the ark were the cherubim of glory which overshadowed the mercy seat — now is not the time to speak of these things in detail.

⁶ Once everything has been prepared in this manner, the priests continually enter the outer tent, performing their liturgical duties, ⁷ but only the high priest enters the inner

---

9:2–5    Ex 25–26 passim. "The mercy seat" (9:5) was made of gold and was where the blood of sacrificed animals was sprinkled by the high priest during the rituals performed on the Day of Atonement.

9:6       Nb 18:2–6.

9:7       Lv 16:2–34. "Once a year," i.e., on the Day of Atonement.

tent, and he goes in only once a year when he takes blood to be offered for the inadvertent sins committed by himself and by the people. 8 In this way the Holy Spirit indicates that the way into the sanctuary has not yet been opened up as long as the outer tent still stands. 9 This is a symbol of the present time, during which gifts and sacrifices are offered that cannot perfect the worshipper's conscience. 10 They only deal with food and drink and various purification rites — regulations for the body which are in force up to the time the new order is established.

11 But when Christ came as the high priest of the good things that have come, he passed through that greater and more perfect tent which is not made by human hands — that is, it's not part of this creation — 12 and entered once and for all into the sanctuary bearing his own blood rather than the blood of rams and bullocks, and thus secured for us an eternal redemption. 13 For if the sprinkling of blood from rams and bulls and the ashes of heifers can sanctify those who are ritually unclean so that their flesh is purified, 14 then the blood of Christ will have a far greater effect! Through the eternal Spirit he presented himself as an unblemished offering to God and will purify our consciences from ineffective practices so that we'll be fit to worship the living God.

---

9:8     The restriction on entry into the sanctuary indicates that as long as the old covenant was in effect there was no open access to God. This will come with the sacrifice of Jesus, and is of key importance in Hebrews.

9:11    Some manuscripts read "that will come" rather than "that have come."

9:13    Lv 16:15–16; Nb 19:9, 17–19.

¹⁵ Therefore, Jesus is the mediator of a new covenant. Those who have been called may now receive the promised eternal inheritance because a death has occurred which redeems them from transgressions under the first covenant. ¹⁶ In the case of a will it's necessary to establish that the person who made the will has died — ¹⁷ the will only takes effect after death; it has no power while the person who made it is still alive. ¹⁸ This is why the first covenant had to be inaugurated with blood. ¹⁹ After Moses had proclaimed every commandment of the Torah to the whole people he took the blood of the bullocks — with water, scarlet wool, and hyssop — and sprinkled both the book as well as all the people, ²⁰ saying, *This is the blood of the covenant God has commanded you to obey.* ²¹ Then he also sprinkled the tent and all the liturgical vessels with blood in the same way. ²² In fact, under the Torah almost everything is purified with blood, and forgiveness is possible only when blood is shed.

²³ Thus it was necessary to purify the copies of the heavenly realities with these rites, but the heavenly realities themselves could only be purified with greater sacrifices than these. ²⁴ For Christ didn't enter a sanctuary made by human hands which only represented the true sanctuary — he entered Heaven itself to appear now before God on our behalf. ²⁵ Nor did he do this intending to offer himself many times, the way the high priest enters the sanctuary every year bearing blood which isn't his own. ²⁶ If that had been

---

9:19–20  Ex 24:6–8.
9:21      Lv 8:15.
9:22      Lv 17:11.

so he would have had to suffer repeatedly, starting from the creation of the world. Instead, he appeared once and for all near the end of the age to remove sin by his sacrifice. 27 And just as it has been ordained that men should die once and then be judged, 28 so too Christ was offered once to bear the sins of many and when he appears a second time it won't be to deal with sin — it will be to bring salvation to those who eagerly await him.

10 1 Now since the Torah has but a shadow of the good things to come rather than their exact likeness, the same sacrifices which are offered year after year can never perfect those who draw near to worship. 2 Otherwise, wouldn't they have ceased to be offered? If those who were worshipping had been cleansed once for all, wouldn't they have lost all consciousness of sin? 3 As it is, these sacrifices are a yearly reminder of sin, 4 for the blood of bulls and rams is unable to take away sins.

5 Therefore, when Christ came into the world he said,

> *Sacrifice and offering You didn't desire,*
> *but You've prepared a body for me;*
> 6 *Burnt offerings and sin offerings*
> *gave You no pleasure.*
> 7 *Then I said, "Behold, I've come to do*
> *Your will, O God,"*
> *as it's written about me*
> *in the scroll of the book.*

---

9:28     Is 53:12.
10:5–7   Ps 40:6–8 (Septuagint).

8 First he says, *Sacrifices and oblations, burnt offerings and offerings for sin You didn't desire, nor did they please You* — these are offered according to the Torah — 9 then he says, *Behold I come to do Your will*. He does away with the first in order to establish the second. 10 That "will" has sanctified us through the offering of Jesus Christ's body once and for all.

11 Every priest daily stands at worship and time after time offers the same sacrifices, which can never take away sins. 12 But when Jesus had offered one sacrifice for sin for all time *he took his seat at God's right hand,* 13 to wait *until his enemies are* finally *made a footstool for his feet.* 14 For with one offering he has perfected forever those who are being sanctified.

15 The Holy Spirit also bears witness to us, for after saying,

16 *This is the covenant I'll make for them*
*after those days, says the Lord;*
*I'll put My laws in their hearts*
*and I'll write them in their minds,*

17 he adds,

*Their sins and misdeeds*
*I'll remember no more.*

18 And where these things have been forgiven, there's no longer a need for sin offerings.

---

10:12–13    Ps 110:1.
10:16–17    Jr 31:33–34.

## F. Culminating Exhortation to Faithfulness

### A Call to Faith

19 So, brothers, since through the blood of Jesus we have the confidence to enter the sanctuary 20 by the new and living way he opened for us through the curtain — that is, the way of his flesh — 21 and since we have a great high priest who has charge over God's household, 22 let us approach with true hearts and the full assurance of our faith, with hearts sprinkled clean from a guilty conscience and bodies washed with pure water. 23 Let us hold fast to the profession of our hope without wavering, for the One Who made the promise to us is faithful. 24 Let us also consider how we can rouse one another to love and good works. 25 Don't neglect your assemblies, as some are in the habit of doing; encourage one another, especially because you can see the day of the Lord drawing nearer.

26 For if, after receiving knowledge of the truth, we

---

10:19–12:29   This culminating exhortation is divided into three sections in an *aba'* pattern. 10:19–39 provides a warning of the consequences of sin, as well as reasons the readers have for being confident. The middle section, Chapter 11, gives examples of faithfulness from the Old Testament. The concluding section, Chapter 12, returns to the general theme of the first section — the author reprimands his readers while exhorting them to persevere in the faith.

10:19         Entrance to the sanctuary should be understood as a metaphor for access to God.

10:25         Absence from the Eucharistic assembly almost certainly signifies serious divisions in the community and may indicate that some members had already apostatized.

10:26–31   The author is clearly concerned here with the possibility of apostasy, comparing a fall from faith in Jesus to a Jew turning from the Torah to idolatry (v. 28 refers to the punishment for idolatry).

sin deliberately, there no longer remains a sacrifice for sins.
27 What remains instead is the fearful prospect of judgment
and a blazing fire that will consume God's adversaries.
28 Anyone who rejects the law of Moses *dies* without mercy
*at the testimony of two or three witnesses.* 29 Think how much
worse a punishment will be deserved by someone who
tramples on the Son of God, regards as unclean the blood
of the covenant by which he was sanctified, and insults the
Spirit of grace! 30 We know Who it was Who said,

> *Vengeance is Mine, I shall repay,*

and,

> *The Lord will judge His people.*

31 It's a fearful thing to fall into the hands of the living
God!

32 Recall the early days of your faith! After you were
enlightened you stood firm through a hard struggle which
involved suffering. 33 At times you were publicly insulted
and mistreated, while at other times you stood by those who
were so treated. 34 You shared the sufferings of prisoners and
accepted the seizure of your possessions with joy, because
you knew you had a better and more permanent possession.
35 So don't lose your confidence, because it will lead to a
great reward. 36 You need to be steadfast if you want to do
the will of God and receive what He promised.

---

10:28    Dt 17:6.

10:30    Dt 32:35–36.

10:32–34  As noted in the introduction, this may refer to the Jewish/Christian distur-
bances in Rome under Claudius in A.D. 49.

37 For in just *a little while*
> *he who is coming will come* — *he won't delay!*
38 *But My righteous one will live by faith,*
> *and if he draws back My soul has no*
> > *pleasure in him.*

39 We aren't the kind of people who draw back and are destroyed — we have faith and will preserve our lives.

## Examples of Faith from the Old Testament

11 1 Faith is confidence in what's hoped for, conviction about things that can't be seen. 2 Through faith the ancients won God's approval.

3 Through faith we understand that the world was created by the word of God, so that what is seen came to be from what can't be seen.

4 Through faith Abel offered God a better sacrifice than Cain's, and thus was approved as righteous. God approved of his gifts and through faith Abel, though dead, still speaks. 5 Through faith Enoch was taken up so that he wouldn't see death, and *he wasn't found because God had taken him up,* for it is affirmed that, before he was taken up, *he had pleased God.* 6 Now it's impossible to please God without faith, because to even approach God you have to believe that God exists and that He rewards those who seek Him.

---

10:37–38  Hab 2:3–4 (Septuagint).
11:5      Gn 5:21–24 (Septuagint).

7 Noah received divine warning of events which were as yet unseen; through faith he took heed and constructed an ark in which his household could be saved. His faith was a condemnation of the world, and through it he became an heir of the righteousness that comes from faith.

8 Through faith Abraham obeyed when he was called to leave for a place that he would receive as an inheritance. He left without knowing where he was to go. 9 Through faith he sojourned in the promised land as a foreigner, living in tents with Isaac and Jacob — co-heirs of the same promise. 10 For he was looking forward to a city whose foundations were built and formed by God. 11 Through faith Abraham received the power to father children, even though Sarah herself was barren and he was beyond the usual age, because he trusted the One Who made the promise. 12 And so from one man — one who was as good as dead — was born a multitude of descendants, *as numerous as the stars in the sky, as innumerable as the sand on the seashore.*

13 They all died in faith without having received what was promised, but they had seen it and greeted it far in advance and acknowledged that they were foreigners and exiles on earth. 14 Those who say such things make it clear that they're seeking a homeland. 15 If they'd been thinking about the land they left they would have had the opportunity to return, 16 but now they're striving for a better land, a heavenly one. Therefore God is not ashamed to be called their God, because He has prepared a city for them.

---

11:12   Gn 22:17.

¹⁷ Through faith Abraham offered up Isaac when God tested him — Abraham had received the promises, and yet he offered up his only son ¹⁸ of whom it had been said, *Through Isaac your descendants shall carry on your name.* ¹⁹ He reasoned that God could raise Isaac from the dead, and so in a sense Abraham did receive him back from the dead. ²⁰ Through faith in what was to come Isaac blessed Jacob and Esau. ²¹ Through faith Jacob, when he was dying, blessed each of Joseph's sons and *bowed in worship over the top of his staff.* ²² Through faith Joseph, as his life was coming to an end, spoke of the exodus of Israel and gave orders regarding the disposition of his bones.

²³ Through faith Moses, when he was born, was hidden for three months by his parents because they could see he was a beautiful child and they didn't fear the king's edict. ²⁴ Through faith Moses, when he had grown up, refused to be called a son of Pharaoh's daughter, ²⁵ choosing to suffer with God's people rather than enjoy the transitory pleasures of sin. ²⁶ From his standpoint, to endure insults for the sake of the Messiah was greater wealth than all the treasure of Egypt, because he kept his eyes fixed on the reward. ²⁷ Through faith he left Egypt and felt no fear of the king's anger — he was steadfast because it was as if he could see the Invisible One. ²⁸ Through faith he kept the Passover and sprinkled the blood so that the Destroyer wouldn't touch their firstborn sons. ²⁹ Through faith they passed through the Red Sea as if it

---

11:18    Gn 21:12.
11:21    Gn 47:31.

were dry land, while the Egyptians were swallowed up when they attempted to do the same. 30 Through faith the walls of Jericho fell down after the Israelites had marched around them for seven days. 31 Through faith Rahab the prostitute survived when those who were disobedient perished, because she had received the Israelite spies in peace.

32 Should I say more? I wouldn't have sufficient time to tell about Gideon, Barak, Samson, Jephthah, David and Samuel and the prophets, 33 who through faith overcame kingdoms, did what was right, obtained what had been promised, shut the mouths of lions, 34 put out raging fires, escaped the ravening sword, drew strength from weakness, were mighty in battle, and put foreign armies to flight. 35 Women had their dead returned to them by resurrection; some were tortured but refused to accept release, preferring to receive a better resurrection; 36 others were mocked and scourged, put in chains and imprisoned. 37 They were stoned, they were sawed in half, they were murdered by the sword, they went about dressed in sheepskins and goatskins, in need and afflicted, tormented, 38 wandering the deserts and mountains, living in caves and holes in the ground — yet the world wasn't worthy of them.

39 They all gained approval through their faith, but they didn't receive the promise 40 because, with us in mind, God had something better in store — only with us were they to be made perfect!

## A Call to Perseverance

**12** ¹ Therefore, since we're surrounded by such a cloud of witnesses, let us put aside every burden and sinful entanglement, let us persevere and run the race that lies before us, ² let us keep our eyes fixed on Jesus, the pioneer and perfecter of our faith. For the sake of the joy that lay before him he endured the cross and thought nothing of the shame of it, and is now seated at the right hand of God's throne. ³ Think of Jesus, who endured so much hostility from sinners, and don't let your souls grow weary or lose your courage.

⁴ In your struggle against sin you haven't yet resisted to the point of shedding blood. ⁵ You have forgotten the words of encouragement which are spoken to you as sons,

> *My son, don't take lightly the Lord's discipline,*
> *nor become discouraged when He punishes you.*
> ⁶ *For the Lord disciplines everyone He loves,*
> *He chastises everyone He accepts as a son.*

⁷ Endure your trials as a form of discipline; God is treating you like sons, for what son is there who isn't disciplined by his father? ⁸ Everyone has shared in this discipline, so if you don't receive it you must be illegitimate and not real sons. ⁹ After all, we had earthly fathers who disciplined us and we respected them; all the more reason, then, to be subject to

---

12:2    "Pioneer." Cf. 2:10, where this somewhat unusual word is also applied to Jesus.

12:4    Some scholars see in this verse a reference to the Neronian persecutions.

12:5–6  Jb 5:17; Pr 3:11–12 (Septuagint).

the Father of spirits so we can live! <sup>10</sup> For our earthly fathers disciplined us for a short time according as it seemed right to them, whereas God disciplines us for our own good so that we'll be able to share in His holiness. <sup>11</sup> For the present, all discipline seems to bring grief rather than joy, but later it will yield the peaceful fruit of righteousness to those who have been trained by it.

<sup>12</sup> Therefore, *lift your drooping arms and strengthen your weakened knees,* <sup>13</sup> *make straight paths for your feet* so that the lame foot will be strengthened rather than twisted.

<sup>14</sup> Strive to be at peace with everyone and seek that holiness without which no one will see the Lord. <sup>15</sup> See that no one lacks the grace of God, that no root of bitterness sprouts up to cause trouble, causing many to be stained by it, <sup>16</sup> that no one among you is a fornicator or an irreligious person like Esau, who sold his birthrights for a single meal. <sup>17</sup> For, as you know, when he later wanted to inherit the blessing he was rejected because he was given no opportunity to change what he had done, even though he tearfully sought to do so.

<sup>18</sup> For you have not come to a mountain that can be touched, to a blazing fire, to darkness, gloom, or a storm; <sup>19</sup> nor have you come to a trumpet blast or a voice whose words caused those who heard them to beg that no further message should be spoken to them, <sup>20</sup> because they couldn't

---

12:12   Is 35:3 (Septuagint).
12:13   Pr 4:26 (Septuagint).
12:15   Dt 29:18 (Septuagint).
12:20   Ex 19:12–13.

bear the command, *If even a beast should touch the mountain, it must be stoned!* 21 Indeed, so terrifying was the spectacle that Moses said, *"I'm* trembling and *afraid!"* 22 Instead, you've come to Mount Zion, the city of the living God, the heavenly Jerusalem with its thousands of angels. 23 You have come to the festal gathering and the assembly of the firstborn whose names are written in Heaven, to a judge who is God of all, to the spirits of the righteous who have been made perfect. 24 You have come to Jesus, the mediator of the new covenant, and to the sprinkled blood that proclaims a better message than Abel's blood.

25 See that you don't reject the One Who is speaking, for if those who rejected the One Who warned them on earth could not escape, what chance will we have to escape if we reject the One Who warns us from Heaven? 26 At the first warning His voice shook the earth, but now He has promised, *"Once more I will shake* not only *the earth* but *heaven* as well." 27 Now the words "once more" clearly indicate that the created things which have been shaken will be removed, so that what is unshaken may remain. 28 Therefore, we who are to receive an unshakable Kingdom should be grateful and should worship God in an acceptable manner with reverence and awe, 29 for our *God is a consuming fire.*

---

12:21   Dt 9:19.
12:26   Hg 2:6 (Septuagint).
12:29   Dt 4:24.

# G. PRACTICAL COUNSELS, CLOSING EXHORTATIONS, AND CONCLUDING MESSAGES

**13** ¹ Let brotherly love continue. ² Don't forget your duty to be hospitable, for some who were hospitable had angels as guests, without knowing it. ³ Remember those in prison as if you were imprisoned with them, and those who are mistreated, for like them you are still in the body. ⁴ Marriage should be held in honor by all of you, and the marriage bed should remain undefiled, for fornicators and adulterers will be judged by God. ⁵ Keep your life free from love for money, be satisfied with what you have, for God has said, *I will never abandon you or forsake you.* ⁶ Thus, we may confidently say,

> *The Lord is my helper,*
>    *I shall not be afraid;*
> *What can mere man do to me?*

⁷ Remember your leaders who proclaimed the word of God to you; consider the outcome of their way of life and imitate their faith. ⁸ Jesus Christ is the same yesterday and today and forever. ⁹ Don't be carried away by all kinds of strange teachings, for it's good for the heart to be strengthened by grace rather than by food which has been of no use to those who partake of it. ¹⁰ We have an altar

---

13:2      Gn 18:1–8; 19:1–3.

13:5      Dt 31:6, 8.

13:6      Ps 118:6 (Septuagint).

13:10    "The altar" is used metaphorically to refer to the victim on it, here, Jesus.

from which those who serve the tent have no right to eat.
11 For the blood of animals is carried into the sanctuary
by the high priest as an offering for the forgiveness of sin,
while the bodies of the animals are burned outside the
camp. 12 Therefore Jesus too suffered outside the gate in
order to sanctify the people with his own blood. 13 So let
us go out to him outside the camp and share the abuse he
bore, 14 for our city here is not a lasting one — we seek the
city which is to come! 15 Therefore, let us continually offer
through him a sacrifice of praise to God, the fruit of lips that
acknowledge His name. 16 Don't forget to do good and to
share what you have, for these are the sacrifices which are
pleasing to God.

17 Obey your leaders and submit to them, for they
keep watch over your souls and will have to give an ac-
counting. Let them perform their duties joyfully rather than
with groaning, for to cause them sorrow would be of no
advantage to you.

18 Pray for us, for we are convinced that we have a
clean conscience and we wish to behave creditably in all
things. 19 I especially urge you to pray that I may be restored
to you quickly.

20 May the God of peace, Who brought our Lord Jesus
— the great shepherd of the sheep — up from the dead
through the blood of the eternal covenant, 21 supply you
with every good thing to help you to do His will, and may

---

13:11   Lv 16:27.

He accomplish in us what is pleasing in His sight through Jesus Christ, to whom be glory forever and ever. Amen.

22 I urge you, brothers, bear with my exhortation, for I have written briefly to you. 23 Our brother Timothy has been released, and if he comes quickly I'll see you with him.

24 Greet all your leaders and all the saints. Those from Italy send their greetings to you. 25 Grace be with all of you!

# PRAYERS

### Prayer for Faith, Hope, and Love

Heavenly Father, you love us and have chosen us to be your own. Help us to live each day in active faith, loving labors, and steadfast hope in our Lord Jesus Christ.

*(Cf. 1 Th 1:3–4)*

### Prayer of Praise

We praise you, O God, for the glorious grace you bestowed upon us in your beloved Son, Jesus Christ. Through him you have given us redemption and the forgiveness of our sins. What a wealth of grace you have poured out upon us.

*(Cf. Eph 1:6–8)*

### Thanksgiving for the Gift of Grace

I thank you, O God, for the grace you have given me through Christ Jesus. In him may we be enriched in every way, in speech and in knowledge. May the message of Christ become so much a part of us that we possess every grace as we await the revelation of our Lord Jesus Christ who will sustain us until the end.

*(Cf. 1 Cor 1:4–9)*

### Fix Our Eyes on You, Lord

Lord, may the temporary afflictions we suffer now produce for us an eternal fullness of glory which is beyond all comparison. Let us never fix our eyes on things which are transitory but rather keep our gaze fixed on the things that are eternal.

*(Cf. 2 Cor 4:17–18)*

### Fulfill Our Good Desires, Lord

Make us worthy, Lord God, of the life which you have called us to live. By your power fulfill in us every desire for goodness and every work of faith so that through us the name of our Lord Jesus Christ will be glorified.

*(Cf. 2 Th 1:11–12)*

### Christ, Our Life

O God, you have raised us to life with Christ your Son. Grant that we may seek the things that are above where Christ is seated at your right hand. Keep our hearts and minds set on the things that are above, and not on the things of this earth, for our real life is with Christ in heavenly glory.

*(Cf. Col 3:1–4)*

## May I See and Understand

Lord God, enlighten the eyes of my heart that I may know the hope to which you call me, understand the rich and glorious heritage you have promised me, and recognize your extraordinary power working in all those who believe.

*(Cf. Eph 1:18–20)*

## Teach Us to Love

Teach us, Lord, to love with patience and kindness, to put aside jealousy, boasting, and arrogance. Teach us to understand that genuine love is never dishonorable, selfish, or irritable, and it does not keep account of past wrongs. Teach us that love never rejoices at injustice, but rejoices with the truth, that real love endures all things and has complete faith and steadfast hope. Love never ends.

*(Cf. 1 Cor 13:4–7)*

## Glory to You, Lord

O God, by your power at work in us, you are able to do so much more than we can ask or imagine. To you be glory in the church in Christ Jesus for all generations, forever and ever. Amen.

*(Cf. Eph 3:20–21)*

## Prayer for Christian Discipleship

Blessed are you, God, the Father of our Lord Jesus Christ, who has blessed us in Christ with every spiritual blessing in the heavens *(cf. Eph 1:3)*.

Through you, Father, in Christ Jesus, we have received grace and our mission as disciples to bring peoples of all nations to faith and obedience in his name *(cf. Rm 1:5)*.

Make us always ready to proclaim to all the boundless riches of Christ... so that the wisdom of God might now be made known through the Church *(cf. Eph 3:8–10)*.

We beg you, Father, to help us always lead lives worthy of the vocation to which we are called: in humility, gentleness, and patience, bearing with one another in love, seeking to preserve the unity of the Spirit by the peace that binds us together *(cf. Eph 4:1–3)*.

Glory to you, Father, whose power working in us can do infinitely more than we can ask or imagine; glory to you from generation to generation in the Church and in Christ Jesus forever and ever. Amen *(cf. Eph 3:20–21)*.

## Prayer for the Gift of Patience

O Saint Paul, from a persecutor of Christianity, you became an impassioned apostle, suffering imprisonment, scourging, stoning, shipwreck, and persecutions of every kind to make Jesus Christ known to the farthest boundaries of the world. You even shed your blood and died for him.

Please obtain for us the grace to understand that illness, hardship, or the everyday difficulties of life can be opportunities to grow in holiness. Do not let the trials of this life make us become indifferent in the service of God, but teach us how to grow ever more faithful and more fervent. Amen.

*Blessed James Alberione*

**Prayer to Saint Paul for Our Nation**

Saint Paul, teacher of the Gentiles, watch over with love this nation and its people. Your heart expanded so as to welcome and enfold all people in the loving embrace of peace.

Now, from heaven, may the charity of Christ urge you to enlighten everyone with the light of the Gospel and to establish the kingdom of love. Inspire vocations, sustain those working for the Gospel, render all hearts docile to the Divine Master. May our nation ever more see Christ as the Way, the Truth, and the Life. May your light shine before the world, and may we always seek the kingdom of God and his justice.

Holy Apostle, enlighten, comfort, and bless us all. Amen.

*Blessed James Alberione*


**Prayer to Saint Paul for the Journey of Faith**

Saint Paul, you traveled the world, never quite knowing where the Spirit would lead you next. You journeyed in faith and accepted beatings, imprisonment, shipwreck, and ultimately execution because of your faith in Jesus Christ.

Help me to accept the great adventure of leading a life faithful to the words of Jesus my Master, the Way, the Truth, and the Life. May I ask myself, "Where does God want me to go today?" On the journey, may I love in the way you taught the Corinthians (1 Cor 13), and be willing to endure all things for the sake of the Gospel. Pray for me, that I may heed the voice of the One who called you on the road to Damascus and set you on the path that leads to life. Amen.

*Rev. Jeffrey Mickler, SSP*

# THE HEART OF SAINT PAUL —
# LIVING "IN CHRIST"

Before utilizing this guide on the Letters of Saint Paul, remember that nothing can substitute for reading the letters just as Paul wrote them. If you have a limited amount of time, you would get a good grasp of his mind and heart by reading the introductions to each of the letters and then concentrating on the text of the First and Second Letter to the Corinthians, Philippians, Ephesians, Galatians, and Romans — in that order.

## Reading Guides for Living "in Christ"

Reading Saint Paul, though a challenge, is immensely rewarding. Understanding his goal for a fully Christian life takes more than one read. It entails holding up the thought of the Apostle as one would hold up a diamond to the light, turning it this way and that, allowing one to admire it from different angles. The Reading Guides below are designed to help the reader to admire, contemplate, and assimilate the guidance of this greatest of apostles who sought not just to imitate Christ but also to become Christ, so that Christ truly lived in him. They are presented in order of development of the Christ-like life.

After reading a passage, ask yourself two questions: *What is Christ saying to me? What is Saint Paul saying to me?*

## *Reading Guide 1: The Summons to Believe*

The summons to believe and the response to the call of God were absolutely essential to Paul's theology. People had to receive what God offered if the process of salvation was to begin.

Reflect on the passages in the topical index (p. 288) under the following headings: *Gospel, salvation, faith, cross, hope, heaven.*

## *Reading Guide 2: Christian Maturity*

Paul immerses the Christian deeply in the power of the cross of Christ, and through this lens we see our Christian life in an utterly fresh perspective.

Reflect on the passages in the topical index under the following headings: *Gospel, baptism, salvation, the Lord's Supper, uprightness.*

## *Reading Guide 3: Growth in Christ*

We are invited not simply to imitate what Jesus did, but also to let Christ live in us, to allow him to think, speak, and act in us.

Reflect on the passages in the topical index under the following headings: *sin, holiness, death, Baptism, transformation "in Christ."*

## Reading Guide 4: Life in the Spirit

The Spirit has a decisive role in Pauline theology in determining and shaping the believer's life.

Reflect on the passages in the topical index under the following headings: *law, freedom, love, Spirit, gifts.*

## Reading Guide 5: Community

For Paul the faith relationship is not only personal, it is also corporate. One cannot enjoy a full relationship with the Risen Christ on one's own.

Reflect on the passages in the topical index under the following headings: *body, unity, love, humility, conscience, uprightness.*

## Reading Guide 6: Building up the Body

Paul envisions a place in the body for each of us, encouraging us to discern each one's gifts, respect each other, remain strong in adversity, and build up the body of Christ in love.

Reflect on the passages in the topical index under the following headings: *vocation, ministry, gifts, preaching, persecution, discernment, joy, reconciliation.*

# Appendix III

# TOPICAL INDEX

This selective, topical index is intended to help readers to get a picture of the Christian life as presented by Saint Paul. The passages listed develop the topic especially in its relation to an individual's growth in Christ. Because this index is selective, the entries are restricted to the topic's role as an aspect of a Christian's growth in "becoming Christ." No doubt some passages may have been omitted that might be very useful. Those included are simply meant to be a substantial introduction to Paul's spirituality.

**Apostle**   1 Cor 4:9–17;
1 Cor 9:9–17; 1 Th 2:8–12

**Baptism**   Rm 6:1–11; 1 Cor
12:13; Gal 3:26–28; Ti 3:4–8

**Body**   Rm 12:5; 1 Cor
10:16–17; 1 Cor 11:24–25;
1 Cor 12:12–27; Eph
1:22–23; Eph 4:15–16;
Col 1:17–18; Col 2:19

**Cross**   1 Cor 1:19–2:5

**Conscience**   Rm 14;
1 Cor 8:7–13; 1 Cor
10:23–33

**Death**   Rm 1:28–32; Rm
5:12– 7:13; 1 Cor 15:54–56;
2 Cor 5:1–10; Ph 3:20–21;
1 Th 4:13–18; 2 Tm 4:6–8;
Heb 2:10–18

**Discernment** Rm 11:33–36;
Gal 5:25; Eph 1:15–23;
Ph 4:8–9; 1 Th 5:19–22

**Discouragement** Rm 5:3–5;
Rm 7:14–24; 2 Cor 1:3–11;
2 Cor 4:17; Heb 4:14–16

**Faith** Rm 3:3; Rm 4:17–25;
Rm 5:1–4; Rm 16:25–26;
1 Cor 15:1–2; Eph 1:13;
Eph 3:16–19; 1 Th 5:23–24;
Heb 4:14–16; Heb 11:1–12:4

**Freedom** Rm 7:4–8:4;
Gal 5:1; Gal 5:13–26

**Gifts** 1 Cor 12:4–11;
1 Cor 13, 14; 1 Tm 4:14–16;
2 Tm 1:6–10

**Gospel** Rm 1:1; Rm 1:16–17;
1 Cor 9:16–18; 2 Cor 13:4;
Gal 2:15–21; Gal 3:1–5

**Heaven** Rm 8:18–25;
Ph 3:20–21

**Holiness** Rm 12:1–2;
Rm 13:11–14; 1 Cor 1:4–9;
1 Cor 3:16–21; 1 Th 4:1–8;
Heb 2:1–4; Heb 12:5–17

**Hope** Rm 5:5, 7–11;
Rm 8:18–25; Gal 5:5;
1 Th 5:23–24

**Humility** 1 Cor 5:6–8;
Ph 2:1–11

**"In Christ"** Rm 6:11; Rm 8:1;
Rm 12:5; 1 Cor 1:30;
1 Cor 15:22; 2 Cor 5:17;
Gal 2:19–20; Ph 2:5;
Eph 3:17; Col 1:27; Col 3:4

**Joy** Ph 4:4–7

**Law** Rm 2:12–4:25, 7;
Gal 3:10–4:31; Gal 5:2–6;
1 Tm 1:8–11

**Lord's Supper, the** 1 Cor
10:16–17; 1 Cor 11:18–34

**Love** Rm 8:31–39;
Rm 13:8–10; 1 Cor 13;
Col 3:12–15

**Mary** Gal 4:4–5

**Ministry** Rm 10:14–17;
1 Cor 4:15; 1 Cor 9:16;
2 Cor 4:1–18; Ph 1:12–26;
Heb 5:1–10

**New creation** 2 Cor 5:17

**Persecution** Rm 12:14–21;
2 Cor 6:1–10

**Prayer** Rm 8:26–27;
Eph 3:14–21

**Preaching** 1 Cor 1:17–25;

1 Cor 2:1–5; 1 Cor 3:5–15;
Heb 4:12–13

**Reconciliation**   2 Cor
5:18–20; Eph 2:11–22;
Col 1: 19–20

**Resurrection**   1 Cor 15;
1 Th 4:13–18

**Salvation**   Rm 5:12–21;
Rm 6:17–23; Ph 3:3–16;
Col 1:21–23; Col 2:10–15;
Col 3:1–4; Tt 3:4–8; Heb
4:14–5:10; Heb 8:1–9:28

**Sin**   Rm 6, 7; Heb 3:7–4:11;
Heb 12:1–4

**Spirit**   Rm 8:1–17; 1 Cor
2:9–16; Gal 5:16–26

**Transformation**   1 Cor 3:1–4;

Gal 2:19–21; Eph 2:1–22;
Eph 3:14–21; Eph 4:14–21;
Eph 4:22–5:20; Col 3:1–17;
1 Tm 1:12–17; Heb 5:11–6:12;
Heb 12:5–29

**Unity**   1 Cor 1:10–16; 1 Cor
12:12–30; Eph 2:11–22;
Eph 4:1–16; Phil 2:1–11

**Uprightness**   1 Cor 6:9–11;
Eph 6:10–20; 1 Th 5:4–22;
2 Tm 4:6–8; Heb 10:19–39;
Heb 13:7–16

**Vocation**   Rm 1:1–7;
Rm 12:4–13; 1 Cor 1:26–31;
1 Cor 3:5–15; 1 Tm 6:11–16

**Weakness**   Rm 8:26–27;
2 Cor 11:16–12:10;

**Pauline**
BOOKS & MEDIA

The Daughters of St. Paul operate book and media centers at the following addresses. Visit, call or write the one nearest you today, or find us on the World Wide Web, www.pauline.org

**CALIFORNIA**

3908 Sepulveda Blvd, Culver City, CA 90230   310-397-8676

2640 Broadway Street, Redwood City, CA 94063   650-369-4230

5945 Balboa Avenue, San Diego, CA 92111   858-565-9181

**FLORIDA**

145 S.W. 107th Avenue, Miami, FL 33174   305-559-6715

**HAWAII**

1143 Bishop Street, Honolulu, HI 96813   808-521-2731

Neighbor Islands call: 866-521-2731

**ILLINOIS**

172 North Michigan Avenue, Chicago, IL 60601   312-346-4228

**LOUISIANA**

4403 Veterans Memorial Blvd, Metairie, LA 70006   504-887-7631

**MASSACHUSETTS**

885 Providence Hwy, Dedham, MA 02026   781-326-5385

**MISSOURI**

9804 Watson Road, St. Louis, MO 63126   314-965-3512

**NEW JERSEY**

561 U.S. Route 1, Wick Plaza, Edison, NJ 08817   32-572-1200

**NEW YORK**

150 East 52nd Street, New York, NY 10022   212-754-1110

**PENNSYLVANIA**

9171-A Roosevelt Blvd, Philadelphia, PA 19114   215-676-9494

**SOUTH CAROLINA**

243 King Street, Charleston, SC 29401   43-577-0175

**TENNESSEE**

4811 Poplar Avenue, Memphis, TN 38117   901-761-2987

**TEXAS**

114 Main Plaza, San Antonio, TX 78205   210-224-8101

**VIRGINIA**

1025 King Street, Alexandria, VA 22314   03-549-3806

**CANADA**

3022 Dufferin Street, Toronto, ON M6B 3T5   416-781-9131

¡También somos su fuente para libros, DVDs y música en español!

**BOOKS & MEDIA**

*A mission of the Daughters of St. Paul*

As apostles of Jesus Christ, evangelizing today's world:

We are CALLED to holiness
by God's living Word and Eucharist.

We COMMUNICATE the Gospel message
through our lives and through all
available forms of media.

We SERVE the Church
by responding to the hopes and needs
of all people with the Word of God,
in the spirit of St. Paul.

For more information visit our website, www.pauline.org.

ST PAULS

The Society of St. Paul is an international religious congregation of priests and brothers dedicated to serving the Church through the communications media.

It was founded by Blessed James Alberione in 1914. Today, with a thousand members, it is represented in thirty countries around the world. The Society of St. Paul is part of the Pauline Family of Congregations, which includes the Daughters of St. Paul and the Sister Disciples of the Divine Master.

ST PAULS/Alba House is the publishing arm of the Society of St. Paul in the United States.

Visit our Web site at www.albahouse.org (for orders www.stpauls.us). To request a current catalog, call 1-800-343-2522 (ALBA).

For information regarding this and associated ministries of the Pauline Family of Congregations, write to the Vocation Director, Society of St. Paul, 2187 Victory Blvd., Staten Island, New York 10314-6603. Phone (718) 982-5709; or E-mail vocation@stpauls.us or check our Internet site, www.vocationoffice.org